THE PASTOR
AND THE
PAINTER

ALSO BY CINDY WOCKNER

Bali 9: The Untold Story (with Madonna King)
Evil in the Suburbs (with Michael Porta)

CINDY WOCKNER

THE PASTOR
AND THE
PAINTER

Inside the lives of Andrew Chan and Myuran Sukumaran –
from Aussie schoolboys to Bali Nine drug traffickers
to Kerobokan's redeemed men

Lyrics from '10,000 Reasons (Bless the Lord)', written by Jonas Myrin and Matt Redman copyright © 2011 Thankyou Music/Said and Done Music/Kingswaysongs and Jonas Myrin/Capitol Paragon (BMI) (Admin, SHOUT! Music Publishing [AUS/NZ]) & Omega Songs (BMI), reproduced with permission from Crossroad Publishing and SHOUT! Music Publishing.

Lyrics from 'Mighty to Save', written by Ben Fielding and Reuben Morgan copyright © 2006 Hillsong Music Publishing, reproduced with permission from Hillsong Music Publishing Australia.

Published in Australia and New Zealand in 2018
by Hachette Australia
(an imprint of Hachette Australia Pty Limited)
Level 17, 207 Kent Street, Sydney NSW 2000
www.hachette.com.au

10 9 8 7 6 5 4 3 2 1

Copyright © Cindy Wockner 2018

This book is copyright. Apart from any fair dealing for the purposes of private study, research, criticism or review permitted under the *Copyright Act 1968*, no part may be stored or reproduced by any process without prior written permission. Enquiries should be made to the publisher.

 A catalogue record for this book is available from the National Library of Australia

ISBN: 978 0 7336 3694 3 (paperback)

Cover design by Christabella Designs
Front cover photographs courtesy of Newspix/Lukman S. Bintoro and Associated Press/Firdia Lisnawati
Back cover photographs courtesy of Newspix/Lukman S. Bintoro
Author photograph courtesy of News Corporation Australia
Typeset in 12/18 pt Simoncini Garamond by Bookhouse, Sydney

*To Andrew Chan and Myuran Sukumaran,
the Pastor and the Painter,
who showed us all that people can change.*

Everyone deserves a second chance.

'As one whose husband and mother-in-law have died the victims of murder and assassination, I stand firmly and unequivocally opposed to the death penalty for those convicted of capital offenses. An evil deed is not redeemed by an evil deed of retaliation.'

CORETTA SCOTT KING

CONTENTS

Prologue — xi

1. Busted — 1
2. Hukuman Mati — 12
3. From Drugs to Jesus — 31
4. Love Your Enemy — 57
5. Respect — 66
6. The Pastor and the Painter — 79
7. Clemency Denied — 92
8. People Can Change — 119
9. A Nation Pleads — 131
10. The Fight Intensifies — 145
11. Mercy, Please — 156
12. The Last Flight — 168
13. Nusakambangan — 181
14. 72 Hours — 201
15. Death Row Wedding — 220
16. The Last Day — 234
17. Preparing the Spirit — 251
18. The End — 268
19. Execution — 275
20. Goodbye — 289

Amnesty and Reprieve — 301
Acknowledgements — 302
Index — 305

PROLOGUE

Myuran Sukumaran and Andrew Chan got what they did not deserve. They did not deserve to be tied up to wooden crosses and shot dead in the early hours of the morning in April 2015. Nor did the six others who were with them in the darkness.

Their parents did not deserve the torture they were forced to endure for months and weeks beforehand and the torment of knowing they had just 72 hours left. They did not deserve that final painful farewell, walking away knowing they would never see their sons again. The jail guards and officials who respected and liked Myuran and Andrew did not deserve, through duty, to be forced to police those final hours.

The 96 men of the firing squads did not deserve their job of sighting the beating hearts, using red laser beams, and then silencing those hearts.

I did not know the six people who were executed with Myuran and Andrew that night but I had met some of their relatives and heard some of their stories. I know they all had families that loved them.

But I did know Myuran and Andrew. I was there in Bali when they were arrested, all full of swagger and bravado and smart-alec quips, full of everything except contrition. And I was there in that small town in Central Java called Cilacap on the night they were shot dead, ten years and eleven days after they were arrested.

True, Myuran and Andrew had been convicted of heroin trafficking. They had admitted their role in attempting to bring 8.2 kilograms of heroin from Bali to Sydney. They had been found guilty of a very serious crime and one that would have brought untold misery to those who used that heroin and to their families. They deserved to be punished and severely. They knew that. They never asked to be freed. All they asked was for an acknowledgement that they had been rehabilitated and for their good deeds to matter.

When I first met Myuran and Andrew at the Denpasar police headquarters the day after their arrest, they were brash and bold. Andrew suggested that what happened to Schapelle Corby happened to him. Back then, I was ambivalent about them. Certainly there were not many reasons to have sympathy for a group of people caught red-handed with drugs. As a crime reporter for most of my career I had seen plenty of criminals come and go, many refusing to admit guilt in the face of overwhelming evidence, lacking in any kind of contrition.

But this story turned out to be different. There was not one moment that I doubted their reformation and rehabilitation was genuine. True, the death penalty provides a powerful incentive to reform or pretend to reform. People would often ask me if I believed the transformation was genuine or an act. I did believe them. And as I got to know them better and better I became more convinced that this was real.

When their jail projects were in their infancy and before Myuran had even picked up a paintbrush, his enthusiasm was infectious. He was so excited he couldn't stand still as he showed me around the jail workshop and computer room. He kept telling me how happy he was to have finally found something worthwhile to do in jail and how he was becoming a better person. He asked me if I agreed he was a better person. I did. Andrew was the same as he talked of helping others through his Christian ministry, giving examples of lives that had turned around and of souls that had been saved. He suggested I talk to those people to get a clearer picture of him. As he said, you can always talk yourself up but the true test is what others say about you. As the projects grew, so too did Myuran and Andrew. They became men of whom their families were proud.

As a journalist my job dictates objectivity and neutrality. I don't have to like or dislike those I write about. I just need to tell the story, accurately and honestly. Of course, it's human nature to feel compassion. And when you spend ten years covering a story like this one, it's difficult not to feel compassion. Myuran and Andrew became more than subjects on whom I was reporting.

For the first few years after their arrest and as their legal cases came and went I saw them regularly at various jail events and at court. They were still brash and not very likeable. They tolerated me but they didn't trust me. After all, I was just doing my job. For my part, I didn't care too much what they thought. It was in 2010 when I got to know them better. The jail boss had allowed me inside for several days to interview the Bali Nine and see how they were beginning to transform the jail. I spent hours with Myuran and Andrew as they showed me around and opened up to me. I was allowed into their cells, in the so-called death tower. Nothing had been off limits. They asked me to bring them McDonald's. I knew they were desperate to be portrayed as real people, doing good in the jail and I left after those visits with no doubt they were changing. They were no longer the two surly drug traffickers I first met in 2005.

Over the next few years I got to know them better and I stayed in touch with them when I moved, from Indonesia to Nigeria to live in 2012–2014. In 2013 I came back from Nigeria to do another series of in-depth interviews with Myuran and Andrew and their families. By this time they were well and truly reformed. From that time on, I communicated regularly with them and as their executions neared, I shared many late-night conversations with them that often turned into counselling sessions. Myuran once asked my advice on making videos for his

PROLOGUE

family to watch after he was dead. With every new announcement from the Indonesian side he asked my advice, he pleaded with me: did I think they were nearing the end, what should they do, how could they save themselves, how much time did they have left? I was a journalist, I wasn't trained for this, this wasn't about me, but I had promised them both I would tell their story. Many times in those last few months I hung up the phone and cried.

Those final 72 hours in Cilacap were excruciating. I had to muster all my strength to hold it together. I will never forget arriving in Cilacap soon after Myuran and Andrew had been read their death warrants. I was directed into the hotel meeting room being used by the legal team and the Australian government. One of the first people I saw was lawyer Veronica Haccou. I looked at Veronica and just collapsed in her arms, sobbing and sobbing. Julian McMahon stood silently and stoically nearby. He knew everyone needed to cry at some stage, even journalists. I just couldn't believe, after all these years, Myuran and Andrew were actually going to be killed. It was like we were all in shock. I was embarrassed that the end of the story was only starting and I was already falling apart in public. Reporters just didn't do that. This wasn't about me. My grief was nothing compared to that of the families. I knew I shouldn't be showing my emotions like this but I just couldn't help it. I didn't mean to cry, it just came out in a gushing torrent. I didn't have time to try to stifle the tears as I have always done on other stories. I scrambled to find a tissue amongst the notebooks and tape recorder in my cluttered handbag. Veronica and Julian were silent. There was nothing to say.

Then there was the dreadful day, the last day of Myuran and Andrew's lives, when, as the family walked through a media and police throng to get to the port to pay their last visit ever, Myuran's sister Brintha howled and cried. She had to be carried through the crowd. It was agonising to hear and watch. A police dog bit me that day. So shocked was I by its savageness that again I broke down in tears. I don't remember it, but someone reported that I was saying, 'I can't believe they are doing this.' And I couldn't. My colleague and friend, Tom Allard, to whom I will be forever grateful, consoled me. I could barely speak as I sobbed and Tom hugged me. The story had become deeply personal. Two people, who I knew so well, were about to die in the most gruesome way.

When they did die, I stood silently at the dusty, hot and noisy Cilacap port, looking to the night sky for a few seconds as the generators whirred around me, phones rang and television reporters did live crosses to Australia and Jakarta and the world. I had no words, just disbelief and a deep, overwhelming sadness, a kind of sadness I still can't adequately put into words. But I can feel it, I can taste it, every time I think about that dreadful night. My Balinese assistant, Komang Erviani, who had been by my side on this journey for so many years, was crying. She was on the phone to Mary Jane Fiesta Veloso's lawyers who were over on the island in the waiting area for families and officials. They were telling her how the authorities had cruelly let Mary

PROLOGUE

Jane's sisters believe, as they heard the shots fired, that she too was dead.

Myuran's brother Chinthu called me from the hotel in town where the Australian families were huddled together, praying and waiting for news. He begged me to tell him, his voice cracking, was it over, was I sure they were dead? I have to tell Mum, I have to be sure before I tell my family. Is it true that Mary Jane was spared? Maybe Myuran was saved too? They are gone, I told him. I knew they were gone. I didn't know what else to say. There was nothing left to say.

It was wrong. The death penalty is abhorrent. Myuran and Andrew were reformed, and killing them was so utterly pointless. By shooting them, Indonesia lost the best anti-drugs ambassadors they could have ever had.

The outpouring of public support for them in Australia in those final days of their lives was amazing. So many people were galvanised to action, calling for an end to the death penalty, attending vigils and lighting candles. Their legacy demands that we continue that fight, here and now, and not wait until the next Australian is on death row overseas and about to be killed. The Pastor and the Painter wanted everyone who cared so much about them to keep fighting. I promised both of them I would do that. This is their story and the story of those who worked so hard to save them.

1.
BUSTED

Something was bothering Raji Sukumaran. Her hair was still wet from the shower when she went out into the street, outside her home in Auburn, in Sydney's west, hoping to see an approaching taxi. Myuran had gone on holiday to Bali but he should have been back. It was about 5.30 p.m. on 18 April 2005, the day after his 24th birthday.

Raji had bought seafood from the market and cleaned it before putting it in to the freezer. She planned to serve it for her son Myuran's birthday lunch or dinner. The family always had a special meal when it was a birthday. And seafood was Myuran's favourite. Raji loved cooking it for him.

Earlier that day Raji had gone to the shopping centre with her sister and her sister's children. Raji's daughter, Brintha, had a university exam. Raji felt down but didn't know why. When she got home, Myuran was not there. Perhaps his flight was arriving in the evening? Raji had made up his bed with fresh linen and cleaned his room. She had folded his clothes and left them on the bed for him. She knew he liked to put them away himself.

When Brintha had got home at 5 p.m. she was keen to know if her big brother was back yet. No, her mum said. Brintha was disappointed.

Outside in the street, her hair wet, Raji couldn't stop thinking how odd this was. Could he have been in a plane crash, or a car accident? No, it wasn't time to panic yet. She should go back inside and dry her hair.

The front door was locked. That was strange – she hadn't locked the door when she'd come out. She knocked again and again but no one answered. She started to worry. The family's dog started barking from the other side of the door, which at last was opening.

Raji saw Brintha's scared face. She was shivering as she reached out and pulled her mother inside. Raji started shaking her, wanting to know what was going on.

Brintha could barely speak. She stood there shaking. 'Myu, Myu, Mum, Bali, Myu, Bali, arrested . . .' It was all she could get out.

A chill ran through Raji's body as the words sank in. Immediately she fainted, collapsing to the floor in a heap.

Brintha had been watching the television news. The lead story was about nine Australians arrested in Bali. Brintha recognised her brother's T-shirt – and there was no mistaking the distinctive tattoo sticking out from under his sleeve. It was Myuran, no question.

As Raji dragged herself up from the floor, her younger son, Chinthu, appeared. At the same moment the phone started ringing: it was the Australian Consul-General's office in Bali. They asked to speak to Chinthu. He went upstairs to take the call, not wanting to talk in front of his mother and sister before he found out what was going on.

At that moment he knew only snippets: he had heard about nine Australians being arrested in Bali on the car radio as he drove home. The consular officer told Chinthu that his elder brother had been arrested on drugs charges, an offence that could send him to jail for at least ten years.

Raji was stunned. She called her parents, and her brothers and sisters. They all rushed over. They cried, prayed and tried to comfort each other. They knew very little except that Myuran had been arrested and was locked up in a police jail. He could get ten years in prison! Raji couldn't believe it. 'What are we going to do for ten years?' she begged Chinthu. 'We have to visit him.'

With the news now out, media started arriving at the Sukumaran house. The family had to get out of there. At 2 a.m. they grabbed some clothes and went to Raji's sister's home. Raji's head was still reeling. She didn't know a single person in jail. She didn't even know anyone who knew someone in jail. Her son lived at home with her and the rest of the family and she never had any reason to suspect that he was involved in drugs.

On that same evening, about ten kilometres away in Enfield, Helen Chan was in shock. Her hands trembled as she dialled her eldest son's number. Michael was in the middle of doing his grocery shopping. 'Your brother's in trouble,' Helen told him. All Helen knew was that Andrew was overseas and appeared to have been arrested. She and her husband, Ken, hadn't even known Andrew was overseas. By the time Michael rushed to the family home, everyone was in hysterics, desperately trying to work out what was going on. Michael left the next day for Bali.

Over the course of a couple of hours that day, nine families across Australia – most of whom had never met and had no clue their children were friends, let alone that they were all in Bali together – were learning about the arrests. In most cases they found out from the media, and soon after received consular calls.

The first letter was written on 8 April 2005. Addressed to the Bali police chief, I Made Mangku Pastika, and copied to the intelligence director, the narcotics director and the director of criminal investigation in Bali and Interpol Jakarta, it was written by the Australian Federal Police's liaison officer in Bali. It had been translated into Indonesian and contained an extraordinary amount of detail about what nine young Australians were planning to do in Bali.

Two days before the letter was sent, four suspected heroin couriers had flown from Sydney to Bali: Renae Lawrence (27),

Matthew Norman (18), Martin Stephens (29) and Si Yi Chen (20). Another three were due to arrive that day: Tan Duc Thanh Nguyen (21), Michael Czugaj (19) and Scott Rush (19). Andrew Chan was already there. He had flown in on 3 April. What was not in the AFP letter was the fact that Myuran Sukumaran was also flying to Bali on 8 April. At this stage, he was not on the AFP's radar at all.

The AFP officers did know, however, that the plan was for the couriers to fly back to Australia on 15 April with heroin strapped to their bodies. They also knew that the couriers would be given baggy clothes to wear, told not to carry any metal and to wear sandals so they would not alert airport scanners; they should also have some souvenir Bali wooden objects with them to declare. They would be told not to smoke leading up to the trip, to ensure they did not appear nervous when the crunch time came and they had to pass security while strapped with heroin.

The point of the AFP's letter was to ask the Indonesian police to conduct surveillance on the eight Australians in Bali: to find the source of the drugs they were to carry, and gather as much intel as possible to catch those higher up the chain. The letter asked the Indonesians to take whatever action they deemed appropriate. It didn't specifically request the arrest of the eight young people, but it was hard to imagine that the Indonesian police would ignore the chance to do so.

A second AFP letter, written on 12 April, provided details about the group's planned return to Australia. Andrew Chan and four couriers – Lawrence, Norman, Stephens and Chen – would fly home on 14 April. Two days later, Rush, Nguyen and Czugaj would follow. The letter suggested that if some of them were arrested on 14 April, the other three would likely become suspicious and abort their mission. The AFP requested that Nguyen, Czugaj and Rush be searched soon after the first group was stopped.

It was Wednesday, 13 April when Bali police intelligence and narcotics police met at the Hard Rock Hotel to arrange a plan for surveilling the Australians. It was a big job and their resources were relatively limited. Two officers checked into the White Rose Hotel in Kuta. Across the corridor, in Room 1022, were Si Yi Chen and Matthew Norman. Two other officers headed to the Aneka Beach Hotel, where Scott Rush and Michael Czugaj were in Room 404. They watched and followed the young men as they went for a day's rafting trip to Ubud, and later met up with other members of the gang – including someone to whom the surveillance team referred as 'the black-skinned man'. This was Myuran. He was staying at the Hard Rock Hotel with Andrew; the pair always seemed to be together. The surveillance team at the Hard Rock was finding it difficult to get any information on Andrew; he had instructed the front desk staff not to reveal his identity or presence there to anybody.

The surveillance team log noted that on Friday, 15 April, at 9 p.m., Andrew Chan walked from the Hard Rock Hotel to the Seaview Cottage. He was there for just ten minutes, then went back to the Hard Rock. At 2.45 a.m. on Saturday, 16 April, Andrew and Myuran left their hotel, carrying two suitcases to a small hotel in Kuta called the Plamboyan. At 3.15 a.m. they arrived back at the Hard Rock without the suitcases. At 7.40 a.m. they went back to the Plamboyan and emerged with two suitcases. This was the handover of the heroin.

When Andrew went to the Sea View Cottage, it was to meet the woman who was supplying the gear. Cherry Likit Bannakorn, a 22-year-old Thai woman, had flown in from Thailand with the drugs, and Andrew had gone to her hotel. The surveillance team, however, had not seen this meeting or even laid eyes on Cherry. The all-important drug handover had been done without them having a clue. It was Cherry's second trip to Bali, and her second meeting with Andrew. The first time she met him had been before the Indonesian surveillance started.

For days the surveillance crews watched the comings and goings of the group, to and from their various hotels. On the final day the Australians converged at the Adi Dharma Hotel. Rush and Czugaj checked out of their hotel and went to Nguyen's room at the Adi Dharma. Norman was already there. Andrew and Myuran arrived with a suitcase and set about strapping the heroin to the bodies of Rush and Czugaj. A little later, in a different room of the same hotel, they did the same with Lawrence and Stephens.

The plastic packages of heroin, strapped to each thigh and around the waist, were secured with a good amount of tape and bandaging. Pepper was used to disguise the smell. The configuration of mules going back to Australia with the heroin was different from what the AFP had outlined in its letter, but the modus operandi was the same. There had also been a delay in the dates of their return: there had not been sufficient heroin, so the group had to wait for more to be transported to Bali.

Rush and Czugaj, both from Brisbane, got into a taxi and headed to the airport. So too did Stephens and Lawrence, from New South Wales. The mules were carrying some 8.2 kilograms of heroin between them. The two groups had been kept apart in Bali: there was no need for them to meet – ever, if all went to plan.

Andrew got into his own taxi and also headed to the airport, giving the driver a hefty tip at the end. He was jovial and at ease. They all checked in for their flights, passing the first wave of security without problem. Andrew wasn't carrying any drugs. He did have a big wooden fish and what was described by police as a voodoo stick. (Years later, he told me there was no particular reason he had these objects; he said he just liked the stick and bought it.)

The five young Australians' journey to the airport had been monitored. When the mules and Chan had checked in and were in the departure area, police pounced. Chan had been sitting in a chair reading a Michael Moore book, waiting to board his flight. The four mules were taken away, and within minutes the drugs had been uncovered.

Back in Kuta, the Indonesian police did exactly as their AFP counterparts had asked and intercepted those not catching that night's flight. Chen, Norman and Nguyen were all in a room at the Melasti Beach Bungalows, in the heart of Kuta, when a knock on the door ended their hopes of heading out on the town to celebrate Myuran's 24th birthday. Myuran was outside the door when police struck. All were placed under arrest. Two plastic bags, containing 334.26 grams of heroin, were found in the Australians' luggage, along with pepper, rubber gloves, medical tape, adhesive tape and cloth tape. They were busted.

Still wearing oversized shirts with flower motifs, which they had bought at the markets for barely nothing, the group found themselves the next day at police headquarters in Denpasar. Before long, word spread that nine Australians had been arrested at the airport with drugs. The arrested young people cowered in the offices and holding rooms of the drug police, attempting to cover their faces as the media tried to get photographs.

Andrew was led out into the car park area, taken from one building to another. 'Whatever happened to Schapelle Corby happened to me,' he declared boldly. Under questioning, he and Myuran had provided little assistance to the investigators, denying any knowledge of the drugs. Of more assistance was Renae Lawrence, whose lawyer encouraged her to tell the truth; doing so was a better bet than clamming up and saying nothing, she was advised. At least it would mean a discount on her sentence.

It emerged that this was not Renae and Andrew's first drug run from Bali. The previous October, with several others, they had succeeded in taking heroin to Australia. Another trip had been planned in December 2004 but had not gone ahead, possibly due to a lack of heroin.

Almost from the moment of their arrest the group was dubbed the 'Bali Nine'. Three were from Queensland and the rest from New South Wales, although some were meeting for the first time at the Denpasar police headquarters. Myuran and Andrew had both attended Homebush Boys High School but had barely known each other at school. Myuran was older. It was not until 2002 that the pair became friendly, meeting through friends of friends at a mate's house. Andrew had worked with three of the others – Renae Lawrence, Martin Stephens and Matthew Norman – at a catering company that serviced the Sydney Cricket Ground. Si Yi Chen and Matthew Norman had been friends, as had Scott Rush and Michael Czugaj, from Brisbane. They became involved in the drug run through Tan Duc Thanh Nguyen.

Raji Sukumaran went into the room where her son was being held. She couldn't believe what was happening; it felt like some kind of dream. It was now several days after the arrests, and she and the family had flown to Bali.

She looked Myuran in the eye but he couldn't bear to return her gaze. He looked away, sneaking glances at his mother when he thought she wasn't looking.

Raji was angry: all she wanted to do was slap her son. But she couldn't. Instead, she hugged him. And she cried, breaking down.

'Don't worry, Ma, don't cry,' Myuran kept telling his mother.

Ken and Helen Chan didn't travel to Bali immediately. They were not well, and it was decided that Michael would go. He ended up spending the best part of a year in Bali. He would fly over, stay 28 days until his visa was due to expire, come home and then go back.

Andrew's parents felt ashamed and embarrassed. Helen couldn't accept what her son had done. She couldn't sleep. It took her a long time to come to terms with her son's crime. To Ken, it felt like a bomb had exploded when Andrew was first arrested. He was shocked. Only 16 months earlier he had finally retired after 40 years in the restaurant business. The couple had barely had time to enjoy their retirement, and now their lives had been turned upside down.

2.

HUKUMAN MATI

When the time came for the nine young drug traffickers to move from the various police holding cells to Bali's Kerobokan jail, three months had passed. During that time both Myuran and Andrew had been kept separated from the others, in the holding cells of two different police stations – Myuran at the Benoa water police base and Andrew at the Sanur police station. The facilities at Benoa were dreadful; Myuran barely saw the sunlight and was on his own for much of the time. At Sanur, Andrew at least had the company of local prisoners.

The separation had been a deliberate investigation ploy on behalf of Bali's drug squad. The police had only a limited time to investigate the case and get it ready to be handed over to the prosecutors in a process known as P21. During the three months the briefs of evidence went backwards and forwards between police and prosecutors, prosecutors asking for more information, until it was deemed complete. Then, once it was ready for court, the Bali Nine all moved to the infamous Kerobokan jail. Some of them, particularly the younger members of the group, were scared and they looked it. They were about to enter a place they had only heard about.

By this time Kerobokan jail was well known in Australia. Eight months earlier its most famous Australian prisoner, Schapelle Corby, had taken up residence there.

There was no doubting the Bali Nine crew knew all about Schapelle and her plight. After all, Andrew had even suggested, in the hours after his arrest, that he was walking the same road as the young Gold Coast beauty-therapy student. Kerobokan prison had become a tourist attraction since Corby got there. Daily, Australian tourists in Bali flocked to the jail, bearing armloads of goodies and the cosmetics they heard she loved. They all sought an audience with her and, after paying the requisite 5000 Rupiah to the guards at the front, were allowed in during visiting hours. In those early days, no one ever really knew what the 5000 Rupiah was for. It was just the way it was. Corby would see almost anyone who came to visit. She was a celebrity, and tourists wanted a story to take home.

Myuran and Andrew both hired the same legal team, led by local lawyer Muhammad Rifan and assisted by Australian expatriate lawyer Peter Johnson. Myuran and Andrew would be tried separately as would each of the four mules caught with the drugs on them. The four mules each had their own legal team. The other three, arrested at the Melasti Beach Bungalows, would face a joint trial, all three represented by the same team of lawyers.

The trials kicked off in mid October 2005, with prosecutors outlining the case against each of the nine, followed by a series of police witnesses who told of the AFP letter, the surveillance, the arrests and the interrogations. With the trials sitting only one or two days a week, they dragged on. What everyone was waiting for was the testimony of each of the nine, to hear what they were going to say in their own defence and about the others. Both Myuran and Andrew adopted the same strategy – deny everything.

It was January of 2006 when Myuran was finally called to testify at his own trial. He spoke softly. His voice seemed at odds with his shaved head and the picture police had painted of the kingpin of this heroin smuggling gang.

He told the judges he had come to Bali for a holiday but had no business with Andrew. What did you do in Bali? 'Just tourist things like shopping, restaurants, to bars drinking.' He didn't strap anything to Renae Lawrence and Martin Stephens, he said, nor did he ever have anything to do with heroin. What about the statements from the mules, that he had strapped heroin to their bodies? 'I did not do that, what they said.' He admitted that he knew Andrew from school, but denied knowing some of the others.

To many questions, he claimed not to know the answer. It became ridiculous. He told the judges he couldn't remember what kind of mobile phone he had at the time. They had had enough. 'Have you ever had the disease of amnesia?' 'Sorry,' Myuran said.

'Loss of memory, forgetting things,' the chief judge said. Myuran now had an explanation. 'Ah, amnesia. I have once, it's so long ago I can't remember. It was more than eight months ago.' The judges were not impressed. 'So, you have forgotten everything, then?' Myuran mumbled something about being under a lot of stress. He ended his testimony, telling the judges he was not guilty.

A week later Myuran was back in court, this time called upon to testify as a witness at Andrew's trial. He was having none of it. Three times he repeated the same thing. 'I don't want to make a statement because I am the same suspect in the same case.' The judge warned him that if someone told him to take an objection or refuse to give a statement it was wrong. Myuran stonewalled. 'I don't know about that.' And that was it. He said no more. Neither did the other three arrested with him – Matthew Norman, Si Yi Chen and Tan Duc Thanh Nguyen – who gave the same objection. It went on like that, each time a case came to court. Myuran and Andrew kept opting not to give evidence, despite the increasingly angry judicial admonishments. It was not boding well.

More than ever the divisions between the group were being laid bare. When Myuran and Andrew were called to testify as witnesses at Renae Lawrence's trial the air was thick with contempt. 'I'm not sitting with Andrew and Myuran and that. Tidak mau,' Lawrence told the judges, using the Indonesian words for 'don't want'.

She sat with her lawyers, at the bar table, to ensure she did not come into contact with the others. By this time the judges were resigned to hear yet another refusal to testify.

When Andrew told the judges he was not willing to be a witness in Renae's trial, they sighed, telling him his initial police statement, after his arrest, would therefore be read to court. It was not true, he said, that he had threatened to kill Renae or her family if she didn't carry heroin. He had only come, with Myuran, to the room at the hotel where the heroin was strapped to the mules to lie down on the bed and watch TV and had only stayed there 45 minutes to an hour. Renae was angry. Asked her response to Chan's statement, she was blunt. 'Bohong,' she said, Indonesian for lies.

Andrew was insolent. The judges persisted. 'Did he understand why he had been arrested?' 'No.' 'Do you mean the police of Indonesia have arrested the wrong person?' 'I don't know.' 'Do you know about a narcotic case called the Bali Nine?' 'I dunno.' 'Did you report to the Government of Australia that you were detained and arrested at the airport illegally?' 'I don't remember.' 'Didn't the Government of Australia object to the detention of its citizen in Indonesia?' 'I dunno.' 'Do you want to revoke your statement given to the police?' 'No, I don't want to make a statement.' 'Can you explain why you don't want to give a statement?' 'Um, I'm in the same case, so no, that's why.' 'Can you explain what case you mean?' 'I don't know.' 'At the time you said you are healthy, physically and mentally, in the police station.' 'Yer.'

It was becoming more than ridiculous. It was the same story when Myuran was called to testify. He didn't want to give evidence. His initial police statement was read to the court. Renae said this too was lies.

Renae, giving evidence at Andrew's trial, painted a very different picture.

When she arrived in Bali she met Andrew and was given a list of dos and don'ts. Don't use the mobile phone to call Australia, don't leave the hotel. 'There was a lot of don'ts: don't do this, don't do that, don't use my phone, he told me when to call my mum and when not to call my mum, he told me not to tell anyone.' Andrew had told her to come to Bali to do something for him but she and Martin Stephens had not known what it was.

Things then got tricky. The judges wanted to know if Renae had come to Bali before, in October 2004, with Andrew and others. They were clearly referring to her earlier police statements. She said she needed to go to the toilet.

Pressed, she said she had been to Bali before, on holiday, and had met others of the Bali Nine. Eventually, after much to and fro with the judges, Renae Lawrence withdrew her earlier police statements.

It became very tangled up. Martin Stephens too was a damning witness at Andrew's trial. It was Andrew who had told him to come to Bali and do as he was told or his family would be hurt or killed. The threats, Martin said, had been made at Andrew's home two weeks before the Bali trip. Martin said he had been offered no reward to come to Bali and carry a package. So why did he do it, the judges wanted to know. 'Coz I had no choice. Coz my family, my mum, my dad and my life was at stake. I celebrated my birthday in the hotel room on April 13 coz I wasn't allowed to go anywhere. So if I was here for a holiday don't you think I would go out and party? But I didn't, we weren't allowed.' Andrew had organised the whole trip.

For his part, Andrew said it wasn't true before being called to testify in his own defence.

It didn't get any better. No, he didn't meet Myuran at the Hard Rock Hotel (where both were staying) and didn't know Myuran as a friend. This was despite police surveillance photographs, taken by Bali police and part of the police brief of evidence, showing the two of them together.

By Andrew's version, he was in Bali to go shopping, clubbing, eating, scuba diving, that kind of thing. He had never met any of the witnesses, the other Bali Nine members, who had testified against him. The judges were not convinced. A rooster crowed loudly. Court staff, who then lived within the court complex, kept roosters in cages for use in cock-fighting and as pets.

A judge raised his voice above the restless rooster. 'You said before that you have never seen, you never met with the witnesses that sit here before, all of the witnesses. Just try to remember, have you ever met with them in Australia?' Andrew was unequivocal. 'I have never met them in Australia, no.'

What about Myuran, did you know him? 'Ah, no.' Renae Lawrence? 'I didn't know her, I have seen her around at work, I have seen her but I have never talked to her, coz it's a big company.' Martin Stephens? 'No, it's the same.'

The judges pressed on. 'Why were you arrested,' they asked him. 'I don't know, I asked the customs officer and they wouldn't tell me. I asked the customs and there was police there.' 'So have you ever been investigated at the police station?' 'I have been questioned but I don't know if it was investigated, like typed up something, I have been questioned but other than that I don't know if it was typed.' It must have been typed since he had signed it.

'So, what about all the witnesses who claimed that Andrew had strapped packages on their bodies,' the judges wanted to know. 'You deny it? Which one is the truth?' 'Um, I never strapped any heroin on their bodies ever in my life.' He denied knowing Renae, Scott Rush, Martin or Michael Czugaj.

'So, as far as you know all of the witnesses are liars?' 'Are liars? From what I believe yes, from what I've heard, yes.' The judges were becoming annoyed now.

'How do you know they are liars, you don't know them, how?' Andrew charged on. 'Well, no, they are saying that they know me but I don't know them.' The judges had had enough and told Andrew as much. 'Please don't tell the wrong story or lies because the judges, the lawyers, the prosecutor, all the people here are not stupid.'

And to make sure that Andrew knew where he stood, the judge instructed the female translator to tell Andrew not to lie to the judges, the lawyers and prosecutors. 'Indonesian judges are not stupid people but we are the people who know the truth, tell him.'

Andrew was not the least bit perturbed. 'Yer, I know they are civilised people and I'm telling the truth.' The judges wanted Andrew to understand that all the other witnesses against him would only make his punishment more severe. 'Um, yer I obviously do,' he replied.

Tell the truth, who owns the packages of heroin? 'I don't know, I don't even know who owns it.' Okay, so does it belong to Renae, Scott or someone else? 'I don't know, I've never seen it until they showed me at Polda (police headquarters). They started throwing it at me, saying it's yours and I've never seen it.'

One didn't need to be a lawyer to know it wasn't a good day for Andrew. The reaction to Myuran's refusal to testify and stonewall was no better.

The pair later said that their refusal to testify, and their constant denial that they had any knowledge of anything, had been on the advice of their first legal team. The approach did not serve them well, in a legal system that places a great deal of emphasis on co-operation, on courtesy and politeness in court and on admissions of guilt and expressions of remorse. The prosecution, when it came time for the closing submissions, saw no reason for leniency for either Myuran or Andrew.

Sentence them both to death, they told the judges. Chan smirked. The translator asked him if he knew what the words *hukuman mati* meant. 'Yes, death penalty, no problem.'

Myuran's and Andrew's lawyers originally believed that both would be given life sentences. But by verdict day, on 14 February 2006, something was going wrong. The lawyers heard, through the judicial grapevine, that both men were going to be given the death penalty that day.

Frantic calls were made to Kerobokan. 'Don't come to court,' the lawyers advised their clients. 'Feign illness, do whatever you can think of, but do not come to court. You are going to get the death penalty.' The lawyers needed time to work out what was going on; once the death penalty was handed down it would be too late.

But it was already too late. Myuran and Andrew could not avoid getting on the bus that would take them from Kerobokan prison to the court that day. They could do nothing but hope that by the time they arrived, the lawyers might have done some fast work and turned the situation around.

Raji and Brintha were in Sydney, watching the live coverage on television. The Sukumaran family had decided that only Chinthu would be in Bali to attend the court that day.

Michael was there to support Andrew. He and Chinthu had never met before the Bali Nine arrests. They came from different worlds, bound together only by the actions of their brothers, and in those early days they had little in common.

Andrew's verdict was handed down first. A huge crowd of anti-drugs protestors was in the court. As far as they were concerned there was only one verdict that would be acceptable. They took their positions at the back of the courtroom, holding up placards. The judges read and read for what seemed like hours, before declaring Andrew guilty and sentencing him to death. It was all conducted in Indonesian.

For Myuran's verdict there was not such a lengthy reading. The judges said that the heroin brought by Myuran's and Andrew's group could have yielded 8200 victims. Myuran too was guilty, and his sentence was death.

Myuran appeared calm as the verdict was read out. Andrew had already got the death penalty before him and Myuran, sitting in the court holding cell waiting for his turn, knew the same fate was stalking him. The anti-drug protestors shouted appreciation, applauding the judges. They were happy.

In different courtrooms of the Denpasar District Court that day two of the mules – Michael Czugaj and Martin Stephens – were both sentenced to life in jail.

The day before, the other two mules – Renae Lawrence and Scott Rush – had also been handed life sentences. Renae had been stunned. The prosecutors in her case had asked for a 20-year sentence, due to the assistance and information she had provided the police about the syndicate after her arrest. She had been led to believe her co-operation would serve her well. She broke down in tears, furious at the shock decision.

The judges in the cases of the four mules rejected their claims that they had been threatened by the ringleaders, saying if this was true they had had plenty of time to report this to authorities.

One day later, the remaining three – Matthew Norman, Si Yi Chen and Tan Duc Thanh Nguyen – were also sentenced to life in jail. Most indicated immediately they would appeal.

Raji was sure the translation she was watching on television was in error. Why had Myuran's verdict been so much shorter than Andrew's? Surely there was some mistake and he hadn't got the death penalty after all, Raji kept thinking. Myuran was angry as he stormed out of court. Something had gone dreadfully wrong. This was not meant to happen. The full extent of what happened would not become evident for many years.

Chinthu was just 22 years old. Already he'd had a lot of growing up to do in a short space of time. He supported his brother, his mother and father, and his sister. Now, after the emotion of the verdict, he retreated to his hotel room. He was exhausted and fell asleep. When he woke up he had 40 missed calls on his phone.

Raji, at home in Sydney, had no idea how the death penalty worked. Would they simply take Myuran away and shoot him dead? She was terrified. A friend from work told her it would be a long road. 'You have to be strong,' her friend said. 'Don't expect him to walk in tomorrow.' Still Raji was convinced Myuran would be home soon.

Her eldest son loved her home-cooked food. His favourites were her crab curry and prawn curry. Once a week Raji cooked prawn curry. But for the first six months after Myu's arrest she stopped cooking altogether. The whole process was loaded with too many memories. Every time she cooked something she knew Myuran liked, she would despair at the fact that he wasn't there. Often, Raji would get out five plates at mealtimes, momentarily forgetting that Myuran was not there. And Sundays were different. Each Sunday Myuran used to make breakfast for the family. Eventually, Raji started cooking again. She realised that the rest of the family was missing out. She kept the quilt cover from Myuran's bed in a special place, intending to put it back on his bed when he came home.

Ken and Helen Chan were heartbroken and struggling to cope. Travelling to Bali was not easy for them, given their frailty and age. Helen suffered terribly. From the day of Andrew's arrest she struggled to get a proper night's sleep.

After the sentence, and as Andrew began finding solace in religion, he started urging his parents to go to church too. Ken and Helen were Buddhists, but as they watched Andrew grow as a result of his religion, they started to think seriously about trying church. In 2007 they were baptised as Christians. They began attending church every weekend, and met a new community of supportive friends. It was another chapter in their changing world.

It was 1955 when a 20-year-old Ken Chan came by ship to Australia. The journey from China took 21 days. His father and brothers were already there; his father was working as a gold miner.

Going straight to Sydney, Ken started working with his brothers in a fruit shop and then the fruit markets. When he started working in a restaurant, he met the woman he would marry: Helen. Soon afterwards, the couple started their own Chinese restaurant. Like many immigrants to Australia, they worked hard, seven days a week, striving to give their children a good start in life.

The Chans had a son and two daughters by the time Andrew came along in January 1984. He was a cute kid, likeable and always willing to help anyone. As Helen remembers, he was also a bit of a larrikin, with a cheeky smile. The Chans mostly spoke Cantonese at home; their English was limited. But Andrew never became fully competent in his parents' native language, meaning there was a communication gap between him and his parents.

The Soper family lived a few doors down the street, and would become lifelong friends of the Chans. As a little boy, Andrew spent hours at their place, and even went on family holidays with them. Shelley and David Soper were both Salvation Army majors; it was through them and their children that Andrew was first introduced to religion, and he began attending services and a Christian youth group.

Andrew went to Homebush Boys High School. He often joked that he was not in the least bit academic; he was a smart-arse, he said. He was not academic but he was good at sport. And he admitted to some stupid choices as a young kid. For a time, Myuran Sukumaran also went to the same school. But he was older than Andrew and they didn't know one another then. They wouldn't meet again until much later on.

Myuran was born in London in April 1981. His parents, Sam and Rajini, known as Raji, were Sri Lankan immigrants. As a six-week-old baby, Myuran was taken to Sri Lanka to live with his grandparents. Sam and Raji were working long hours in London, and sending him to childcare at such a young age was not possible. Two years later, Sam and Raji went back to Sri Lanka, and then took the family to Sydney.

As a little boy, Myuran loved Lego. When he grew older he loved to watch action movies and read comic books. Myuran told a forensic psychiatrist, employed to write a report for the court, that at school he had suffered racist bullying that was so bad his parents decided to move him away to a new school. He was nervous and shy, and felt isolated from his classmates. He was also a chronic asthmatic. Myuran only started to make friends in his early adolescence; many of his mates were from various ethnic backgrounds and had experienced racist abuse themselves. It was an anti-social group who truanted from school regularly. But Myuran managed to rise above it and did well enough to be accepted into university.

Even as a young boy, Myuran had a strong sense of social responsibility and wanted to help others. He was keen to donate blood but was too young to do so without parental consent, so he got Raji to sign the form for him. He donated $30 a month to Unicef: on the calendar in his bedroom he circled the date each month the money was due. (For a long time after his arrest, Raji kept paying the money for him each month.)

Myuran told the forensic psychiatrist that he felt isolated at university and could not cope. None of his school friends had gone on to university and he found it hard to find a new social group. The isolation led him to leave university at the end of his first year, moving into clerical jobs, for six months at a time. The work was easy but he would become bored and then quit.

He told the psychiatrist he had been painfully shy in the company of young women. After he left university he drifted back to his old school friends, many of whom were unemployed and involved in petty crime. But, he told the forensic psychiatrist, he was too anxious and law-abiding to get involved in the theft from cars and other crimes that his friends participated in.

He started doing odd jobs at clubs and dance halls, putting up posters and delivering leaflets to publicise their events. He became part of the group again. Myuran told the psychiatrist that it was through his old school friends that he first became involved in the drug trade. He was flattered the group accepted him; he felt safe and important in a way he had not done before. He knew the group's activities were illegal but had never really faced up to the potential consequences. By the time he did, it was too late.

Most of the Bali Nine decided to appeal the verdicts to the next court of appeal, the Denpasar High Court. For Myuran and Andrew there was little to lose. They were already on death row. But for the others the stakes were high.

Appeal courts in Indonesia can decrease or increase a sentence. They faced having their sentences upped to the death penalty. It was a chance they were willing to take. For Matthew Norman, Si Yi Chen and Tan Duc Thanh, the gamble paid off and the Denpasar High Court reduced their sentences to 20 years. It did the same for Renae Lawrence and Michael Czugaj. The judges found they had only been couriers, acting on the instructions of the masterminds. Inexplicably, Martin Stephens lost his appeal and the life sentence stood. Scott Rush had not appealed.

Within months the group appealed again, this time to Indonesia's highest court, the Supreme Court in Jakarta. The gamble was the same. Sentences could just as easily be increased.

For some, the news in September of 2006 was dreadful. Scott Rush, Matthew Norman, Si Yi Chen and Tan Duc Tanh Nguyen, all had their sentences increased to the death penalty. Michael Czugaj's 20 years was increased to life. Martin Stephens' term remained at life and Myuran and Andrew remained on death row. Renae Lawrence had not appealed and her sentence remained at 20 years.

The decisions were hard to explain. Three of the four mules had life and 20 years while Scott Rush got death. The traditional appeal process had been exhausted and all that was left was what is known as a judicial review to the Supreme Court, a review of the cases which would normally require new evidence to even get off the ground.

All nine were held in Kerobokan prison together. Renae Lawrence was in the women's block where she shared a testy friendship of sorts with Schapelle Corby. The other eight were in the men's section, all bunched together in what was known as the 'death tower' or 'super maximum security'. It was a group of cells together, located underneath an old water tower near the front entrance, and dubbed the death tower due to its previous occupants, the three Bali bombers, who had been sentenced to death for orchestrating the 2002 Bali nightclub bombings. The bombers – Amrozi, his older brother Mukhlas and Imam Samudra – had been held there from shortly before their trials in 2003 until October 2005, before they were moved to Nusakanbangan prison island, off the coast of Central Java ahead of their executions four years later.

The Bali Nine moved around in the different cells, depending on personal differences, of which there were many. The evidence given in court against Myuran and Andrew by some of the mules did not help relations. The blame game was on. Some blamed others for their sentences. Some blamed legal advice.

After the appeals Myuran slumped into depression. He was angry and down on the world all the time. He found little to smile about. He had a quick temper and a fist to match. Others found solace in the ready supply of drugs inside the jail, drowning their sorrows in a drug-induced haze day after day. The eight men fought and bickered amongst themselves constantly. Andrew was a much more jovial personality, always quick with a one-liner. The other prisoners thought he was funny. For Myuran and Andrew, something needed to change.

Melbourne barristers Lex Lasry QC and Julian McMahon, along with a group from Melbourne's legal fraternity, first got involved in Myuran and Andrew's case on a pro bono basis in 2006, about the time that the last Supreme Court appeal confirmed their death sentences. In December of the year before, the two men had been in Singapore when their client, Melbourne man Van Nguyen, was executed by hanging after being arrested with 396 grams of heroin. They had fought his case and against the death penalty for years. Now they were taking on another death penalty case.

Myuran and Andrew dispensed with their previous legal team and embraced the Melbourne lawyers. On board with them was respected Jakarta lawyer and human rights activist Todung Mulya Lubis. Julian had asked people in a number of countries who the best lawyer in Indonesia was and who would be willing to take on a case like Myuran's and Andrew's. All of them said Todung Mulya Lubis. Deciding to take on the case had not been an easy decision for the charming and affable Mulya, as he was known, who was well connected in Jakarta society. He knew it would not make him friends and would see him railing against those in powerful political circles. He had been there before – representing *Time* magazine in a defamation suit brought by the Suharto family. It took him a month to decide to take the Australians' case.

3.
FROM DRUGS TO JESUS

Everything has a price in jail. You want 1 kilogram of marijuana brought in? That's about Rp 3 million, or around $300. Heroin costs more: about Rp 5 million for a kilogram. That's not the cost of buying it. That's the cost of paying a jail guard to bring the drugs into the jail for you. At least, that's what it cost back in the early 2000s, when Matius Arif Mirdjaja was a drug dealer operating with impunity inside Kerobokan prison.

Arif, as everyone calls him, had a bright future. He studied law in Bali and got his degree. In 1997 and 1998 he was arrested for subversion for his involvement in the widespread student protests of the time calling for the ousting of President Suharto. Indonesia was in a period of upheaval, and its students had found their voice. Arif was jailed for three months for his first offence in Jakarta. The next year, in Bali, he got six months.

The drugs had started before then. He began using when he was a student on campus, about 1995 or 1996. He was studying philosophy, learning about revolution as he worked towards his law degree. Students were afraid of the regime, and selling drugs and running illegal lotteries were lucrative ways to finance the protest movement. In 1999 Arif found himself in East Timor, working for the United Nations during the region's historic independence referendum, in which the East Timorese voted overwhelmingly to separate from Indonesia.

Within a couple of years, though, Arif was back in jail for selling and using drugs: in 2002, 2004 and again in 2006. This time he decided to pay Rp 150 million for a light sentence. He shelled out another Rp 5 million for a doctor to testify in court that he was rehabilitated. In fact, he'd never met the doctor who testified on his behalf. Arif's case was not unusual. Everyone knew that was how it worked: if you had the money, justice was for sale.

During his 2006 term in Kerobokan prison, Arif met Andrew. They lived in different worlds, though, and he had little to do with the Australian. At the time Arif considered himself a businessman. He was making about $4000 a month selling drugs, both inside and outside the jail. He had seven people working for him on the outside. The guards would bring the heroin in for him, he would cut it into straws, and when he got an order Arif would tell his man where to drop the drugs. He would then instruct the buyer where it was: 'Walk five metres from the traffic lights and turn left . . .' When the buyer turned up, Arif's man would watch from nearby. If customers tried to claim the drugs weren't there, they were caught out.

Arif himself was using – heavily. It took nine straws of heroin a day to feed his own habit. Kerobokan was his safe haven: it was guarded 24 hours a day, there were no police inside, and with the guards paid off he was in no danger of being arrested. Generally, if a police raid was planned, they got ample notice of it beforehand to get rid of the gear.

Lizzie Love wasn't a woman to be messed with. She had started her working life as a schoolteacher at a migrant school in Australia and had been living in Bali since June 2003. Lizzie had a good knowledge of how things worked, and understood the Balinese culture. She first went to Kerobokan jail in 2007 with a group from the Bali International Women's Association, which had organised a dentist to see female prisoners. One of the first prisoners she met was Renae Lawrence. Lizzie asked what she could do to help.

Renae said she and the other sentenced prisoners were okay, but the new arrivals were sleeping on concrete and had little more than a sarong.

Lizzie asked Renae to count how many prisoners were sleeping like that. Later, she was out shopping for a single bed for her house. She saw a pile of mattresses. 'How much are they?' she asked the shopkeeper. The answer: Rp 150,000 each. 'I'll take

27 of them,' she said – the number Renae had reported back to her. The 27 mattresses were delivered to Lizzie's home. Next she priced pillows and blankets, before putting out a call to her network for donations to pay for it all.

When the mattresses arrived at the jail, the Australian prisoners helped bring them in. They showed Lizzie the jail medical clinic and the other facilities they had.

Lizzie walked beside Myuran. 'Don't get me wrong,' she told him, 'but I'm old, and I can't remember how to say your name.'

'Just call me Myu,' he replied.

She asked how to spell his name so she could google him.

'Oh, God, don't do that,' he warned her. 'They've said terrible things about me.'

Lizzie suggested that they make a deal, there and then. 'How about our relationship starts here, right now?'

Myuran was thinking aloud. 'You're just going to turn out like the rest,' he told her. 'You do a documentary about yourself and then leave. It's a bit like getting a divorce and nobody tells you why.'

Lizzie knew he was serious, and it got to her. She hadn't yet decided if she was going to commit to helping at the men's block, and she told Myuran that if she gave her word, then she would return. She continued helping out at the jail after that in the women's block. Every week she went in to help run cooking classes, reflexology, sewing and pattern-making classes.

Once he committed to their case, Julian McMahon sat down with Myuran and Andrew in jail. They verged on being cocky, not really understanding or grasping the reality of their situation.

Julian told them they had to look into themselves and face up to how stupid they had been. It was a tough love speech. They had to grow up and behave like men if they were going to cope in prison in a meaningful way. They had to prove themselves as worthy of some kind of mercy or re-sentence.

There was one conversation that struck a chord with Myuran. You have to choose the dark or the light in the way that you live, Julian told him. From 2006 to 2007 Julian had a series of similar conversations with both of them. At one stage he put a lot of pressure on Myuran to embrace the fact that he had the capacity and almost the standing to lead the community that he was in. He had to take positive and concrete steps and decisions to make the transition into being someone worthy of being a leader.

Julian and the other lawyers watched as Myu made those decisions. It wasn't just Julian. It wasn't his project alone. It was a group effort from a team of committed and passionate lawyers, who donated their time free of charge, to fight for Myuran and Andrew. Some of the other lawyers too were impressing on them the seriousness of their situation, in long and profound conversations.

For the first time since they had been arrested Myuran and Andrew were beginning to have a purpose. Changing the way they lived in Kerobokan wasn't easy. They were surrounded by the worst of humanity 24 hours a day. Only those who have been there know just how soul-destroying that can be when you have already been told by the state that your life is worth nothing.

The new legal team embarked on a bold action, lodging an appeal against the death penalty with Indonesia's new Constitutional Court, which then was still in its embryonic stages and finding its place in Indonesia's legal hierarchy. Lawyers for Scott Rush also filed the same appeal. Their argument was that the death penalty was in contravention of the right to life that was enshrined in the Indonesian Constitution. They pointed out that Indonesia had ratified the International Covenant on Civil and Political Rights (ICCPR), which states: 'Every human being has the inherent right to life. This right shall be protected by law. No one shall be arbitrarily deprived of his life.' The ICCPR did give leeway for capital punishment, for the most serious of crimes, particularly crimes of genocide. But Indonesia had yet to ratify the Second Optional Protocol that expressly forbids capital punishment. The legal team called a host of world-renowned experts to testify on the matter.

The Indonesian Attorney-General, in opposing the petition, argued that narcotics crimes were within the category of the most serious crime because narcotics threatened security and national stability, disturbed social and economic institutions, and narcotics crime indirectly caused the death of its victims. The National Narcotics Board argued before the court that narcotics were within the most serious category of crime. Narcotics criminals, they argued, vanished the right to life of their victims.

Myuran's and Andrew's legal team had their work cut out for them — and it was definitely going to take a strong team effort to fight for the lives of the two Australians. They needed the right people.

Solicitor Veronica Haccou, from north eastern Victoria, read an advertisement in a Law Institute of Victoria publication. It sought an Indonesian speaking Australian lawyer. She sent an email, offering herself. It was 28 May 2007. Born in Indonesia, Veronica had studied in Australia and stayed, establishing a life and career for herself. She was exactly what the team representing Myuran and Andrew wanted — a native Indonesian speaker who could navigate the Indonesian legal system and who could understand the intricacies of Indonesian society and the language. Veronica became an indispensable member of the legal team, sometimes working for 40 hours straight translating documents and providing legal counsel. She stayed in the background, at least publicly, shunning media attention. She was a private person and one whom Myuran and Andrew respected greatly and trusted implicitly. In the years that followed, when they spoke of her it was always with great respect and fondness.

Fellow solicitor Joel Blackwell had earlier worked closely with Julian on the case. He had lived in Indonesia as a teenager, spoke Indonesian and conversed with the jail guards using local slang, something they loved. But when he left private practice to work for the government, he had, for practical reasons, to leave the case. He hadn't wanted to, but Julian didn't want his future career prospects inhibited by his involvement. Lex Lasry left the team in October 2007 when he was appointed a judge on the Victorian Supreme Court. The core legal team also consisted of Melbourne silks Michael O'Connell SC (now a Victorian County Court Judge) and Peter Morrissey SC, and solicitors Alex Wilson and Megan Tittensor, barristers Scott Johns and Tony Trood. They worked as a collective on the major tasks. At least four or five others also assisted from time to time with particular issues. In Sydney, barristers Peter Strain and Christopher Ward SC also worked with the team, assisting with family liaison and international law. In addition, ten to 15 law students and young lawyers helped with translation, drafting documents and analysis.

It was 30 October 2007 when the Constitutional Court, with Chief Judge Jimly Asshiddiqie at the helm, convened to deliver its decision on the constitutionality of the death penalty. Death penalty opponents hoped against hope that the court would be brave and bold enough, in Indonesia's anti-abolitionist political environment, to rule for change. It didn't. In a six to three majority, the court ruled that the death penalty was constitutional.

It was a crushing blow to Myuran and Andrew and the legal team. But some tiny steps had been gained. The judgement suggested that the country's Criminal Code be amended so that death row prisoners, after a ten-year period of good behaviour, could have their death sentences commuted to life or 20 years in jail.

Judge Asshiddiqie would later reveal that he actually agreed with the minority, to abolish the death penalty for drug crime, but as the Chief Judge had sided with the majority to give the judgment legitimacy; he saw that as the role of the chief. Had he gone the other way the decision would have been five to four and things may have been very different in the death penalty debate. Change was so close but so far away.

As the legal team regrouped, in the face of the Constitutional Court defeat, to work on the next strategy, Matthew Norman, Si Yi Chen and Tan Duc Thanh Nguyen got a new lawyer and launched a judicial review with the Supreme Court in Jakarta.

In contrast to their earlier cases, when they had denied any role in the Bali Nine, they now accepted responsibility, admitted their guilt and apologised, saying they were turning their lives around. The Supreme Court accepted their appeal and their death penalties were reduced to life in jail. They could breathe again. Scott Rush also apologised and received the same good news and had his sentence reduced to life in jail.

With Julian's words, that they needed to look into themselves and face up to reality, ringing in their ears, Myuran and Andrew set about trying to make some changes. It wasn't easy.

Myuran knew he needed a purpose. He wasn't getting out of jail anytime soon – nor did he deserve to – but he felt compelled to do something with his time. He was waking up angry every day. There was nothing to do and he was always in a shitty mood. It was the same thing all the time, day after day, week after week. Sitting around the cells, waiting – but not knowing what for. For the lunchtime rollcall . . . for the day to end . . . for the night-time lock-up. Watching other prisoners shoot up or smoke drugs, lying around with glazed eyes and dull expressions, doing nothing but seeking out money to buy the next hit. Or trying to avoid the gangs when they owed money and couldn't pay.

Myuran felt directionless. There were only so many books you could read before you needed something more to fill the hours. And he was so grumpy. He said so himself. So did others. It was time to seize control of his life and shake off the heavy cloud that hung over him.

On a more practical level, Myuran and Andrew both had to change their lives if they were to have any chance of winning a reprieve. They needed something positive to tell the court when they applied for a judicial review of their cases.

The Melbourne legal team started the change when they donated 13 computers to the jail so Myuran and Andrew could set up and run computer courses for inmates. The jail's governor, Siswanto, was impressed, and he encouraged the rehabilitation courses proposed by the two Australians. When the idea to run the courses was first raised, he had invited Myuran and Andrew to see him straightaway. Previous governors would have made them jump through hoops to even arrange a meeting.

But Siswanto was all for the idea – he loved it. A Christian and a pastor himself, he was just the kind of jail governor the Australians needed in order to begin their active rehabilitation. And over time Siswanto became one of their biggest supporters.

A computer teacher from outside was brought in two days a week, and all those enrolled got a certificate at the end of the course. Myuran already understood some of the computer programs, so he helped the teacher, as well as throwing himself into getting English and first-aid courses established, again with certification. Andrew and Matthew Norman also helped out with teaching the courses. The idea was that the skills the prisoners learned would help them find work when they were released, breaking the cycle of crime and jail. They would have hope.

Indonesian prisoner Lukman Agus had done two stints in jail. His third, for possessing 19 ecstasy tablets, was harsh – six years. He tried to commit suicide by injecting himself with bleach. But he missed the vein and didn't die.

Lukman turned out to be another of the catalysts that got Myuran out of his malaise.

Lukman knew how to paint and had started working with coffee and egg. He showed Myuran some of his designs, and Myuran could see he had real talent. He was inspired: they could turn this into something. Besides, Myuran was deeply affected by Lukman's bid to kill himself. It was such a waste. The man had a family, children who needed him. People like Lukman needed help and nurturing – they needed a purpose. They also needed skills to help them once they were released from jail.

Myuran was thrilled at the prospect of helping Lukman to paint. It was March 2010 and things were finally looking up. I went into the jail for several days running, invited inside by Siswanto. Nothing had been off limits as I interviewed the Bali Nine, saw inside their cells and watched the computer and English classes in action. Myuran's eyes danced with excitement as he talked about Lukman, about how he wanted to start an art space at the jail where prisoners could come to paint and how much he himself had changed. He was desperate to start a program, making and screen-printing T-shirts. They already had some sewing machines but they needed a screen-printing machine. Myuran's plan was to sell some of Lukman's coffee and egg paintings to help fund the screen-printing business.

The next day, when I went back to see him, Myuran was happy to tell me he had sold some of the paintings to a former art gallery owner who was due out of jail shortly. It was all coming together. He also needed funds to run a second and third phase of a first aid course for guards and prisoners. After the first phase of the course it paid off. The life of a Dutch prisoner, who had a seizure in the middle of the night, was saved because guards and other prisoners knew what to do. Without that knowledge he would certainly have died. Myuran felt like there weren't enough hours in the day. At night, in his cell, he sketched designs for the T-shirts he wanted to print and thought of new projects.

Andrew too was becoming more focused. He had started doing a bachelors degree in theology and a certificate in ministry.

He had recently got a High Distinction for an assigment. He laughed, telling me that back in high school he couldn't get an HD even if he cheated. Andrew said he hadn't been the smartest chap in life but he couldn't change the past. 'I'm not going to blame anybody. I'm not going to blame anybody but myself,' he said. 'I'm not going to turn around and say because I have been sentenced to death everybody should feel sorry for me, give the sob story. I'm not going to cry, I'm not going to complain. I get along with life, that's it you know, I'm not going to let it stop me from whatever I need to do.' He talked, sitting at his desk in the tower block as he read and studied a Bible. His faith was what sustained him the most.

'When you look outside, what do you see?' Sandy Elliott wanted to know.

The answer was simple: a wall, barbed wire. Myuran didn't need to visualise too much. These things surrounded him every day.

'But you don't have to paint the wall exactly like the wall,' Sandy prompted. 'What colour is the wall? What about the barbed wire?'

'The wire is like blood,' he said. 'That's how I visualise it.'

So that's how he started painting it. Fiery-red barbed wire and a drab wall. It was Myuran's first ever attempt at painting. It was mid-2010 and not long after he first met Sandy.

A visual arts teacher from Brisbane, she had taken long-service leave to spend a year in Bali. She found herself helping the women of the 'Lipstick Brigade' taking mattresses into the prison after Lizzie Love's buying spree. When she was in there that day, someone, knowing she was an art teacher, asked if she had seen the remarkable coffee and egg paintings being done by Lukman. Sandy decided to meet this Lukman, and Myuran, and see what they were about.

Myuran told her he really wanted to organise art classes. 'I'm an art teacher,' Sandy told him, and they went immediately to the jail governor's office to get permission for her to come in and teach. Siswanto was more than happy for it to happen, and Sandy put out a call to her friends for donations to get started. The response was overwhelming and soon they had enough money to buy a bulk lot of canvases and paints in June 2010. Together with a local gallery owner, who also helped out by translating, it was decided to get everyone to paint some works that could be exhibited and auctioned to make more money and keep the program going.

Several of the Bali Nine were keen, despite never having painted before. Andrew leapt into it with gusto, painting a series of works. One of them he called 'Andralia' – a play on his name and Australia. But Myuran was reluctant. He had never painted before, and was adamant that he was doing this for the others. Sandy encouraged him: now the others were painting, he should too. Just a few for the auction. By this time she was teaching art twice a week inside the jail.

At Sandy's urging, Myuran finally picked up a paintbrush. Art was a form of escape, she told him. When he decided to paint the wall and the barbed wire, Sandy encouraged him to respond to his subject matter. What colour should he use? What did they represent for him? What did he feel when he gazed at it? But the result was too bleak – too depressing. He painted over it after Sandy left that day.

When Sandy returned for the next class, she wanted to know what had happened to the painting of the wall. 'It's underneath,' Myuran said. He didn't want to be depressed. He wanted to paint something nice. Flowers.

Sandy was surprised, and suspected he was covering up his feelings by taking an easier option.

Myuran spent hours on a painting of jasmine flowers. But he was always coy about its significance. The first time I met him, before the auction, he showed me the jasmine painting and told me that its meaning was a secret. The flower had a meaning, he revealed; it was more than just a flower. It symbolised something, and the purple he used was also significant. But it was his secret. He laughed shyly at my suggestion that it was something to do with a woman.

The truth was that Myuran had looked after a jasmine plant once, at the jail, but it died and he'd never smelt jasmine since. That jasmine flower was Myuran's first ever artwork. Well, the first artwork he shared with the world. The wall and barbed wire had been first, but he had painted the jasmine flower over the top of that one. Raji still has the jasmine painting at home. Sandy still has a photograph of Myuran painting the wall.

After Sandy left, in 2010, Myuran approached Lizzie Love and asked if she would come in and do a beginner's art class. Lizzie had already been thinking about Myuran and her vow to him that if she committed to helping him she would be there for the long haul. Lizzie, a self-taught artist, began researching how to teach beginner art to others. She had been a maths and science teacher in a previous life and knew how to teach.

Lizzie started a beginner's course – how to mix paints, that kind of thing. Every participant got a box of art supplies and a folder. The first classes were held in the jail's small library. It was a huge success. Lizzie kept getting calls from Myuran, wanting more art boxes for more inmates who wanted to take part. But there was one steadfast rule: anyone with glazed eyes was not allowed. Every participant had to be drug-free. That was Myuran's rule and there was no bending it.

Myuran asked Lizzie to teach sketching and pencil portraits. He wanted people to get out of jail with a skill they had learned inside, but he knew many of them would never have the money to buy paints and canvases. Lizzie got permission to bring a camera into the jail so she could take a photo of each student, so they could see the beauty in their faces and paint it. Myuran attended every art class run by Lizzie. The classes were held every Friday afternoon in the jail's modest library. They started with 12 students and quickly grew to 30 as more and more inmates asked to join.

About six months after Lizzie started her classes the son of expatriate Dutch artist Nico Vrielink, who lived in Bali, was arrested and locked up in Kerobokan. Lizzie suggested to Nico that he come to the jail and teach art. He was a realist artist, and Myuran had been keen to find another artist to run classes for those who showed promise and graduated from Lizzie's classes.

By this time Myuran was hooked on art and was desperate to learn as much as possible. Lizzie also helped out by selling paintings from the art room to raise money to buy more paints and canvases. Myuran too attended every one of Nico's classes.

Myuran was arranging for more courses to be run. He was absolutely loving it. The joy sparkled in his eyes as he explained all the projects already up and running and those he planned for the future. He spoke of how many people were being helped. He could barely stand still, so excited was he to show off the artworks and programs. And he was not angry anymore. He was starting to feel happy. He was finding purpose in his life, and he felt like he was becoming a better person.

He started graphic design classes, with the plan to set up a T-shirt screen-printing business; he would call it Kingpin Clothing, a tongue-in-cheek reference to the name given to him by police after he was arrested. Police had claimed Myuran was the 'kingpin' of the Bali Nine, and Andrew the 'godfather'. The monikers stuck for a long time.

Myuran arranged for a T-shirt printing machine to be brought in. He was dismayed when it didn't work properly, and frustrated to realise he had been ripped off. But he didn't stop forging ahead. In fact, being ripped off inspired Myuran to ensure it never happened again. His error was partially due to his inadequate understanding of the Indonesian language. Never one to do things by halves, Myuran arranged for a tutor to come to the jail and teach him Indonesian. He wanted to know every aspect of the language, from street-level slang to the formal Indonesian used in courts and government circles. He had been initially slow to learn the language, in the early days when the cloud of depression hung over him. But with the tutor he soon became proficient.

Before he was arrested and put in Kerobokan prison, Myuran didn't know any drug addicts. Then he met plenty. He saw them shooting up. He saw them overdosing. He saw them almost dying, and helped save their lives. He saw the depths to which they would sink to get their next hit. He saw three or four men kill themselves. Some had run up drug debts, and to escape them they opted to suicide.

Once, when an inmate drank mosquito repellent in a bid to end his life, Myuran rushed to his aid, clearing his mouth and airways. They managed to resuscitate him. Then there was the time he saw an inmate tortured to death by 13 prisoners. He had ripped off someone on the outside, and a family member of the aggrieved happened to be in jail – and in the same cell.

Andrew remembered that day well: it was his birthday. He woke up and saw the body lying in front of his cell. 'What's wrong with him?' he asked.

'He's dead.'

Andrew, too, had seen countless people die around him – from AIDS, drugs, suicide.

Myuran had tried cannabis as a young man but hadn't liked it. As an asthma sufferer, he didn't like smoking tobacco. He tried cocaine back then but didn't enjoy that either. And he had never injected anything. Andrew, on the other hand, had been a chronic cannabis user before his arrest. Afterwards, he became drug-free for the first time since he was 16 years old.

Both men admitted they had never thought much about the effects of the heroin they were bringing to Australia, or about the countless families who would be affected. Back then it wasn't relevant to them. They lived for themselves: they were only concerned with the here and now, with the payday they'd have at the end of a successful drug run. The rest wasn't of interest to them.

But being in jail, with a death sentence hanging over their heads, was the ultimate wake-up call. If things didn't change, they stood no chance of mercy. So in 2010, with the projects and programs all underway – with Andrew studying to be a pastor, with the art room going so well, and teachers from the outside coming in regularly to run programs – it was time for

Myuran and Andrew to launch their last court appeal, known as a judicial review. The plan was to show the court that they were rehabilitated, that they were remorseful and had become a force for good within Kerobokan prison.

For the first time since their 2005 arrests, Myuran and Andrew were going to admit their guilt publicly. It was a big step. From the night of their arrests, through their police interrogations and their trials, both had steadfastly claimed innocence. Unlike the seven couriers, who were caught with the drugs either strapped to them or in their possession, neither Myuran nor Andrew had been caught with any drugs. Both had prepared statements they wanted to read to the court. By now they were fluent in Indonesian. It was a good move, and the judges were impressed by their language skills.

Five years earlier, Myuran had not been willing to admit his guilt. Now he launched into a heartfelt plea for his life. It was the first time he had spoken in public like this since he was a boy at school. He was a different person now, though, and he realised how many people his drug dealing had hurt along the way: his mother, his family and the families of many drug addicts.

> I know that I cannot take back the wrong I have done, but I am now leading a life which helps other people. Since I was arrested I have had plenty of time to think about the error of my ways, and with the support of Almighty God I have tried to change the way I behave, to help others and to lead a generous and not a selfish life. For this reason I respectfully

ask the court to consider that my punishment should be imprisonment and not execution . . .

I cannot say enough how truly and deeply sorry I am for what I have done. It was only after being in prison for several years that I realised that I must make up for what I have done. I also want to say publicly that I truly feel ashamed about how disrespectful I was in court in 2005. I was stupid and thoughtless enough to listen to bad advice, and as a result I deserved to be treated harshly at that time. I cannot make up for all the things that I have done. But with the support of Almighty God I have learnt to change my behaviour and I now spend my time working on projects to help other prisoners, including helping to set up projects that benefit them. One of those projects that I am most proud of is the computer course that I set up.

Myuran listed the courses that were now running at the jail, and spoke of his pride in the first 20 students who had graduated from the computer course. Setting up these courses was the best achievement of his life, he said. And he meant it.

Andrew, too, was now at the mercy of the court.

Your Honours, when I was first arrested in 2005 I stupidly thought I knew everything, and in my previous trials, on the advice of my old lawyers, I pleaded my innocence. I stupidly thought I could walk out of here despite the crime I committed. However, I now know much better and it feels good to be able to speak the truth, to apologise and to ask for the forgiveness of Your Honours.

I also want to apologise for my behaviour in 2005 when I was in front of this honourable court. At that time I did not have the proper respect for the court. However, I have learned a lot about myself and about Indonesian society during the last five years since then, and I feel very embarrassed about my behaviour.

I know that I did some stupid things when I was younger, and I know that I can't change my past but I have genuinely changed my behaviour and I really want to focus on what I can do, now and in the future. I understand much better now the devastating effect that drugs can have on people and their families, and God has shown me that a person who has done bad things in the past can make amends once they can accept responsibility for their actions.

Andrew told the court about the jail programs and how he was studying theology and a ministry certificate, and how he tried to support prisoners in need of help.

I am doing these things to help others because I believe I have a purpose in life, not just to be held in prison and then executed. Once again, I want to say how deeply sorry I am for what I did in the past. I accept that I deserve to be punished for my crime but I beg the court not to be executed.

I feel that I am still young. I am only 26 years old. One day, when I have served my full sentence, I hope to have a family and become a minister or a counsellor so that I can work with young people to prevent them from making the same mistakes as me. I hope that the honourable court will give me that chance.

The Australians' Jakarta-based lawyer, Todung Mulya Lubis, said he found their statements both touching and emotional. He was especially impressed by the way both spoke so eloquently in Indonesian, a mark of respect. Julian McMahon said it had been a big day in terms of everything that had happened in the previous four years. Myuran and Andrew had done what they could. They had finally taken responsibility for their actions.

When the court resumed two weeks later, it was to take evidence from an unlikely character witness – the governor of the Kerobokan prison, Siswanto. He had agreed to testify on behalf of both Myuran and Andrew. This was a remarkable development; normally Indonesians in positions of authority and power within the bureaucracy – prison governors, guards, the police and their ilk – would never speak out against government policy. Their job is to carry out government policy without questioning it, particularly in a public forum such as a courtroom.

The gentle and clever Siswanto had been so accessible to Myuran and Andrew when they sought his permission to set up their various programs. He had fostered their enthusiasm and supported them, and had welcomed a succession of teachers into the jail. The testimony he gave at their judicial review was from the heart. He gave glowing reports about both men, telling of the good they were doing for the jail community. It was the first time that Siswanto had testified on behalf of any prisoner.

The governor made plain his own personal objection to the death penalty, and questioned why Myuran and Andrew could not be forgiven. The death penalty was too harsh for them, he said. If the pair were executed he would feel very sorry, because only God had the right to take someone's life. As an individual, Siswanto recognised he could not challenge Indonesia's use of the death penalty, but his heart asked, 'Can't they be forgiven? God is merciful.'

His words struck a chord. So they could listen to his evidence, Myuran and Andrew had been allowed to sit in the court's public gallery area like free men; such was the trust they had built up with their guards. (Later, after being transferred away from Kerobokan prison, Siswanto died in a motorbike accident. He had touched a lot of people's lives, and many prisoners were upset at his passing.)

Also testifying that day was a former Indonesian Supreme Court judge, Yahya Harahap. He spoke about a key plank of the duo's defence in this new hearing: that the original court had made an error by convicting Myuran and Andrew of exporting heroin from Bali. For the heroin to have been exported, he said, it had to have left the airport's departure lounge and be taken onto the plane, passing the last customs check. In this case, of course, it hadn't, as some of the Bali Nine were arrested in the airport departure area, and others at a hotel.

There was also the fact that a long-running revision of Indonesia's Criminal Code contained an important clause which had also been recommended by the Constitutional Court: that, after ten years of good behaviour, a death sentence could be commuted to life or 20 years in jail. But this revision was still only at draft stage, and was subject to a great deal of political argument at the time.

The Australians' chances of prevailing in the judicial review increased substantially a few months later, when the three judges in Bali who had heard the evidence wrote a report and recommendation to the Supreme Court in Jakarta. It is the Supreme Court, the highest court in Indonesia, which determines the outcomes of judicial reviews. But it does not hear the applications. A lower court, the District Court, actually hears the evidence and submissions; it then sends all the documents, along with its own summation, to the Supreme Court for determination.

In a six-point written conclusion, the three Denpasar District Court judges argued that the right to life was a fundamental, lasting and universal human right that could not be ignored, reduced or taken away. The death penalty must be used only selectively. The judges pointed out that Indonesia had, in 2006, ratified the International Covenant on Civil and Political Rights, which stated that the death penalty should only be used for the most serious crimes. However, Indonesia had not yet ratified the second, optional protocol, which expressly forbade capital punishment.

In mid 2011, almost a year after Myuran and Andrew had first made their judicial review application, the Supreme Court returned with its decision: they had lost. The court found no errors in the original judgements and no reason to reduce the men's death sentence.

It was a crushing blow for Myuran and Andrew, their lawyers and their families. There was only one option left: a plea for clemency to President Susilo Bambang Yudhoyono, a man not usually minded to show clemency.

4.
LOVE YOUR ENEMY

In 2011 Matius Arif Mirdjaja got another one-year sentence, this time for robbery. Back in Kerobokan prison, he knew something needed to change. After seeing what he thought was a ghost, he was introduced to Andrew; another prisoner thought the Australian might be able to help Arif get rid of his vision. Andrew told him it was not a ghost – it was Jesus.

Arif railed against him, accusing Andrew of idolising a statue of Jesus. Andrew suggested to Arif that he should start fasting in a bid to rid himself of drugs. And stop selling them. For three days Arif was weak, drinking water but taking nothing else. When Andrew finally visited him, his assessment was blunt: 'You look like a dead dog.'

Arif went without drugs for a week. During previous withdrawals, he felt like he had been hit by a truck. This time was different. Andrew asked him to pray and give thanks to Jesus.

Andrew read to him from the Bible – the verse about Peter walking on water. 'You can do miracles, Arif, when you focus on Jesus,' Andrew told him. 'If you don't, you will sink.'

Nobody could believe Arif had quit drugs. Some of the jail gangsters – the gang leaders who ruled the place with violence – came to him, suspicious. 'You're not getting it from other sources, are you?' They didn't want to be undercut. That would mean trouble. When word spread that Arif really was drug-free and had given up the trade, others came to him. They wanted to quit as well. So Andrew convened a meeting in the jail church.

He told the gathered inmates that he would help them, but he had one condition. 'You have to tell the truth. I'm not asking you to quit suddenly but you have to tell me the truth. How many drugs are you taking every day? Where are you hanging out, and who with?' These things mattered, Andrew said, so they could identify a pattern of consumption. He also wanted to know where the users were when they didn't take drugs. Some said they were sleeping in the church. So a decision was made that the group would gather together every day, there in the church. It was a place they didn't associate with drugs.

Andrew knew that if these men were to conquer the temptation of drugs, they needed activities. He loved cooking, a passion instilled in him from his parents' years of running their Chinese restaurant. He had always enjoyed mixing spices and the aroma of great food. Now he decided to start cooking so the men could share food together. He spent hours cleaning fish and mixing spices, and they all cooked it together and ate together. No one used drugs while they were cooking and eating.

After a while, Andrew started a formal cooking class, for which inmates could receive certification. And the jail authorities agreed to build them a proper kitchen.

By this time Arif was moving towards Christianity. He planned to be baptised in jail, but he couldn't completely leave his old ways behind. He knew that gangs ran the jail, and so decided to start a Christian gang.

Andrew was angry. According to the Bible, he told Arif, anyone who lived by the sword would die by the sword.

'So what should we do?' Arif wanted to know.

'Love your enemy,' Andrew told him.

'That's rubbish,' Arif shot back.

Andrew organised a meeting in the church, and told everyone to love one another, not attack one another. And that was how the church cell groups started. With Andrew at the helm, they helped many people.

Jason was a prisoner whom the gangs were about to bash because of an unpaid debt. Arif got everyone ready at the church. The Christians would fight the gangs. Andrew wanted to know what was going on. 'There is no need for violence,' he said. He walked calmly to the block where Jason was about to receive the gang's punishment. Smiling, Andrew said he was picking up Jason to take him to worship. He never got bashed up.

In this way, Andrew became like a guardian angel for his fellow inmates.

By mid-2012 Myuran knew he could get a lot of artists to come to Kerobokan to teach the prisoners. But he wanted someone who really cared – and who would care especially for the female prisoners. Myuran and Andrew cared deeply for the female prisoners, whose opportunities in jail were far more limited than the men.

Tina Bailey was an American pastor who had lived in Bali since 1997. She was not a traditional art teacher. She liked to be with people on their journey, and watch them grow and learn to believe in themselves. Myuran liked that. It was what he wanted too. So Tina agreed to come in once a week, from 9.30 a.m. to midday.

Next Myuran asked if she would consider running a dance class for the female prisoners. She agreed.

Like Lizzie, Tina had googled Myuran to find out more about him.

'What did you read?' he asked tentatively.

After reading about how Myuran had guarded the prison officers' weapons during a recent jail riot, Tina thought he must have been a decent guy. Myuran insisted it wasn't a big deal. He just hadn't wanted to get shot – and if the prisoners had got their hands on the armoury it would have been a bloodbath. Nevertheless, Tina was impressed, and from that moment on she became one of his closest confidantes and teachers.

Around the same time American yoga teacher Denise Payne also started going into the jail, teaching yoga. Myuran loved it and practised regularly with her.

It was in February 2012 that gang violence at the jail had spilled over into rioting. The angry prisoners easily overpowered the handful of guards on duty, using anything they could find as weapons. When they set fire to the administrative block, Andrew and Myuran made a decision to act.

They could not allow the rioting gangs to get into the jail's armoury; that would mean weapons in dangerous hands, and certain bloodshed. The women's block, locked separately to the men's, was so far unharmed, but if anyone got their hands on the keys to it, things could turn very ugly indeed. The rioters had rape on their minds.

The two Australians, along with an Iranian prisoner called Moshen, who adored Myuran, got iron bars and guarded the armoury, stopping the rioters from getting anywhere near the weapons held inside.

Later, Andrew was over at the women's block, standing guard to ensure that the rioters could get nowhere near the female prisoners. Andrew and Arif also stopped the rioters from burning down the jail's cafeteria, which was about 50 metres from the women's block.

By now the police riot squad was shooting at the prisoners who were closest to the front door. Four prisoners were shot and wounded. All the jail guards had retreated into the lobby area of the prison. When a police officer came in, past the lobby, with a megaphone, urging the prisoners to calm down, Arif suggested they take him captive; if things got too hairy they could always shoot him. The officer he had in mind was crying by this stage.

Myuran was appalled. How could a man who had repented and found Christianity want to kill a policeman?

Myuran's demeanour shocked Arif back to reality. His suggestion to take a policeman hostage and then shoot him was a throwback to his criminal past.

'Release him,' Myuran demanded.

From that moment, Arif's relationship with Myuran was restored. He thanked him.

By now the electricity in the jail had been shut off, and there was no food or water. Andrew and Myuran contacted Lizzie Love. She called around all her contacts – restaurants, pizza joints and the like – and was able to collect leftover food from the previous day. She brought it to the prison, forcing her way through the throngs of heavily armed police and army. She wore her jail ID pass around her neck; nobody stopped her. Perhaps they thought she was a harmless granny.

On the second night of rioting, Myuran and Andrew were instrumental in getting the prisoners to negotiate, which ultimately ended the riots. Just as police were about to storm the prison, Myuran called Lizzie, who was outside. 'Stop,' he said. 'They will negotiate.'

Thanks to Myuran and Andrew a bloodbath was averted.

Later in 2012 Christie Buckingham and her husband, Rob, both pastors from Melbourne's Bayside Church, began visiting the jail and met Myuran and Andrew.

Christie's old friend, Gail Dwije, with whom she had gone through Bible college, was now living in Bali, a pastor at C3 church and married to a Balinese man. Their Arms of Love foundation worked with the jail, conducting church services inside. Andrew had recently been baptised. He was now studying theology, with a view to becoming an ordained minister. Christie and Rob were in Bali running a women's and men's ministry conference, and Andrew heard about it. He asked Gail to see if they would like to visit the jail, and they agreed.

By this time, Arif had been released from jail, and he returned with the Buckinghams and Gail. Together they met Andrew and Myuran, and visited the workshop to have a look at the various projects.

Andrew told them that he now felt freer inside Kerobokan than he did on the outside. When he felt down, he said, instead of telling God how big his problems were, he told his problems how big God is. Christie and Rob were in no doubt that Andrew was a changed man. As they prepared to leave the prison that day, they told both Andrew and Myuran to let them know if there was anything they could do for them.

Within two weeks Christie had received a big list from each of them. Andrew's requests were for the church and kitchen. Myuran's related to art supplies and computers. The Arms of Love foundation helped organise what they needed – six more computers – and paid for English and computer teachers. Next they brought in 150 kilograms of men's clothing, and 1000 hygiene packs for the prisoners.

Myuran had always shaved his head; Raji regularly had to buy him the shaving gear he needed. That prompted another idea. One of the prisoners had been a hairdresser; perhaps they could open a barber shop inside the jail, and at the same time teach others how to cut hair?

Then there was an idea for a bakery, so prisoners could serve an apprenticeship and become bakers. Chinthu investigated how they might source a bakery oven, getting costings and looking for places to set up a shop.

There were many funny times as Chinthu did absolutely everything he could to help his big brother. Once he sourced mannequins that could model Myuran's Kingpin T-shirts for a catalogue. People watched, puzzled and amused, as Chinthu carried the two mannequins into his hotel room, and then the next day into the jail. Tourists bought a lot of odd stuff in Bali, but what on earth did a grown man want with two mannequins? He couldn't help but laugh.

Andrew, meanwhile, came up with a scheme to breed ducks in the jail. He received permission from the governor, set up a pen and had some ducks brought in. All that they needed now was for them to start breeding. But nothing happened – the ducks just wouldn't breed, or couldn't for some reason. Andrew complained to Christie Buckingham, who was helping with the project. 'I've done everything and I just can't get them to have babies,' he said, stumped.

Christie was amused. 'They won't breed without a drake,' she told him.

Andrew put on the puzzled, quizzical look he used when he couldn't quite understand. 'What do you mean?'

Christie laughed and laughed. Andrew had totally overlooked the fact that he didn't have a male duck.

5.
RESPECT

In May 2012 the legal term launched its last throw of the dice: a clemency appeal to the President of Indonesia, Susilo Bambang Yudhoyono. This came at the same time that SBY, as he was known, controversially granted Schapelle Corby a five-year cut from her 20-year term.

Corby's clemency bid had been on humanitarian grounds: that she had suffered a mental illness since being incarcerated. One month earlier the Justice and Human Rights Ministry had recommended, as part of the clemency process, that her sentence be reduced by ten years. When SBY's decision was announced, it met with severe criticism, not least because the president had previously said he would not grant clemency to drug traffickers. His reversal seemed a good omen.

Much of the same material that was presented in the judicial review application was submitted now for clemency. Under the clemency system, all documents and legal decisions are submitted to the president's office, along with recommendations from the various government ministries. Raji Sukumaran wrote a letter to Yudhoyono, as did Chinthu. Michael Chan did likewise.

Raji had thought long and hard about what to say. She wanted SBY to know how she, as a mother, felt about the frightening prospect of losing her eldest child.

> I am the mother of Myuran Sukumaran, who is in Bali Kerobokan Prison sentenced to death, and I am writing to you to beg you to spare my son's life. I have been living for seven long years with the knowledge that my son might be executed because of a stupid mistake that he had made. I go to sleep thinking about it and I wake up in the middle of the night thinking about it. I have not been able to sleep properly since he was given the death penalty. I cannot really explain what this feels like but I have this incredible pain in my chest all the time. It is an unbearable fear and sadness – a feeling of desperately wanting to help my son – but I am helpless to do anything.
>
> In order to cope I have to keep praying to God and tell myself that it is going to be all right. My son will be all right. Please, Mr President, let it be all right, give him a chance to make up for his mistakes. Forgive him and give him another chance to live. He has turned his life around: he has worked so hard to help other people since his arrest and will never look back.

My son was so young when he committed the crime for which he faces the death penalty. He has grown and matured in prison [while] awaiting his fate. He understands now fully the impact of the drug trade – the grief and harm it causes to victims and society as a whole – and he is deeply ashamed and remorseful for his part in it. He uses all his time and energy to help others – and uses his own experiences to counsel and caution others not to make the same mistakes he has.

My husband has been suffering with depression for most of Myuran's life. During the period when Myuran was arrested, his father was going through a lot of problems and was in and out of hospital. It was a burden on the family as he was unable to work. Now he is a little better and was able to make his first overseas trip to Bali in January this year to visit Myuran. The family try not to tell him too much about Myuran's situation as this will trigger his illness: he now suffers from Parkinson's and dementia.

My other two children have been affected terribly since Myuran has been given the death sentence. My daughter was just twenty years and my other son was twenty-two years; they have put their lives on hold to support their big brother. We struggle and have not been able to think about anything more than Myuran's situation. We travel to Indonesia as much as we can afford to in order to visit Myuran. Your country is a very welcoming and accepting one, but we always leave it with such a heavy heart. It is a sign of Myuran's inherent goodness that when the time comes for us to leave to go back to Australia, a time when he feels extremely sad, he tries to make it easier for us to leave.

Of course Myuran was sad and confused when he was first arrested. But after a little while the real Myu, the son that I know and love, began to emerge. In the past seven years I have seen my son grow as a human being inside the walls of Kerobokan prison, and I thank your country for that. I am not sure that he would have been allowed the same opportunities in an Australian prison or in any other countries.

Myuran thinks very little of his own needs anymore – his own needs are met by making life better for others. He has helped so many other prisoners over the past seven years. He has been a driving force behind making Kerobokan a model prison, providing inmates with much better qualifications and prospects [for] when they are released into the community, allowing rehabilitation to truly work inside Kerobokan. He has set up a number of programs for others to better themselves.

Myuran started a program to teach his fellow prisoners different computer skills. He started this because he saw how it could help heal people and give them a chance to not make the mistakes that sent them to prison. Myuran has set up classes teaching basic Microsoft Office, including Microsoft Word, Excel and PowerPoint.

Myuran set up computer design classes that teach Adobe Photoshop, Illustrator and Corel Draw. This program provides real skills that can be used to get jobs. Myuran has found a love of art, painting and drawing. Myuran has set up a small business that uses screen-printing to make T-shirts, with the money coming back to the prison to help fund these classes. Myuran also wanted to teach language and life skills so he set up first aid and philosophy classes. Myuran has also organised auctions through the different teachers, with profits used to make the prison better and buy materials for the classes. I have become so proud of the work he has done to try to make up for his mistakes. He has learned a lot and has apologised for his crime.

Myuran has made a lot of friends in the prison by helping them and has a lot of respect for the prison guards, who see him as a role model for other prisoners. When I visit Myuran in the prison I meet other families who tell me how much their loved ones have benefited with Myuran's encouragement. This makes me so proud of my son, and I thank you for giving my son this opportunity in the Bali prison – I only hope and pray that you can find it in your heart to grant clemency and spare my son the death penalty.

The prison governor spoke very highly of Myuran's work with prisoners and how he has helped so many people. Pak Siswanto surprised everyone when he came into the court and asked the court to spare the life of Myuran because it would be a waste of his life. Myuran has so much to give. Please read the testimony of Pak Siswanto; it is here that I see how much my son has tried to fix the mistakes he has made and atone for his crime.

Myuran always wanted to help people. He was a blood donor and was involved in different charity work as a young man, [but] unfortunately he got off track and made a huge mistake, for which he pays a heavy price every day.

Myuran made his huge mistake by getting involved with the wrong people. As a parent you try hard to guide your children but sometimes they make a mistake. His mistake has changed his life. He was young and foolish. He was going through a tough time while his father was sick and things at home were getting too much for him to handle. He was trying to get away.

Myuran has done all in his power to make up for it since. His goal is to [set] a good example [for] all the young children who are in [a] similar situation. Myuran played a big role in helping to stop the recent riots. Myuran was able to control the inmates and play a key role in bringing peace to the prison. Myuran helped to get food and water to the women's block during the riot, and was able to do this because he was respected by everyone in the prison.

Now my son – who has truly turned his life around, learned quite a lot about life and wants to do good for everyone – has his life in your hands.

Myuran is my eldest son. He is everything to me and my other children. Even though he is not much older [than] his siblings, he took care of them during the time their father was sick. His plight is shattering for all concerned.

I'm humbly asking you with all my heart not to execute my son. It would be an excruciating loss and would destroy our family.

Thank you, Mr President, for reading this letter, and thank you for all the good things you have done to the Australians and other prisoners from other countries that are in similar situations.

May God bless you and your family.

Yours sincerely,

Raji Sukumaran

Michael Chan's letter to President Yudhoyono was equally heartfelt:

I am writing this letter on behalf of my family to beg that you grant my brother release from the death sentence to a lesser sentence. My name is Michael Richard Chan and I am Andrew Chan's older brother. Our parents, Ken and Helen Chan, had four children. Andrew was the youngest. We have two sisters.

My father, Ken, migrated to Australia in the 1940s so he could start a family and give us a better life. Our father and mother, Ken and Helen, have worked extremely hard, seven days a week, all their lives in order to ensure we had all the basic things in life such as a proper education, food and a roof over our heads.

We are an average family that live in Australia. We do not have many relatives here as my father is the only person left on his side of the family, and my mother's family mostly reside in Hong Kong. I currently work . . . for a retail company. My two younger sisters are good hard-working women. I am married and have been for the last four years. We don't have any children – it is hard for anyone in the family to consider the future when we face daily the prospect of my brother's death. My parents [are] find[ing] [it] very hard to cope. They blame themselves for Andrew's situation – when he was growing up they were at work a lot, he was the youngest and was perhaps allowed to get away with things, and not given the level of discipline and guidance given to the rest of us.

Andrew has been in Indonesia's Kerobokan prison since April 2005 for attempting to traffic drugs to Australia. The family try to visit Andrew as much as they can. My parents are elderly and are not able to travel much anymore. This is excruciating for them. My sisters and I visit every year. Since his imprisonment in Indonesia we have seen him grow from a young immature man with no aspiration in life to a mature fully grown adult. He has deepened his faith in God and is helping and inspiring others with his strength and tenacity for life. He has grown into a man that we are proud of.

We do not attempt to downplay the serious nature of what Andrew has done. My brother talks about the gravity of what he has done. He recognises the destruction that drugs cause to individuals and the community. He is ashamed that he ever got involved with them. He is ashamed that he has put all the people that care about him through this ordeal. He knows he has hurt his parents very deeply.

Andrew now knows what he wants in life. If by your grace he is given the opportunity to live, he will devote his life to helping the community. He wants to counsel and teach others, in particular young children, of the dangers of becoming involved with drugs. He is already doing all he can in this regard, counselling those around him and writing letters to others outside the prison.

He helps the Indonesians inside the prison by teaching them the English language and computer skills, enabling the prisoners to gain life skills and help them to look for employment, which will deter them from committing crimes and returning to prison.

Andrew has found his faith again inside Kerobokan prison. He attends every Sunday service. For the past several years Andrew has also studied theology via correspondence. This has been a life-changing experience for my brother. He aspires to be a pastor and to one day lead his own church or congregation. Andrew has run church services inside Kerobokan prison. He believes he can give something back to the people of Indonesia by encouraging the inmates to lead a better life and not to return to prison through prayer and faith in God.

We would like to thank your country for at least allowing us to see what kind of man our son and brother can be. Andrew is a real example of the successful rehabilitation programs that your country allows. The genuine nature of my brother's reformation was apparent when, at the last appeal, the governor of the prison, Pak Siswanto, came and urged the court to spare his life, because of the good work and influence he has now brought to the prison.

We ask that you please recognise that my brother was a young man who made a terrible decision, that he has truly repented for his crime, and that his life has great value and meaning to others.

We humbly beg of you to please allow Andrew to continue on his path to improve the lives of others. Please let him be a son and a brother to us.

Please let him live.

With respect,

Michael Chan

Chinthu, too, wrote a letter, describing how his father's illness had impacted the family, how his mother had worked two jobs to support the family, and how Myuran had taken the responsibility, as the eldest child, to look after them. Chinthu told how his little sister, Brintha, seemed to have put her own life on hold since Myuran's arrest. She too felt like a criminal, like no one would want to marry her, her life lived under the shadow of Myuran's crime and punishment. Chinthu wrote too about the good works Myuran had done while in jail.

He has lived in the shadow of death for so long now yet he has not crawled away and hidden, but has sought to turn his life around. Myuran has grown so much as a person. He has become wiser. When I see him spending time helping others, I see the real Myuran, the true Myuran. He is the big brother that I have always known. These actions are his truth today. I thank the prison and I thank Indonesia for allowing him the chance to turn his life around. I do not believe he would have been given such an opportunity in prison in Australia.

All I can do as a family man is ask you to consider all of this. I humbly ask you to grant him mercy and to permit him to live.

Yours sincerely,

Chinthu Sukumaran

With the clemency appeal lodged, there was nothing to do except wait and pray that President Yudhoyono would reply with a favourable answer. For a year nothing happened – nothing at all.

It was in late 2012 that a woman named Mary Farrow sent a Facebook message to the renowned Australian artist Ben Quilty. Mary had joined the campaign to save Myuran and Andrew after meeting Julian through a separate campaign in Victoria, and soon she was visiting Kerobokan jail. She threw herself into helping Myuran and Andrew with their various projects, and was particularly passionate about Myuran's artistic journey.

Ben replied the very next day. He vowed to help, and in December 2012 they were walking through the prison doors in Bali to meet Myuran. Ben was amazed they had got in so quickly, with so little security checking; they could easily have brought in contraband, he commented. 'There's already guns and knives in here,' Myuran said, laughing.

Myuran was stunned and delighted when Ben agreed to mentor him in his development as an artist. According to Myuran, when Ben first came to the jail he 'blew my mind', and it was clear that after Ben's arrival his painting style changed. Being in jail was a gift for a painter, he joked. The experiences and the emotions were so raw; you didn't need to look far to find inspiration.

In late 2013 something disastrous happened. It was revealed that Australian intelligence had been tapping the phones of Yudhoyono and his inner circle back in 2009. Perhaps most galling to many Indonesians, and to SBY himself, was the revelation that the phone of his wife, Kristiani Herawati, known nationally as Ibu Ani, was among those being tapped.

The president was furious, and Indonesians everywhere reacted angrily. It was one thing to spy on the leader, but to be spying on his family was another matter. In Indonesian culture family is all-important, and women are revered in households.

A diplomatic row erupted. Amid claims that Australia was treating Indonesia like its enemy, Yudhoyono recalled his government's ambassador from Canberra. Calls for Australia's prime minister, Tony Abbott, to apologise went unheeded. Abbott claimed that Australia should not have to apologise for reasonable intelligence-gathering activities.

It was not until almost a year later, in August 2014, that the issue was finally put to bed. Indonesia and Australia signed a code of conduct on intelligence cooperation, and Australia pledged not to use its spy agencies in ways that could harm Indonesian interests. By this time Yudhoyono's second term as president was coming to an end; he was not eligible to stand again, and in July of that year Joko Widodo was elected to replace him. Widodo was sworn in on 20 October 2014.

The Sukumaran and Chan clemency pleas were still languishing somewhere in the president's office. What impact the spying scandal had on Yudhoyono's intentions to grant them is unknown. He may not have intended to deal with them before leaving office. He has never spoken publicly on the matter.

6.

THE PASTOR AND THE PAINTER

Myuran wrapped the cord around his neck. In the dark, alone in his cell, he wanted to know what it felt like, what the sensation would be if he decided to end his own life. He wasn't planning to do it then and there. But he often wondered, if it came to it and the execution was imminent, whether it would be better to do it himself rather than get lined up, tied up and shot. Might it be better to go on his own terms, rather than be paraded around like a circus animal in the final hours and minutes? Maybe. His family would be spared the trauma of those final 72 hours.

This was years ago, after he was first sentenced and lost his initial appeals, and before he chose to lift the fog of depression and make something of his life. He never seriously contemplated it but he did think about it.

Being on death row, for Myuran, felt like having a gun held permanently at the side of his head, and not knowing when it would go off. Or walking on a sheet of glass day in and day out, never knowing when it would crack and he would fall through. Never knowing how long he could keep walking on it.

Andrew felt like he was playing Russian roulette, and the gun had already gone off five times. He was still alive, but next time he wouldn't be. He, too, had thought about suicide, in the very beginning. But that was a long time ago, before he and Myuran had made the conscious decision to own up to their crime and start leading meaningful lives.

Andrew often found himself counselling others out of suicide. Like when British woman Lindsay Sandiford was, in a shock decision, sentenced to death in 2013 for smuggling 4.8 kilograms of cocaine from Bangkok to Bali. The prosecutors had requested only a 15-year sentence; when the judges announced the death penalty everyone in court was stunned. Her co-accused received far lesser sentences.

The jail governor asked Andrew to go and talk to Lindsay when she came back from court, to calm her down. She was in a state of shock and panic. She was depressed. Andrew told her it was a process – to remember that God's strength and her family would hold her together. 'Your family is your number one priority,' he said. 'By killing yourself it will only sadden them more.' Lindsay was one of many prisoners Andrew counselled and prayed with in this way. (At the time of publication, Lindsay Sandiford is still on death row.)

Back then, in 2013, Andrew believed that if he hadn't got caught when he did, he would probably still be involved in drugs.

Or dead. It was the lure of the easy money that had attracted him to it in the first place. He hadn't thought about the consequences. He'd felt invincible. Back then he believed the odds of getting caught were two in ten. And he was only thinking about himself.

He said he didn't blame the Australian Federal Police, whose controversial tip-off in 2005 led the Indonesian police to intercept the nine Australians. Andrew was clear: he had made his own choices and had no one but himself to blame. He felt responsible for some of the other nine, who may never have been involved had he not brought them into it. While he had never coerced any of them, he said, he nonetheless felt some responsibility. To those he believed he owed an apology, he had apologised long ago.

Before being arrested, Myuran didn't really have a life plan. The future seemed a long way away. He didn't really have any aspirations either. Perhaps a car. But after he went to jail he realised that a car wasn't even that important. Family and good friends were precious. The money he would have made from the drug run could never compare to the suffering and strain that was bearing down on his family. When he committed the crime, Myuran had been young. He saw the money he was to be paid as a lot. Reflecting on his life, Myuran knew that if he had stuck at one of his early jobs he would likely have ended up as a manager and been earning good money. But youth meant he wanted everything instantly. He had been so short-sighted. Eight years in prison had taught him one thing: when it comes to drugs, nobody but those at the top get rich. Most get caught and end up in places like Kerobokan.

When the pair was first arrested, they got hate mail from people in Australia who abhorred drugs, whose sons or daughters had been addicts and died from the kind of heroin Myuran and Andrew were bringing from Bali to Australia. Back when they were running the drugs, they hadn't thought about their effects. But when they found themselves living among drug addicts, that all changed.

Andrew started thinking about how badly his drugs could have harmed people. He had been young, selfish and obnoxious back then, by his own description. What didn't affect him directly didn't matter.

Andrew felt especially saddened at the effect of his crime on his parents. They had worked hard to give their four children a better life. He felt he had repaid them with nothing but pain and agony. He couldn't tell his mother not to care, that everything would be alright. He didn't know if everything would be alright. His parents were not well. His dad's health was poor, and the trip to Bali was arduous. Andrew had never thought too much about things like his father's health, their financial situation. But after years in jail he recognised the impact his crime was having on the whole family. And he now appreciated how precious life is.

He wanted his family to see how much he had changed. He got his strength from God, but it was because of his family that he got up every day. What would hurt them more than he already had? If he didn't get up and carry on. That's how he thought of it. He was still a son, and still part of a family – he had a lot to live for. He saw every day as a chance to help someone else, to change the course of someone's life, to help others.

This was how both men felt as their jail projects became more popular and garnered more applause. Andrew was keen to get a first-aid course going, with professional teachers, with the eventual aim of having two trained prisoners per block. Lives could be saved. A man in his 50s had died from a stroke when simple first aid might have saved him, Andrew said. Personally, Andrew was relishing completing something he set his mind to.

People who came into the jail for stealing generally left knowing how to cook crystal meth or sell drugs. Now they were building their self-esteem and gaining positive life skills they could use in the outside world.

Myuran, too, had learned the harsh reality of jail. 'Education for criminals, that's what it is,' he told me once. 'People send their kids to Harvard for the connections and the networks they make. It's the same in jail. You meet criminal connections in jail. You get better at crime.'

Myuran wanted to become a better person – and he wanted the same for everybody else in the art classes. It was a vehicle for them all to travel in, he said one day. Guards often peeked in the windows, watching them work. They sat as subjects for the artists and sometimes even took up the brushes to paint themselves.

These projects were Andrew's and Myuran's pride and joy. The workshop where classes were held had once been legendary as a methamphetamine factory. Now it had become a sanctuary for prisoners who wanted something more from life. They all wanted to pursue learning, either to pass the time and avoid the dull boredom of jail, to develop skills to help them get jobs once they were released, or to keep their personal demons at bay. Sometimes you could even forget for a moment you were in jail.

Julian McMahon says Myuran displayed a huge amount of courage. Daily or weekly he had to resist the jail gangs who tried to infiltrate his space. Many times he had to physically keep them at bay. They were not happy at the power and respect Myuran had earned in the jail. He walked around with the keys to the jail workshops. Traditionally, it was they who ruled the jail, not some Aussie prisoner who had an art workshop. Myuran also had to give the guards, who helped him at the workshop, the courage to keep the gangs away. And he had to lead the inmates and show them how to do it as well. It was a massive burden and he struggled with it. It took a lot of physical and emotional fortitude, day after day. Like everyone, he wasn't flawless. Sometimes he would lose his temper and resort to thumping someone.

Andrew, Julian says, inspired inmates in an evangelical way, more of a healer in the wider prison environment, not just the church. He counselled many people about drugs. And it wasn't just the inmates. He ensured their families on the outside were okay. If they needed money for their kids' schooling, it was forthcoming from within Andrew's circle in the jail. If they needed money for medical reasons, it was always there. No one was ever hungry or left bereft. Andrew was running an efficient NGO from behind bars. And people loved him for it. The church was his sanctuary, and no one was ever turned away.

Myuran's sanctuary was the art workshop. In one corner was Myuran's desk. On it sat a computer, his art text books and office equipment while his paintings adorned the wall behind. It looked for all the world like a normal Balinese office. A painting he had done of his mother hung on the wall behind the desk. Other paintings by Myuran were on the wall, alongside the works of many of the other prison artists. Easels were dotted around the wall, paint brushes in buckets, tubes of paint. On first glance it could have been any art workshop anywhere. The only sign it was a prison was the guards in their uniforms.

Every prisoner in that workshop had nothing but praise for Myuran. They loved him. So too did Hermanus, the guard in charge of the area. In 28 years as a prison officer, he had never met a prisoner quite like Myuran. Hermanus was amazed at his ability to motivate his fellow prisoners, who before had done very little with themselves. Now they were creative and disciplined. So trusted was Myuran that he held the keys to the workshop area.

He was constantly looking for new courses to run – the aim was to keep inmates so busy that they had no time for drugs. Myuran knew from experience that once you started having negative thoughts, it was easy to spiral out of control.

In his early days at Kerobokan, Myuran had been greatly burdened by his guilt – primarily over the impact his crime was having on his family – and descended into depression. He kept a journal. Although he said it contained nothing profound, he shared one deeply moving page with me. In it, Myuran lamented that no matter how much he did at the jail, it felt like it was never enough – that something was always missing. He felt worthless and useless, a burden on his family, friends and country. He tried to keep himself busy in order to suppress those feelings.

As his art progressed, under Ben Quilty's tutelage, Myuran became more confident. He became the man he wanted to be. He said Ben helped him do that. The only thing he wanted now, he told me, was for his mum to be proud of him. Nothing else mattered.

Fellow Bali Nine members Si Yi Chen and Matthew Norman, both serving life sentences, were also involved in the jail projects. Si Yi ran a highly successful silversmithing course, and made silver jewellery that was marketed as Mule Jewels – a reference to the drug mules. With the help of expatriate woman Joanna Witt, who runs Yin Jewellery, Si Yi teaches inmates how to create and make silver jewellery.

Matthew Norman helped teach English and run the computer courses. He had been the youngest of the gang when they were arrested – just 18. He had to grow up quickly behind bars.

Like Myuran and Andrew, both Si Yi and Matthew were turning their lives around, and hoping that this would earn them some reprieve from their sentence. In the Indonesian justice system, life means life – no parole date is set. But after six years of good behaviour, prisoners can apply to have their sentence reduced to one of 15 to 20 years. Year after year, Si Yi, Matthew and the other Bali Nine members have applied for reduced sentences, but so far none has been forthcoming. The president's approval is required. When a sentence is reduced from life to 20 or 15 years, inmates also become eligible for twice-yearly sentence remissions, which can shave eight months off for each year served. Those on life sentences get no remissions whatsoever.

In 2013 Andrew penned a letter to school students, warning them against drugs. He wanted it to form part of an anti-drugs program for use in schools in Australia more broadly and was working with a filmmaker on making an anti-drugs documentary, *Dear Me: The Dangers of Drugs.* He deeply wanted to be an anti-drugs ambassador – so he might be able to deter young people from taking the path he had. Andrew sent his letter to me.

His life, he wrote, was a perfect example of an absolute waste. The hurt he had caused his family was agonising to him. 'A simple touch such as a hug is not possible for a condemned man like me,' he lamented. 'I have nothing but iron bars to hug, rather than be embraced by those I love and miss.' He urged young people who might be slipping into the grip of drugs to seek help – go and see a school counsellor, even if you didn't like him or her. Churches and youth centres could also help. Telling no one was akin to digging your own grave.

> I was once 15–16 years old, and it wasn't too long ago that I was sitting in class just like you guys. I was an average kid, and let me tell you, my teachers obviously didn't like me for I was no teacher's pet.
>
> To cut a long story short, I got mixed up with drugs at a pretty young age. By the time I was about 15 I was fully addicted. I was just like most of you, trying to hide these things from my parents and family, but in the end things spiralled out of control. I have seen many friends die in the past, and I'm sure if they had a second chance to do things differently now they would.
>
> I have done things which I'm not proud of in my life, and made some pretty stupid decisions. I'm the right person to say this; all you need to do is type me into Google and I'm sure you'll get the results – sentenced to death.

Andrew went on to say that if he had thought about the consequences of his actions, he wouldn't be where he was today. 'Every criminal thinks they won't get caught, but your past comes to catch up with you,' he told the students. 'You are still young, with decisions to make.'

> If you want to be a thug and the big bad wolf, I'll see you very soon. But for those who want something in life, I would like

you guys to see how important it is that you put your head down and study hard.

At the end of the day, I'm 29 years old. The truth is I might not be able to even see my 30th. How many want to follow in my footsteps?

I hope that these words will penetrate through your minds and hearts and that most of you if not all of you will achieve more than I ever did.

They were powerful words from a man who, as a teenager, had embarked on a self-destructive path, and whose life now hung in the balance.

As well as being earnest when preaching and warning others, Andrew was exceptionally funny. He was always good before a crowd. One time, while fundraising for victims of a natural disaster in the Philippines, he addressed his companions. 'The good news is we've got the money,' he told them. 'The bad news is it's still in your pocket.'

Andrew led the jail's Christmas services for the Christian inmates, and was always involved in organising the day's celebrations. One year he told a story about a greedy boy who wanted a bike from Santa. His mother was poor and didn't have any money. She told him to pray and to ask God for the bike. So the boy prayed and promised God that if he got a bike, he would be good for a year. That night he couldn't sleep, and began praying again; now he promised to be good for six months in exchange for a bike. Finally, he looked to the left of his bed and saw a statue of Mary. He grabbed it and stashed it under his bed. 'God, if you want to see your mother again, you'd better give me a bike,' the boy said. Everyone laughed. Andrew was reminding his fellow inmates not to forget the real meaning of Christmas – not to hold God for ransom.

He was the pastor of Kerobokan.

Myuran's art skills were developing. He devoured art books, asking anyone who came to visit to bring him more texts and tomes to read. He wanted to learn so much so quickly. He still couldn't believe that Ben Quilty was teaching and mentoring him and he was so grateful. He sometimes found it hard to get his head around the fact that someone as revered in the art world as Ben was actually coming to the jail to teach him. In June 2014, at Ben's urging, he entered a self-portrait in that year's renowned Archibald Prize.

Showing me the self-portrait he joked with me that Archibald entrants often paint famous people. He was painting an infamous person – himself. 'Look where I am,' he said as he looked around the jail visiting area that day. 'There are not exactly famous people in here for me to paint.' He used a mirror to paint himself. He admitted this technique – which he started using after meeting Ben, who told him to stop painting from pictures in magazines – made him think a lot about himself as he looked at his own image. 'Sometimes you like what you see, sometimes you don't,' he said of gazing at himself for so many hours. And he told of learning about himself. 'I have learned a lot. I have been focusing on what my flaws are, so I really know what they are. It is not the best place to work on your flaws. You get frustrated, you get angry, you get jealous, you get depressed.' The most important thing, he said, was to know your flaws.

This was something that Lizzie Love had helped him with. Lizzie had many discussions with him about his lack of impulse control. He told her it was a different environment in jail, you had to establish yourself as top dog. It wasn't like the outside world, he lamented. It was always him breaking up fights inside. Sometimes his temper got the better of him. Lizzie tried to give Myuran ways to use his brain and his mouth to resolve problems and issues, and, for the most part, it worked.

7.
CLEMENCY DENIED

It was back in December 2014 when Joko Widodo, newly elected as president, first revealed what he had in store for drug criminals. There would be no mercy, no clemency, he told university students. He vowed to reject all 64 clemency requests from those convicted of drug crimes. Indonesia, he said, was in a drugs emergency, with victims dying every day. He produced a set of figures – apparently drugs statistics – which he used as justification for his stance.

Myuran and Andrew had lodged their clemency pleas during the second term of President Susilo Bambang Yudhoyono, but he had failed to respond. During the 2014 presidential elections, they had put their hopes of salvation in Widodo, known popularly as Jokowi. A former furniture maker from Solo, who had become his town's mayor and then the Jakarta

CLEMENCY DENIED

mayor, Jokowi was not part of Jakarta's political and military elite. The Australians were optimistic that he would show clemency – especially given that his opponent for the top job, Prabowo Subianto, was a military strongman with a chequered human rights history.

Yet the former Jakarta mayor quickly surprised many with his hardline stance on drug crime. He spoke frequently of the dangers of narcotics, and of his desire to start executing people. It was a long December for the Australians and their families.

Myuran's world came crashing down. It was 7 January 2015. An aide from the Presidential Palace flew from Jakarta to Bali carrying a letter confirming that Myuran's clemency plea had been denied. (The President, Joko Widodo, had actually signed the clemency denial on 30 December 2014.) The aide went first to the Denpasar District Court, which had handed down the initial sentence. After this, she went across town to Kerobokan, delivering a second copy of the letter to the jail authorities, who were to pass it on to Myuran.

'After carefully considering clemency pleas from convicts listed in this Presidential Decree,' the letter stated, 'it is assessed that there is not enough reason to give clemency to those convicted.' No reasons were given as to why the bid was rejected.

Myuran was speechless. He felt lost and angry.

In Melbourne, Julian McMahon was busy with a local case when I told him the news. I sent him a copy of the letter. He called the rest of the legal team, the government and DFAT, and broke the devastating news to the Sukumaran family. Raji was in tears. She couldn't stop crying. Nor could Brintha. Chinthu could barely speak. Everyone was in shock.

Soon after getting the letter, Myuran opened up to me in a long missive, spelling out his despair.

> Me and Andrew don't want to be executed just about some political thing. How do you compare us, young and stupid attempting to smuggle 8.3 kilograms to Oz between the nine of us to seasoned smugglers, big people who do 1000 kilograms, 800 kilograms, 600 kilograms, and they only get a life sentence or 10–15 years. Why are we so evil that we deserve to be taken out and shot? This is so, so messed up . . . Is there no such thing as rehabilitation? Or is it not possible for people to change?
>
> In the world of all incarcerated people on drugs offences, no one has worked harder than me to rehabilitate not just me but many people around me. I haven't bullshitted or pretended to be good, I did it. I spoke out against drugs within the prison, against the drug bosses and the gangsters; I've been threatened and intimidated and many, many times attacked for it. I stood my ground. With the help of the Kerobokan prison guards – a few good ones in particular – we did much good work here. Does that not mean anything?

We [have] been living under the shadow of death for so long, and it's killing my family. It's eating us slowly. It's a miserable way to live. I feel completely lost about this decision and really don't know.

But I won't let them break my spirit. I will keep doing what is right, and at the end of the day when I stand before judgement I will be judged on who I am and what I've done.

I think in this world everyone can bullshit and play politics and accept bribes and corruption, squashing the little fish and taking money from people to let them do what they do. All the people in Indonesia are dying from drug overdoses – when are the lawyers, prosecutors, judges, police and politicians going to take responsibility for their part in this?

I was attempting to smuggle drugs out of Indonesia! I failed, and I know what I did was wrong. I am trying to make up for it. I live everyday trying. I've pushed more than anyone to set up programs until the guards got sick of me asking. I honestly don't know why they won't give me and Andrew clemency. They've given other people clemency who have not earned it. They gave Corby clemency. And they gave an Indonesian woman clemency in 2012 who was running a drug ring from inside the jail.

Me and Andrew led a push for rehabilitation within this jail – we changed the prison from within – and they execute us? It doesn't make sense. What do they want to show the world – that they have no rehabilitation?

In his message Myuran touched on something that he and Andrew and others in the Bali Nine had long felt: that public opinion in Australia had supported Schapelle Corby but not the Bali Nine.

> If I was white, blonde hair, blue eyes? If I was a huge mega-kingpin drug lord who could afford to pay millions of dollars to bribe people?

Myuran was speaking from his heart. He was angry and hurt and felt let down. He thought he had done enough to be spared death.

> Please take a closer look at my and Andrew's case; please see that we are different; please give us a second chance. Please show us mercy. I am absolutely terrified that my mum and brother and sister will have to experience my execution. We are the best examples of the good points of the Indonesian justice system. We show the potential of what the Indonesian justice system can do. Why destroy that?

Inexplicably, Dutchman Ang Kiem Soei's bid for clemency was rejected along with Myuran's – in the very same letter. There was no explanation for why the two cases had been linked in this way. In other cases, co-defendants were linked on the same decree, but there was no relationship whatsoever between Myuran and the Dutchman. Was it an error? Should it have been Andrew Chan, not Ang Kiem Soei? No one knew. Myuran wanted to know if it was a typo or a mistake – or perhaps the president simply was not really aware of who he was. It just added to the sense that the executions were being organised in a shambolic fashion, with little regard for detail.

'This is insane. Things are moving so fast.'

Before the president's rejection letter arrived, Myuran had been doing some paintings of a young female prisoner who had a tumour in her uterus, for which she urgently needed an operation. Medical services are not free for prisoners in Indonesia. In order to be treated in a hospital, they must first pay the costs upfront. Those who can't pay simply can't be treated. Indeed, it's no different for anyone in Indonesia, where health services, especially good ones, are not free and there is no social safety net.

Maria Cecilia Lopez, a Filipina prisoner, had been arrested for attempting to take 250 grams of methamphetamine from Thailand to Indonesia; she was sentenced to eight years and six months. Myuran had got to know her after she participated in some of his rehabilitation programs, including the computer workshop and dance class, as well as learning reflexology. Now she was gravely unwell and he wanted to help her.

Her story was a sad one. Pregnant, she began suffering from a uterine disease; she decided to smuggle drugs in order to pay for her health problem and to care for her unborn baby. A month after she was locked up in jail in Bali, she lost the baby and the disease got worse. The only cure was an operation, although that might render her infertile. And the cost was prohibitive: at Bali's Sanglah hospital the medical fees would reach about $4000. Myuran made it his business to raise the funds for Maria's operation by doing what he did best: he would paint portraits of Maria and himself to be sold. By this time his art was becoming better known. Many Aussie expatriates in Bali were happy to buy them, especially to support such a good cause.

At the time he learned his clemency was denied, Myuran had already raised Rp 10 million, he said; they still needed another Rp 20 million or Rp 25 million. Despite his own desperation, he kept painting. Nothing was going to interfere with his determination to help Maria.

Given the gravity of what was happening, though, he couldn't concentrate. He sent me a picture of a portrait he was trying to complete, but which he said he'd messed up.

> My idea is to do four more paintings and try to sell them at $500 a pop to get the money for her operation. The last Rp 25 million will come from my pictures; I've just got to finish four more paintings.

Lizzie Love set to work selling the paintings once they were done. In a bid to sell the works, Lizzie paid tribute to the work both Myuran and Andrew had done in starting co-educational classes at the jail, to ensure that women as well as men were able to participate – something that had previously not been allowed. 'Maria is important to them both,' she wrote in a flyer. 'They are clucky at times in their protection and concern for the women in the jail. Prospects for the women in the jail are grim if these two lads are executed.'

She had been out of contact with Myuran for the previous three months after a disagreement over a new project to keep dogs inside the jail. Lizzie, a dog breeder, had donated some of her dogs to the inmates to raise but had taken them out after a disagreement over the way the program was running. With his clemency blow, Myuran asked Lizzie to come and see him. It was gut-wrenching for Lizzie. The last words she said to him as she left the jail that day were: 'I am so scared for you Myu.' She stood on her tippy toes and hugged him for the first and last time.

Raji Sukumaran's heart was breaking. Her worst fears were being realised. She just couldn't understand how it was possible that all her son's work at the jail could count for nothing. All she wanted was to have one chance to meet President Widodo, to plead her son's case before him.

'I am sure if the president knows what Myu has done inside, I am sure he will grant him clemency. I know that he would not take my son's life away,' she told me on 10 January. 'I am angry, I am terrified, I don't know what to do, I feel helpless. I am really scared, really scared.'

Raji spoke about her feelings on learning that Myu's clemency bid had been denied: 'I was shocked. I thought that with all the good things that he has done in the prison, the president will grant him clemency. There are so many things he has done – he has helped so many people. Every day he is looking for something to do to make somebody's life better. He is rehabilitated and still they want to take him and kill him, and it's not fair.'

The close-knit Sukumaran family rallied to support each other. As always, Chinthu was a rock for Raji and Brintha. As Raji sobbed that day in Sydney, Chinthu was standing nearby, ready to comfort his mother if she faltered. But Raji was determined. She wanted to talk about her eldest son and the injustice that killing him would be, no matter how much her heart ached. Hers was the pain any mother would feel at the prospect of losing a child. 'If they want to kill him, they should be killing me first, because I brought him to this world,' she sobbed.

Chinthu approached to comfort her. It was hard to watch and hear her despair. She couldn't do the one thing she wanted to do: hold her son and tell him everything would be okay.

'I can only say that I love him,' she continued. 'What else can I say to him? I can't tell him that I will bring him home. I can't promise him that everything is going to be okay. I just want him to be alive somewhere so that I know that he is okay. I don't want to live like this. I wish they kill me first. He doesn't deserve to die.'

Raji cried and cried.

CLEMENCY DENIED

Myuran was desperately scared. In fact, he was more afraid than he had been in the ten years since his arrest. Unable to sleep, he was haunted by thoughts of his own death, of being tied to a pole and shot through the heart, of saying goodbye to his beloved family, of what it would do to his mum. It was just eight days after he'd learned that President Joko Widodo had denied his clemency plea.

There had been no word yet on the fate of Andrew's clemency bid. But given that his and Myuran's cases had been identical – in their arrest, conviction and rehabilitation – few believed the result would be anything other than a denial. The president had already indicated as much: Indonesia was pushing ahead with plans to execute six people that month, and more later. Myuran had heard that several of the six were already being moved to the execution island of Nusakambangan.

At 7.30 a.m. on 15 January 2015 he sent me a message:

> There's a rumour going around that a Nigerian and
> Brazilian have been taken to the island to be executed.
> I didn't sleep last night – it was the most terrifying feeling
> I've had since I've been in jail.

The prison grapevine was alive with news of the upcoming executions. Everyone knew it was a bad sign.

Later that day, Attorney-General Muhammad Prasetyo held a press conference in Jakarta. He announced that in the early hours of Sunday, 18 January, six drug convicts would be executed: five foreigners and one Indonesian. No Australian names were on the list.

'The execution of the Bali Nine cannot be done yet,' Prasetyo told the media. 'We are still waiting for one other person, named Andrew Chan.' Under the law, he explained, if a crime had been committed by more than one person, the executions of all those involved should be done at the same time. Myuran would not be executed until the outcome of Andrew's clemency was decided, he added. If Andrew got clemency, then Myuran would be executed. But if Andrew's clemency plea was rejected, they would be executed together.

Prasetyo listed those who would die: Brazilian Marco Archer Cardoso Moreira, Nigerians Daniel Enemuo and Namaona Denis, Dutchman Ang Kiem Soei, Vietnamese woman Tran Thi Bich Hanh and Indonesian woman Rani Andriani (alias Melisa Aprilia). The Vietnamese woman was to be executed alone, in Boyolali in Central Java. The others would die together at Nusakambangan. News of the imminent executions sparked an outcry from the nations of those involved, and from human rights organisations.

Myuran and Andrew were desperate to know what the attorney-general was saying. 'Please update me,' Andrew messaged when I told him the press conference had just started. 'Please let me know ASAP,' Myuran wrote.

Both men kept a close eye on the news, watching every article that appeared, especially those with information from the Indonesian side. Myuran sent me a link to a story reporting Indonesia's response to Australia's pleas for the lives of the Bali Nine duo, which had emphasised their rehabilitation. The Republic understood Australia's response, but noted that the Australian prime minister had said the matter should not affect bilateral relations between the neighbouring nations.

Myuran had also seen a story in which the Indonesians said there had been no pressure applied by Australia. 'It doesn't look good,' he told me. 'From what I'm hearing things will move quickly.' Nor had his Indonesian legal team, led by Todung Mulya Lubis, been very positive:

> He said that there is a big chance that the Supreme Court won't accept our PK [judicial review], and that if that happens then things will move fast. They could accept and recommend the sentence be upheld. Before he left he hugged us . . . he didn't seem confident.

Myuran felt their fate now rested on whether the Australian prime minister, Tony Abbott, could persuade his Indonesian counterpart to be merciful. 'We still don't know but from everyone's indications the only thing left is from Abbott,' he told me.

He said everyone thought the second judicial review was a slim chance.

'All the lawyers and consulate think that it is meaningless and won't work. It's now entirely up to Abbott.'

Myuran was desperately trying to think of options. 'Somebody suggested that I stay away from asking for mercy and focus on how good the Indonesian justice system is in Indonesia and how they could rehabilitate prisoners, especially the Australian ones who cause so much trouble. Appealing to their pride rather than their mercy,' he messaged. He said an Indonesian had also suggested it might be better to praise and thank Indonesia.

After hearing Attorney-General Prasetyo declare that six executions would take place that weekend, Andrew messaged me suggesting an article about his case: 'My headline for my article is "What Does It Take?"' He was referring to all the rehabilitation work that he and Myuran had done in jail, to all the inmates whom they'd helped find purpose and meaning, and to their own deep remorse and their continued work to make amends for their crime. What else did it take to get a second chance? Despair was setting in.

The next morning Myuran felt like the end was nearing. 'Honestly, after talking with everyone I think we are close to the end,' he wrote. What could I say to that? His desperation was heartbreaking.

Think positive, I urged him; things are fluid and change quickly in Indonesia.

He responded:

> Can you do an article on the hypocrisy of everything here? I know we did bad and made a mistake but what about the 800-kilogram bust three weeks ago? Why's nobody calling for their execution?

He also pointed out a story about an Indonesian policeman caught importing 4 kilograms of drugs from Malaysia.

So many cases had obvious anomalies. One of those to be executed on 18 January was Rani Andriani. She had been arrested in 2000, part of a drug syndicate convicted of attempting to smuggle 3.5 kilograms of heroin and 3 kilograms of cocaine to the United Kingdom. Also arrested were her cousins Meirika Franola (alias Ola) and Deni Setia Marhawan. Ola had been arrested at home; her husband, Tajudin, was shot dead during the police raid. All three women had been sentenced to death by the Tangerang District Court in West Jakarta.

Eleven years later, President Susilo Bambang Yudhoyono granted clemency to Ola and Deni, reducing their sentences to life in prison. This was one year before Myuran and Andrew lodged their own clemency pleas.

Ola was dubbed *Ratu Narkoba*, or 'Queen of Narcotics', by the Indonesian press. A mere ten months after her clemency was granted, she was arrested in jail, accused of masterminding a drug-smuggling syndicate that moved 750 grams of crystal methamphetamine from India to Bandung, West Java. Granted a second chance at life, Ola had been dealing drugs from inside jail.

The cases of Rani Andriani and another Indonesian woman, Edith Yunita Sianturi, were joined with those of Andrew, Myuran and Scott Rush in the 2007 challenge against the death penalty in the Indonesian Constitutional Court. Eight years later Rani Andriani's punishment was about to be finalised. (Sianturi died in prison in 2009, apparently having contracted tuberculosis and HIV.)

The story of Namaona Denis, another slated for execution on 18 January, was also replete with anomalies. Firstly, it was said he was from Malawi, but he was in fact Nigerian. His name was not actually Namaona Denis but Solomon Chibuike Okafor. The name under which he was convicted was the name on the false passport he was carrying at the time of his arrest. He had been sentenced to death in 2004 for smuggling a kilogram of heroin – in 73 capsules, which he had swallowed – into Jakarta airport. He had been promised US$3000 if he successfully delivered the heroin to its destination. He had originally received a life sentence, but it was upgraded on appeal to the death sentence. In 2009 his lawyers had filed for a judicial review of his case, based on the incorrect identification; that was turned down, and he remained known by the Indonesian authorities as Namaona Denis.

His tearful Indonesian wife visited him on Nusakambangan, and afterwards read a letter he had written:

> My name is Namaona Denis, a poor man that has been bankrupt and forced to be a courier. I am not a drug dealer. The change of my sentence from the life sentence to [the] death

sentence . . . has robbed [me of] the justice that I have fought for until now. I plead to all people to understand my struggle to get justice, so that other people will not face the treatment that I have faced. Because apparently having good behaviour and being obedient to the laws in this country was not enough to get justice.

He asked forgiveness from the Indonesian people.

Denis's lawyer, Choirul Anam, was angry. So too was his client. They claimed he had been tricked and lied to about leaving the Tangerang prison, where he had been held, to be brought to Nusakambangan for execution. Anam said that Tangerang prison guards had told Denis there was a new case involving his name, and that he needed to leave the prison to meet that person. Instead, he was taken to Nusakambangan to die. Anam argued that it was illegal to kill his client, who had recently lodged a judicial review of his case, which was yet to be finalised. The Indonesian National Human Rights Commission had also written a letter on Denis's behalf, asking for the execution to be delayed as the judicial review was incomplete. These pleas were ignored.

Another of the 18 January group – Dutchman Ang Kiem Soei – also complained about the arbitrary nature of the death penalty. Lawyers for Soei, who had been convicted over an ecstasy factory, told the Indonesian media that their client's judicial review had not been fully considered by the Supreme Court. Lawyer Harry Ponto told Indonesian newspaper *Kompas* that the judges had considered only one of the three points made in the review, and that Soei's rights had been violated as a result.

Moreover, Soei had shown clear evidence of rehabilitation. While many drug convicts continue their illegal activity in jail, Soei had developed a herbal therapy treatment that had been registered as a legal medicine by the Food and Drug Agency, and had even received a patent. Ponto claimed that Soei had treated many inmates and Nusakambangan locals.

In the evening of 17 January Andrew messaged me: 'Heard they'll be taking Marco out very soon.' He was referring to rumours now circulating that the condemned were being readied for execution.

At 1.02 a.m. on Sunday, 18 January 2015, Attorney-General Prasetyo announced that all six scheduled executions had been carried out. The prisoners had been shot dead at 12.30 a.m. Five had died on Nusakambangan and one in Boyolali.

According to news portal Detik.com, Tran Thi Bich Hanh had worn white clothing and a hat of her choice for her death: she had been 'beautifully dressed up', according to the prison's governor. She had apparently been ready to meet her fate, telling guards it was her life's path.

Marco Archer Cardoso Moreira had not been accompanied by his spiritual adviser, the Catholic priest Father Charlie Burrows, who had been based in the St Stephen's Church in Cilacap since

1973. Father Burrows had been ministering death row prisoners since 2007 and was outspoken in the fight against the death penalty. In this case, the priest had inexplicably been barred from being with the prisoner during his final hours, and from comforting him in his final moments. The Brazilian government was angry.

The United Nations Human Rights Commission called execution a barbaric practice, and argued that narcotics offences could not be considered among the most serious crimes for which the death penalty might be used. Ahead of the killings, Amnesty International had called on the Indonesian government to cancel its plans, claiming the death penalty was a human rights violation:

> Indonesia's new government took office on the back of promises to improve respect for human rights, but carrying out these executions would be a regressive move. Rather than putting to death more people, the government should immediately impose a moratorium on the use of the death penalty with a view to its eventual abolition.

Amnesty International's Research Director for Southeast Asia and the Pacific, Rupert Abbott, criticised the Indonesian leadership:

> It would be a huge setback if the government goes ahead with its plans to execute as many as 20 people during the year. Tackling rising crime is a legitimate goal of President

Widodo's administration but the death penalty is not the answer and does not work as a deterrent to crime . . .

The plans for a new spate of executions come at a time when the government is actively seeking to protect Indonesian nationals who face the death penalty overseas. If the death penalty is wrong elsewhere, it is surely wrong in Indonesia too.

In the early hours of the morning, after the executions had been confirmed, Andrew was angry:

> U gonna bash out that story now with the one in Jakarta 840kg? Someone needs to cover that story or nothing will be done. Also what's that terrorist's name that gave up the Bali bombers? Where is he now?

He was referring to an 840-kilogram methamphetamine bust, recently captured in West Jakarta.

Myuran was downcast about his and Andrew's prospects. 'I think the outcome is already set,' he said. Now that the Indonesian president had acted on his promise to execute drug traffickers, he could feel the net closing around them.

Andrew meanwhile was trying to remain positive. The day after the executions I asked how he was coping. 'As dandy as one can be,' he quipped. I commented that he had had some church visitors that day. He wanted to know who was spying.

'They were spotted like the Big 5 in Africa,' he joked. He loved figures of speech. Used them all the time. He wanted to know why there were so many reporters in front of the jail. 'Do they actually know I'm limiting my press releases to only you? Stupid people. I have limited who I speak to media wise. If I have something to say I will go through you.'

It was the afternoon of 22 January when an official from the president's Jakarta office again arrived in Bali bearing a letter. This time it was Andrew's clemency rejection. It was handed to the Denpasar District Court about 1.20 p.m. The official then headed to Kerobokan. At the time he arrived, Andrew and Myuran were taking Norway's ambassador to Indonesia on a tour of the prison, pointing out the rehabilitation programs they had set up.

The letter had been signed by President Widodo on 17 January; it read:

> After carefully considering the clemency plea from the convicted that is listed in this Presidential Decree, it is assessed that there is not enough reason to give clemency to the convicted.

It was not a huge surprise. Many had predicted the outcome would be the same for both the Bali Nine applications.

The Australians' legal team was in Bali, planning their next moves. Julian McMahon and Veronica Haccou had been at the jail that morning but had left before the letter arrived. When Julian heard the document was on its way to the jail, he ordered his car to turn around and return immediately. He needed to be with his clients.

When he arrived, he couldn't find Andrew and was worried. Eventually he spotted him comforting a fellow prisoner who had passed out, as they waited for an ambulance to arrive. The man's arm was paralysed from a stroke and he was struggling. It was a mark of the man Andrew had become: during one of his darkest hours, he was helping a fellow prisoner in need. Andrew's faith was sustaining him, and he wanted to keep ministering.

'I'm still alive and he was in bad shape, so he needed more help than me,' Andrew later wrote. 'It's the human thing to do – if someone needs help and you can help, we as humans should help.'

Myuran, meanwhile, continued to show the dignitary around the jail programs.

At the same time, lawyer Todung Mulya Lubis was at the Denpasar District Court, meeting with the chief judge to work out how to apply for a new judicial review (known as a PK – *Peninjauan Kembali* – or case review) on behalf of Myuran and Andrew. The problem was that, under the law, both men had to be present at court when the PK was lodged; given the amount of security required, this appeared to be impossible. Mulya was trying to work out another way to lodge the appeal.

By the end of that day both Andrew and Myuran were deeply sad. Julian felt the sadness and resignation as he spoke with them that afternoon. The combination of statements by Indonesian authorities and rumours and messages people were hearing led to a sense that it was all over and that they would be dead within days or possibly a week or two.

Just days earlier, President Widodo had spoken again about the drugs emergency. 'Why do I say the country is in a state of emergency over drugs? Because the number of [illegal drug users] who need rehabilitation is nearly 4.5 million people,' he said. Widodo claimed that 1.2 million drug users could not be rehabilitated, and nearly 50 died each day. Indonesian clerics must spread the word about the dangers of drugs. Jokowi himself would continue to reject clemency requests for the 67 men and women on death row, locals and foreigners alike.

The president was confident in his approach. Heads of state of countries with citizens whose clemency had been rejected had been contacting him, he revealed. But he was being backed by parliamentary committees, whose members were urging him to resist the pleas of foreign governments. His policies were popular: everyone from fellow politicians to taxi drivers and shopkeepers were parroting his statistics about the country's drug crisis in order to justify the executions.

Despite the blow, Andrew was trying to keep his spirits high. He had set up a kitchen at the jail, and begun teaching inmates to cook. It was a decade now since he had lived at home and enjoyed the superb Chinese cooking of his parents, Ken and Helen, who had run their own Chinese restaurant. But he still knew a thing or two about cooking, and loved whipping up dishes and photographing them. For a while, he sent me photos every day of what he had crafted for dinner that day in the jail's kitchen.

Andrew was always on the lookout for ingredients, encouraging his visitors to bring this or that spice, meat or vegetable into the jail. He once convinced me that he needed a leg of ham that he would glaze and bake. He could taste and smell it before he even got it. I searched Bali for the ham and after he cooked it, Andrew sent me photos of the glazed leg. And he always wanted Chinese Five Spice – he was forever convincing people to bring it over from Australia.

Helen and Ken Chan were urgently planning to visit Andrew, who by then hadn't seen his parents in three years. Their health was ailing and the trip would be arduous, but with the clemency bid now denied, Helen and Ken were not staying away from their son. Andrew was anxious about his mum, in particular, coming to Bali. 'She is going to have 50 million questions for me and I won't have the answers,' he said.

Still, he hadn't lost his sense of humour. 'I'm as busy as an escort agency that's just hired George Clooney,' he joked of all the things he had to do and all the people who wanted to see him. At the time Andrew was reading *The Four Loves* by C. S. Lewis, which explores aspects of love from a Christian perspective – affection, friendship, erotic love and the love of

God. Andrew fancied himself as a writer and often joked with me about writing a Pulitzer Prize–winning piece: 'Lol, Cindy, as I said, you saved my ass that many times, I'll give you a golden piece after. Let's just see how things go.'

Some had suggested he was a good creative writer, he told me, but he confessed to having been hopeless at school: 'Lol . . . the only A on my papers was my name starting with an A, Andrew.' He suggested the Lord had blessed him with the ability to write.

Myuran was worried about the future. 'It's not about the bullets,' he told the lawyers. 'It's about leaving family behind, leaving things unfinished.'

He was thinking deeply. He talked a lot about his art and about how proud he was to be learning from Ben; he was conscious of how much he was learning, and of how much he still had to achieve. He now knew what he had to do to get to the next level. He wanted to keep living so he could make it there. 'If I didn't have people like you,' he told the lawyers, 'I'd probably be like them too,' referring to Nigerians in the jail who continued to deal and use drugs.

Myuran was trying to paint portraits of his family members each day. He tried to paint his mum but she couldn't sit still. He too was having trouble concentrating, with all that was going on. He had told his family when they first arrived that he was being selfish; he wanted it to be a happy, fun visit. 'I don't want them to remember us sitting around crying and being miserable,' he wrote to me. 'I want my Mum and family to see me happy and doing what I love.'

His belief that he was meant to be a painter was growing. He loved it so much. It was too hard to talk to his mother about his feelings, he said; he wanted to make her laugh instead. They talked a lot about when they were little kids, about the good old days, telling funny stories. It was a means of self-preservation, given things were now dire. Myuran had heard that the Australian government was making no progress in Jakarta. 'It's just not looking good,' he said. 'Everything is on a razor's edge.'

The impasse over the request for a second judicial review was resolved when the court agreed to come from Denpasar to the jail and receive it there. Myuran and Andrew joked with their lawyers – if I was in a coma for six months the doctor's certificate could say 'no shooting today'.

Support for Andrew and Myuran back home was building. Word came through that a concert titled 'Music for Mercy' and a candlelight vigil were to be held in Sydney's Martin Place on Thursday 29 January, organised by Ben Quilty and hosted by actor David Wenham. But Myuran and Andrew, after ten years in jail away from Australia, appeared not to know who Wenham was.

'Didn't he play some kind of lawyer? Some kind of overweight lawyer?' Myuran asked.

'I don't know who he is,' Andrew said. 'Was he in *The Castle*?'

'The one who played the fat lawyer?'

'The one who died?'

There were many times in Kerobokan prison that January when it was just Myuran, Andrew, Veronica and Julian spending time together. They called them the verandah conversations – they sat on a verandah area together. They were precious times. There were lots of laughs. They had more fun in that time than they had ever had since knowing each other. There was a running gag about Julian's weight. Myuran and Andrew called him 'The Fat Man' and joked with him about how much weight he was putting on. Once he was jesting with Myuran and Andrew about how much weight they themselves had put on since the clemency was denied and they were eating so much junk food. 'You two could be plus-size models,' Julian told them. Myuran didn't miss a beat. 'Yes, and you can be the first customer.'

Myuran lamented that since his clemency had been denied, many of the prisoners in his art classes had stopped coming to class as they were too distressed. He was running around trying to get them to come back.

'I don't want to be counselling people about my execution,' Myuran said one day. He wanted Jokowi to take another look at their case. 'We did wrong. If you don't give people incentive to change, then why would they change?'

As the lawyers left that day, Myuran farewelled Veronica. 'Thank you, Veronica,' he said. 'I don't want to die, Veronica. Remember that.'

8.
PEOPLE CAN CHANGE

'Whether you have three days, three months or three years to live really doesn't make any difference to the kinds of steps you should be taking in regards to how you live,' Julian told Myuran. 'You have to stand up and lead, and stop feeling sorry for yourself. There are a lot of people fighting for you.'

Before he left Myuran that day, Julian said he wanted to see a new painting by the next morning. As he walked out of the prison, though, he wasn't sure that Myuran would take up his brush again.

But that talk had stopped Myuran from falling into an abyss. He embraced Julian's words. That evening, he decided to send a message. A powerful message. He hoped it would reach the eyes of the one person who now mattered. He started painting: black hair, parted on the left side and neatly swept over . . . a chiselled jaw . . . dark eyes.

The painting Myuran produced that night was good – very good. It was an impressive likeness of a man he had never actually laid eyes on, but whom he'd seen often on television, and whose image appeared regularly in the Indonesian press.

Satisfied with his portrait of President Joko Widodo, the next day Myuran showed it to Julian.

The lawyer urged him to give the painting an inscription. 'If you could speak to the president right now, what would you say?' They got a black pen.

Myuran turned the canvas over. On the back, in cursive script, preceded by a little arrow, he wrote three powerful words: 'People Can Change'. He underlined them. The portrait was simply titled 'Jokowi'. He signed it: 'Myuran Sukumaran, Kerobokan Prison, Bali, 23/01/2015'.

As he left the jail Julian clutched the still-wet painting, with a blank canvas over the top to hide its contents. It was the most important blank canvas he had ever carried. (He still has it.) Julian didn't want the painting unveiled to the media just yet. He thought it was a wonderful painting, in no way negative about the man who had just ordered Myuran's death. Julian thought the painting had the potential to be weaponised at some point in the future and it was kept under wraps.

From the time the lawyers lodged the clemency pleas in mid-2012, they had decided not to pursue any other legal avenues, believing this would be disrespectful to the president as he considered their requests. But it was now clear that the issue was politically charged. The comments from Jakarta were a signal to the legal team that legal and due process was being replaced by politics. It was very concerning to hear comments that all the death row prisoners would be executed regardless of legal actions. The team began to shape its legal responses, looking at the comments of the president and the attorney-general. Julian remained optimistic that reason and representations at a political and diplomatic level could ultimately prove sufficient to save 'the boys' as he called them.

At the same time as shaping their next move, the legal team was trying to keep up Andrew's and Myuran's flagging spirits. Myuran, in particular, was at risk of falling into depression. He had always had what Julian said was a melancholy disposition.

It had been a dreadful few weeks and Myuran had struggled to do any painting; he was haunted by nightmares, he was emotional and stressed. Many times he wondered whether he should go on.

Julian and Veronica were straight with him: he needed to pull himself together. The lawyers couldn't do their job if he was falling apart. Julian was concerned that at the very time they needed to be ready to fight on many fronts, Myuran might sink. He was deliberately forceful with him, in a supportive way.

Andrew finally had some good news. As the culmination of six years of study, he was ordained as a pastor during an emotional ceremony held in the jail's chapel.

Helen was in Bali to celebrate her youngest son's achievement. She hugged him – both were in tears. She was so proud of Andrew. For him it was a dream come true, and he was thrilled to conduct a service for his family and friends.

Pastor Christie Buckingham was there too. She had helped supervise Andrew's study and his work, and now she presented him with a Bible. Inside was an inscription in beautiful handwriting:

Presented to Andrew Kenneth Chan on the occasion of his ordination as a minister of the Gospel of the Lord Jesus Christ. 'Preach the word of God. Be prepared whether the time is favorable or not. Patiently correct, rebuke and encourage your people with good teaching.' 2 Timothy 4:2.

And in a letter dated 27 January 2015, Brian Medway, the national chairman of Crosslink Christian Network, confirmed that Pastor Andrew Kenneth Chan was duly ordained as a minister of religion at Kerobokan Prison Church. It was a big achievement for the man police had once called the godfather of a heroin racket.

On 29 January, the Martin Place vigil went ahead. More than 1000 people gathered to protest Andrew's and Myuran's executions. A petition calling for mercy already had 135,000 signatures.

But, within days, there was more bad news. On 4 February the Denpasar District Court announced that the judicial reviews lodged by Myuran and Andrew just a few days earlier had been rejected. The legal team had hoped the Supreme Court in Jakarta would allow them a second PK. But the court in Bali said that neither Australian had fulfilled the primary requirement for a PK – that there be new evidence. For this reason, their requests could not be accepted.

It was also unclear whether prisoners were allowed more than one PK. Both Andrew and Myuran had already run one PK, back in 2010, which they had lost. Attorney-General Prasetyo argued now that no more than one PK was allowed. The Supreme Court concurred.

But others, including the Constitutional Court, held that there was no limit on the number of judicial reviews possible. It seemed that the Supreme Court did not consider itself in any way bound by the decisions of the Constitutional Court. Others disagreed, saying the Constitutional Court was the highest court in Indonesia. It was clear as mud – and, like so much of the Indonesian legal justice system, what was written in the law books was not necessarily the way things worked in reality. Had the Constitutional Court's view prevailed, Myuran and Andrew and the others on execution lists may have been allowed to lodge their second PK.

As part of their application, Myuran and Andrew had written letters, in Indonesian, to President Widodo and to the Supreme Court, begging for a second chance.

In his letter Andrew acknowledged that he was guilty of the crime, and said he was not attempting to justify or minimise that. But he had changed, he wrote, and was teaching others not to make the same mistakes. He was training to become a priest. 'I hope from the bottom of my heart for a second chance,' he wrote.

Myuran apologised for what he had done ten years ago, and wrote that he had been working to right the wrong by helping those around him. He felt ashamed of how he had hurt his family and his country, and he had tried to become a better person. It is difficult to be a good person in jail, he wrote, but after he learned Indonesian and built trust with his guards, they had shown him kindness and compassion and patience, and had helped him start a program to teach inmates computer skills. Myuran listed all the programs that were now running at the jail.

Then came crushing news. The Australian consul-general to Bali, Majell Hind, visited Kerobokan jail early on 6 February, to tell the men that the Australian Embassy had been advised the previous evening by the Indonesian Foreign Ministry that Myuran and Andrew would be executed that month.

It was the worst possible news, and the first instance any timeframe had been articulated. There was no date, just the month. Given it was already a week into February, the clock was now ticking loudly.

Myuran and Andrew were in shock. Within hours, both their mothers would be arriving at the jail to visit. Myuran wanted to tell Raji himself, and Andrew would tell Helen.

Raji was inconsolable as Myuran broke the news.

Myuran messaged me, saying that his mother might make a statement to the media when she left the jail that day. 'Can you ask them not to be aggressive?' he wrote. It was all becoming too real now.

Helen, too, was devastated, breaking down as Andrew gently told her what they had been advised. Ken, who had not been well enough to travel with her to Bali, would now come within days. Helen was herself suffering from an eye condition, which was exacerbated by the heat and the dust, and all the crying. Michael Chan was in Sydney and would fly back to Bali the next day. All were hoping and praying for a miracle.

Michael felt like they had already done everything they possibly could. Andrew, he told me, was in a good headspace and was holding up pretty well, considering. They still had hope. What else could they do?

Raji and Brintha did speak to the media as they left the jail that day. For days they had come and gone silently, keeping their counsel despite the entourage outside the jail. But now there were some things they needed to say.

Raji's message to the Indonesian government was simple. 'They have rehabilitated,' she said. 'They are doing a lot of things here. They are good children. Please don't kill them. Give him a second chance.'

Brintha begged the government to spare her big brother. 'Please don't kill my brother,' she said. 'Please, he is a good person. He has rehabilitated and we love him so much. Please don't kill him. Please, please.' Brintha spoke about how her brother was selling paintings to pay for Maria Lopez's operation. 'He is doing everything he can to help people inside. No one is listening to us. It's not fair. He is scared. I could see it in his eyes.' Now Brintha was in tears. She loved Myuran desperately – he was her rock. He always had been, since she was a little girl.

Later that evening, locked down in his cell, Myuran was alone with his fears and his nightmares. At 8 p.m. he started painting. A dark background, half-finished. Over it was a stark white wooden cross, with red streaking down it. He sent me a picture, and the message, 'Work in progress'.

I knew exactly what it was. I had first seen that dreadful scene seven years earlier. It was the kind of wooden cross to which two Nigerian drug traffickers were strapped before they were executed in June 2008 at Nusakambangan. At the time I was researching a story about the death penalty and how it was carried out, as the three Bali bombers – Mukhlas, Amrozi and Imam Samudra – were due to be executed soon. I had seen a series of haunting images, taken by officials, of the two Nigerians as they were led out to be formally given their 72 hours' notice, and measured and weighed for their coffins. There were also night-time photographs of the crosses set up at the killing field. Myuran had seen the images.

At 6.50 a.m. on 7 February Myuran sent me a photo of the finished painting: a pitch-black background, the blood-streaked cross and stand. 'I just finished that,' he wrote.

I asked why he had decided to paint such a bleak image, which was haunting and powerful.

'I dunno. It feels like one of the last things I would see.'

Later that day something strange happened. A man neither Myuran nor Andrew had spoken to in years – in fact, since their first verdict and appeals back in 2006 – arrived at Kerobokan prison. It was their first lawyer, Muhammad Rifan, who had represented them after their arrest and at their trial. They had not parted on good terms, but now, the day after officials had told the Australians they would die that month, here was Rifan at the jail, asking to see them. What could he possibly want?

Rifan spoke to both men and spent almost an hour at the prison. He talked at length with Myuran. Andrew spent less then 30 seconds with him; he had church work to do, he said.

I asked Andrew how he felt about Rifan now, given that he was part of the original legal team which supported his initial plea of innocence which went so badly.

'I forgave him a long time ago,' he said.

When he emerged from the jail, Rifan gave some clues to the waiting media as to why he had come, hinting that he had new evidence that could save them. The lawyer claimed that both Myuran and Andrew were meant to be sentenced to life in jail, but there had been an 'intervention' that had seen them get the death penalty. The judges had told him, he said, that they had not wanted to sentence the men to death – but the government had. Now Rifan wanted to pass on information that might save Myuran's and Andrew's lives.

While Rifan was promising new information, the families were trying another avenue. They were travelling to Jakarta to see if they could make the difference.

The day on which Raji, Chinthu, Helen and Michael were to fly from Bali to Jakarta was beset by one major problem: nature. The sky had opened and Jakarta was experiencing a tropical downpour that flooded the streets and jammed the traffic for hours on end. Traffic is dreadful at the best of times in Jakarta, but many times worse as soon as it starts raining.

It was 9 February and the plan had been for the families to go to the Presidential Palace to plead their case. They were desperate to get their words to President Widodo and the others making decisions. But the flooded streets and pouring rain made that impossible. So instead they held a press conference at a Jakarta hotel.

Raji read a statement on behalf of herself and Helen Chan, begging the president to take the time to look properly into their sons' cases. She spoke eloquently of the good works the two young men were now doing inside Kerobokan prison, and of how they had become role models within the jail system. They were desperate for someone in the president's inner circle to understand the work the Australians were doing, not just to make amends but also to help other prisoners, especially Indonesians.

Next the families met with representatives from Komnas HAM, the Indonesian human rights commission, who promised to do everything possible to pressure the government to call off the executions.

After a wet and frustrating Jakarta day, the two exhausted mothers, with their sons, caught an evening flight back to Bali. They had said what they could. Now they just needed someone to listen.

At this time the legal team was doing everything it possibly could to save the lives of Andrew and Myuran. A letter to President Widodo was prepared, articulating what the lawyers had been arguing all along – and what Myuran and Andrew themselves had always believed: that they deserved not freedom or a massive sentence cut, but simply the chance to remain alive, as recognition that their rehabilitation could assist Indonesia in its fight against drugs. The plan was to send this letter directly to the president. If it did not make it all the way to him, at least his inner circle might see and read it.

The lawyers argued that people like Myuran and Andrew, if they weren't executed, could be an asset to the Indonesian state in its war against drugs. If prisoners who were successfully rehabilitated were nevertheless executed, it gave the impression that the government was simply not serious about the value of rehabilitation. And if those on death row had no incentive to change, the result could only be more violence inside prisons, making the job of guards harder and more dangerous.

The lawyers called on President Widodo to show wisdom and courage. They proposed postponing the execution of prisoners who had demonstrably been rehabilitated. Rather than weakening his anti-drugs reputation in Indonesia, they wrote, this would earn him respect. A policy that offered no prospect of mercy could only harm his attempts to rid Indonesia of illicit drugs. They urged Widodo to adopt a 'midline' position.

Whether the president ever read it or saw the 'Midline Letter' is unknown.

9.
A NATION PLEADS

After farewelling his family, Myuran headed back to his cell. The afternoon of 12 February had been lovely. For the first time in a long time he had seen his mum smiling during her visit. The family had even joked around, teasing Myuran. They were all laughing.

That day the Australian foreign minister, Julie Bishop, had made a powerful and moving speech to the House of Representatives during debate on a bipartisan motion calling for a stay of execution. She pledged to continue to work tirelessly for clemency for both Myuran and Andrew. What was happening to the two men was a grave injustice, she said. She asked people to put themselves in the shoes of Myuran, Andrew and their families. The heroin they attempted to smuggle would have brought untold misery, and possibly death, to many Australians. That was true. But she also paid tribute to the extraordinary reformation both men had achieved, and of the tireless work they were doing at Kerobokan prison. Both were paying their debt to society with dedication and commitment, improving and enriching the lives of other prisoners. So profound was the effect these two Australians had had that fellow inmates had come forward to support them, writing to President Widodo, even offering to take their place in front of the firing squad.

During her honest and emotional speech, Bishop also touched on something that was a major irritant to the team working to save Myuran and Andrew: a poll, done by Roy Morgan Research, which suggested that a slim majority of Australians were in favour of the death penalty. The results, broadcast on the ABC's Triple J radio station, on its *Hack* program, showed that 52 per cent of the 2123 people polled by SMS agreed that Australians convicted of drug trafficking overseas and sentenced to death should be executed.

The pollster's question had not used the names of the two Australians at Kerobokan. When the result was announced, Andrew and Myuran's legal team were furious. Soon Indonesian politicians, including Attorney-General Prasetyo, were quoting the poll's findings, saying that even Australians thought the two men should be put to death. This gave the Indonesians confidence they were not making a mistake, he said.

Triple J was accused of supplying ammunition to the Indonesians. The radio station defended its decision to publicise the poll results, saying it would be a dangerous precedent for journalists not to report such matters because they were fearful of how politicians might react.

Bishop addressed the issue directly, saying serious doubts had been cast on the poll's legitimacy, and that the results, which she did not believe represented the views of the Australian public, had been irresponsibly misused. She said it was deeply discomforting that out-of-context polling might be relied upon by authorities in Jakarta.

Hundreds of supportive emails had flooded into Bishop's inbox. More than 30,000 Australians had written to the Indonesian president and government. Five successive Australian prime ministers had, over the years, made representations. Since 7 January, when Myuran's clemency was denied, Prime Minister Abbott and several senior ministers had sent 11 written representations to their Indonesian counterparts as part of a high-level advocacy campaign. In addition, Abbott and Bishop had joined with the Opposition and the Greens and more than 100 parliamentarians to petition the Indonesian ambassador. The letters emphasised Australia's respect for Indonesia's sovereignty, and pointed out the special aspects of Myuran and Andrew's case that warranted mercy. Indonesia could be in no doubt about Australia's position.

In her speech, Bishop pointed out something the Sukumaran and Chan camps had been highlighting for some time now: the fact that the Indonesian government was working hard to save the lives of up to 200 Indonesian citizens who faced the death penalty abroad, in countries such as Saudi Arabia. It was incongruous for Indonesia to execute foreigners while striving to save its own. There were some 360 Indonesians on death row overseas, according to Migrant Care and other NGOs. 'We urge the Indonesian government to show the same mercy to Andrew and Myuran that it seeks for its citizens in the same situation abroad,' the Foreign Minister told parliament.

Myuran was humbled by Ms Bishop's words – and by those of her opposite number, Tanya Plibersek, the deputy Labor leader, who delivered her own moving and personal speech calling for clemency. For the first time in a very long time he started to feel better about himself, less ashamed – as though people were finally seeing him and Andrew for who they had become, not who they had been almost a decade earlier. It seemed unbelievable that his and Andrew's names were being spoken in parliament with such emotion and support. Finally his family could hold their heads up again. For years Myuran had lived with the burden of the shame he had visited upon his mother. He loved her desperately, and all he wanted was for her to be proud of him.

Walking back to his cell, Myuran felt lighter. Ben Quilty was visiting the next day and was planning for Myuran to do a big painting. He had asked all the other prison art students to come in and watch. Perhaps they had more time. Perhaps it wouldn't happen after all.

But his optimism drained away the minute he was back at his cell. Myuran and Andrew looked at each other, taking it in. The authorities in Bali had just announced that Jakarta had told them to prepare to move Myuran and Andrew to Nusakambangan. They had only just read the urgent text messages I had sent them the minute the announcement was made. I had promised them I would tell them everything I knew, good or bad.

Myuran's heart dropped like a stone. There had been a meeting in Bali that day; another was planned for the next day. As soon as Myuran heard about the meetings, he called Majell Hind; she was already on her way to see and brief them. Myuran and Andrew were starting to feel desperate all over again. The dark shadow that had been hanging over them was back.

Myuran messaged me that night:

> Yesterday they looked like they were backing off this.
> Now full steam ahead. Do you have any idea whatsoever how we get ourselves out of this?

On 12 February, reporters Michael Bachelard and Nick McKenzie published a story in the Fairfax press about two Indonesian judges who had been involved in Bali Nine cases: they had subsequently been sacked for corruption or manipulation of cases.

Achmad Yamanie was a Supreme Court judge who had been on the panel that, in 2011, had rejected Myuran and Andrew's appeal. A month later he was on a panel that reduced the death sentence of an Indonesian drug lord to 15 years' imprisonment.

Yamanie was later discharged from the court after falsifying documents to reduce the sentence further, from 15 to 12 years.

Another judge, Putu Suika, the chairman of the panel of judges who had dealt with the judicial review of one of the Australian cases, was later found to have violated the judicial code of ethics when, midway through a trial, he met the defence lawyer in a karaoke bar and accepted money. The cases called into question the integrity of the Indonesian legal system.

'Can we say because we didn't have enough money we got the death penalty?' Myuran asked me. 'Yeah, can we scream it?'

For a while Myuran had been thinking about making video messages for his family to watch after he was gone. Chinthu had encouraged him, but Myuran had avoided the task, hoping it would never be necessary. Now, with the latest news, he decided he needed to get it done.

I spoke to him on the phone that night. His voice was sad and listless. He sounded defeated, gutted, like he was ready to give up. 'I am speechless,' he told me desperately. 'I don't even know what to say about this. I don't believe this is happening.' Each day seemed to bring new hope, but then it would be dashed, sometimes within hours. It was traumatising.

Myuran told me he had heard about people who were dying of cancer or other diseases who made videos for their families. He wanted to know if I thought it was a good idea to make them, and what he should talk about. He knew what he wanted to say, but he didn't know how to do it.

I wasn't sure how to answer. Eventually I told him to speak from his heart. 'Tell them all the things you would want them to know if the worst happens and you are executed.'

'You said *if* it happens,' he said. 'You don't think it's going to happen? Do you think there's hope?' He was desperate for something to hold onto.

The truth was that, at that time, I did think there was some hope – but I was also a realist. I knew that Indonesia was unpredictable. Just when you thought you understood it, you realised you knew nothing. I struggled to answer Myuran's questions. I wanted to be honest, without crushing all hope in him.

Andrew was more controlled that evening. A very different man to Myuran, he was hiding his fears, trying to make light of the bad news. Putting on a mask. In a text message he asked what I was writing, and why I was taking so long: 'Come on now, Mrs Wockner, get a crack on – I wrote my last piece in 20 minutes! LOL.'

It was about football, his great love, and his team, the Penrith Panthers. He had penned a piece headlined 'Why I Love Rugby League and Penrith Panters'. He sent it to me:

> I'm a Westie – not just your average class Westie, but a Westie born and bred. When we think of a Westie we have an image of a wife-beater, a pair of footy shorts and a stubby in one hand. Welcome to my life in the West! That's right, folks, the heartland where rugby league thrives, with the smell of meat pies and hotdogs warming up at Centrebet Stadium.

We are almost at the kickoff of the season at Penrith, a club that's been around since 1967, when it first entered the competition. I was fortunate enough to watch them win both premierships and minor premierships.

I was born in the 1980s, a time when Parramatta was at its best and the Newtown Jets had just been relegated. My first taste of league was at an early age: I use to watch Mal Meninga storm over, and players like Jonah Lomu went through the whole English team. The game is a lot different to what it was in the '80s and '90s. It's a lot faster, tougher and the athletes just get bigger and stronger. Just ask 'Fat Man' Vautin, who use to play for every pay cheque – he could tell you our game has now changed and become a dynamic national sport, and is slowly hitting the international waters. It's amazing to see how much rugby league has spread, not just in the West but internationally.

I'm always going to be a Westie at heart. I love my Panthers, even though for several years they were on the brink of collecting the wooden spoon. The club has now grown; having the likes of Jamie Soward leading the team around the park has been one of their best buys.

When Phil Gould released Michael Jennings and Luke Lewis, every Panther was searching for him like they were searching for Bin Laden. The members didn't understand what Phil was trying to bring, and how he wanted a coach to dynamically bring through juniors from the biggest feeder clubs in the competition. In the last three years Phil has turned the club from wooden spooners to (almost) silver spooners. He intelligently recruited Ivan Cleary, a man who took the New Zealand Warriors to many finals. There's a saying: 'What would Jesus do?' Well, what will Phil do? This is what every Panther speaks.

Andrew's knowledge of rugby league was incredible. He followed all the games every season, and knew every player's form. Apparently, some players had visited him in jail when they were on holiday in Bali. Andrew even knew the gossip. He loved being on top of it all, despite being locked up in a Bali jail on death row. At one stage the prisoners had their own tipping competition in the death row tower, the block where Andrew and the other Bali Nine were kept. He also loved getting copies of newspapers and magazines so that he could devour rugby league stories. Another thing he loved was the shopping catalogues that come in newspapers.

But right now he was preoccupied. Helen and Ken would leave Bali in a few days. The health of both his parents was deteriorating in Bali and they really needed to get home. Helen's eye condition was worsening; she'd had to seek medical treatment three times already during the trip. And it had been a miracle that Ken had made it to Bali this time at all: his trip had been delayed initially, and then, just before he was due to board his flight, he had another fall. But both Andrew's parents were determined to be there for their son. Their last meal at the jail before they left had been the first time in nine years that the whole family – Mum, Dad, siblings and partners – had been together. 'So basically it's goodbye for them,' Andrew told me. 'Ahh, not much you can do. It's not goodbye forever.'

Ever since the clemencies had been denied, the jail had allowed the Chan and Sukumaran families to visit each weekend, as well as each weekday. Under normal circumstances, weekends were non-visit days. Helen and Ken were due to leave on Sunday evening. This week the jail was not allowing any Saturday visits due to a meeting. There were doubts that they would be allowed in on the Sunday, too. Andrew told me his mum and dad didn't know if they would ever see him again:

> My mother wanted to stand in front of the prison for the next two days if she didn't get to see me just so she could make sure I knew how much she loved me and didn't wanna leave my side.

Thankfully, in the end the visit was allowed. When it came time for them to go, Andrew didn't say the word *goodbye*. 'See you later,' he told them.

Andrew asked me if I had seen the movie *John Q.*, starring Denzel Washington. It's the story of a father who is desperate to save his young son's life, after learning the boy has an enlarged heart and needs a transplant, which is not covered by insurance and which the family can't afford. 'Watch it. That's just how my mother and father feel,' Andrew told me.

A NATION PLEADS

Before his parents left Bali, Andrew felt privileged to conduct one last prayer service with them.

Myuran didn't make the videos for his family that night. He told me he felt sick – he hated it. The guards were now being distant, he noted. Perhaps they knew the execution would be soon.

He was starting to get depressed. One afternoon he sent me a photo of a self-portrait he had tried to paint that day. It was not good and I struggled to know if it was him or someone else. The look in the eyes was one of defeat. I asked him what it meant. 'I don't know. Maybe it's how I feel.' He wanted to know what I thought would happen next. 'I think they're very committed to this. I don't think they will back down.'

Andrew was devouring the press. He forwarded me the link to a story about the brother of an Indonesian maid whose life had been spared from the death penalty overseas by the Indonesian government's program of saving its own citizens. The maid's brother had accused Indonesia of having a double standard, given its program of executing foreigners at home. He asked how to get the story into the Indonesian press.

When, in mid-February I told Myuran that the government had delayed plans to move them to Nusakambangan jail, he was overwhelmed. He felt like he could breathe again. His mum Raji, who had been visiting when he got my message. 'She screamed, but in a good way,' he told me of Raji's overjoyed reaction. He was so grateful to have more time with his family. He started painting, another self-portrait, and sent me a picture of it. He hoped the news the next day was not bad again so he wouldn't ruin it. At the time news of the delay came through he had been clearing out his art studio, organising his art books and personal belongings.

Earlier that day the Australian Consulate briefed the families on logistics, how to get to Nusakambangan jail when the men were moved, what to expect, what to collect from the jail in Bali. Myuran and Andrew had been told to prepare. They each gave the lawyers a set of clothes in case, at the time of the move, they were not allowed to take anything with them.

Myuran was exhausted and fell asleep at 8.30 that night without finishing the painting. 'Yesterday was too hard. It's hard going from such extreme emotions, from really sad to happy,' he told me. Until hearing of the delay, Myuran said he felt like it was all over.

The next day Myuran wanted to know if I thought they would go ahead with the executions. He sent me the link to a story in the Indonesian press. His sleep was erratic, his emotions were all over the place. He found it hard to get into the zone to keep painting but when he did, it provided him with an escape from the reality, he told me. 'I love being a famous painter, not a famous criminal.' He wanted to do three or four big pieces, including a landscape of Nusakambangan, and asked me to send him photos of it.

When I told Myuran a day later that the Indonesian Vice-President had indicated the executions would be delayed three weeks to a month, he was more desperate. 'But are they still going to go through with it?' he wanted to know. He asked me to send a photograph of my son so he could do me a painting.

Every day there was a new story. The latest was reports that they would be transferred to Nusakambangan by a fighter jet escort. Myuran shook his head. He was trying to focus on his painting but it was getting harder and harder. He had felt like he had some space to breathe 'But I'm scared that it's only really technical reasons [for] why they want to delay the executions and then they go at it again. I've heard they say it was a messy execution last time and they want to do it precisely this time. They're also scared the media will get on the island.'

By that evening there were new reports that the fighter jets were already in place at Bali airport, ready for the transfer. 'What do you think of this? I think they are serious. I think I'm going to lose the plot soon.' He said he couldn't help but scour the local media for any news of what was going on. I told him to stop reading everything so much. He was nervous and scared. He wanted to know if the fighter jets had left yet.

Andrew continued counselling people and running church services. And he joked about wanting to write a sports column for us in exchange for free newspapers for his family and a lifetime NRL pass to all games. He was having takeaway Indian and it cost him a 'bloody bucketload' he complained. When I suggested someone in his position deserved some treats, he laughed: 'With them prices it set me back four years.'

As well as the ongoing legal challenges, Veronica Haccou was now dealing with the practicalities of the situation. A year earlier, well before the clemency was denied, and before any talk of executions, she had helped Myuran and Andrew to make their wills. Myuran had been gloomy about it but she told him it was normal – everyone should have a will. Now it was more serious. She needed his and Andrew's instructions on what to do with their bodies if they were executed.

Veronica also briefed them on the practicalities of the execution. They must not be embarrassed if they lost control of their bodily functions, she said. Veronica never sugar-coated anything; she wasn't that kind of person. She had promised to always be upfront with them and tell them the truth.

Myuran wrote a letter in Veronica's notebook:

> After they kill me, I would like the following steps to take place in regards to my body. That my body be released immediately to the Australian Embassy staff/my lawyer/my family for burial in Australia. I don't wish for my body to be dealt with by the Indonesian authorities. I do not want them to conduct a post-mortem in Indonesia. I do not want my body to be cremated.
>   Myuran Sukumaran

Andrew wrote and signed an identical letter.

10.
THE FIGHT INTENSIFIES

Myuran didn't know whether to laugh or cry. Two fighter jets were flying menacingly low over Kerobokan, their engines screaming. It was absurd.

Raji, though, was terrified. She pulled her son inside the nearest room, desperate to hide him from the soldiers who, she was sure, were about to snatch him away for execution. She was trembling, panicking. Was it all about to happen? For weeks now, she and the rest of the family had visited Myuran every day as the authorities talked tough. Apparently, he and Andrew were soon to be moved to Nusakambangan in Central Java, but no date had been given.

Three Sukhoi fighter jets, from Indonesia's military, and based in South Sulawesi, had arrived at the airport, along with a CN-295 transport aircraft and helicopters. For days the military had denied they would be involved in the transfer of the two

Australian prisoners. The presence now of all this hardware, according to military spokesmen, was a coincidence. Another said it was for a joint exercise with air force personnel based in Bali, or for routine patrols securing Indonesia's borders. But the jets flew so low over the jail that day, scaring people witless, that no one was in any doubt about what was happening: the transfers would be conducted by the military.

Myuran ran out to look at them. 'They are crazy, they are crazy,' he said to his family, shaking his head. 'What are we going to do? We are in prison!' To Chinthu he said, 'Only weak men need to put on shows of strength like that.'

Police and justice ministry officials went to the airport to inspect the transport aircraft to see if it could be used to fly the Australians and the entourage of officials who would accompany them to Java. If it was unsuitable, a commercial jet would have to be chartered. There were rumours that the transfer was turning into a tussle between the police and the military, long-time adversaries; the organisation that ran the operation would receive a bigger slice of the budgetary pie.

It was 24 February, seven weeks after Myuran's clemency had been denied, and it seemed everything was coming to a head. Myuran was stressed. It was a bit much, he said, using the military for two low-level criminals like him and Andrew. 'It really shows how insecure they are,' he told me. 'They must feel really small.' It was weird, he said, how the whole country was jumping on them. Myuran felt like he and Andrew were being used to show how tough Indonesia could be on Australia.

The scariest thing was not knowing when the authorities would come and take him and Andrew. It could be any time at all.

Was he giving up hope?

Living day-to-day like this was difficult. 'In the morning you just do your normal thing and get ready to be shipped off somewhere,' he said. 'It's like a sudden thing, back and forth. Tuesday last week feels like so long ago.'

He was feeling dejected. They had done so much but it wasn't making any difference.

'You know what really upsets me?' he continued. 'We got a really good lawyer, we did all the right things, we rehabilitated, we did everything, but they would not give us a reduction of sentence. And worse people get out.' Drug criminals came and went from Kerobokan, many who had been caught with far more drugs than he and Andrew. People with 20 times more had received remissions or been freed.

Myuran had been told by a lawyer (not one from his own legal team) that, on appeal, for $200,000, he could have got a light sentence. He wished so much that they had taken a different road at the very beginning. Myuran wished that, instead of denying any knowledge of the drugs and refusing to give evidence, he had admitted guilt from the moment he was arrested. Things would be so different now, he said, if he had done that.

Andrew heard the jets fly over the jail again that night. He joked that the pilots would have needed night-vision goggles. On the inequitable system that was determining his fate, Andrew offered this observation:

> Laws are like spider webs: if a fly or mosquito gets near, it gets trapped, but if a wasp or a bee goes near, it breaks it and leaves. The same applies to the law: if a poor man strays he gets caught, while the rich and powerful exempt themselves from the law and walk away.

Andrew was reading the Christian book *Traveling Light*, by Max Lucado, which focused on Psalm 23 and the release of our burdens. He told me he only read Christian, history and medical books. 'I like to learn, not imagine,' he said; novels were a waste of space in the head.

I asked why he read medical books.

'Coz I don't like being checked by a vet. I would rather operate on myself.'

Sometimes Andrew's comments, in our chats, were out of left field. Just after we talked about the books he was reading, he wanted to know: was he unique among other prisoners I had come across? 'I'm not exactly Ted Bundy,' he said, referring to the American serial killer, a man who confessed to 30 homicides and was executed in 1989.

That day, as the lawyers and family visited the jail, Andrew took Veronica's notebook and penned a note for only her: 'Can I discuss marriage?'

She nodded, and motioned that they go for a walk to speak privately.

Andrew had decided he wanted to marry Febyanti Herewila, a young Indonesian pastor he had first met back in 2012 inside Kerobokan prison. Feby, from Yogyakarta, had come to minister to the prisoners. She had run prayer groups and youth ministries in Indonesia and in Singapore, and a friend asked her to visit Kerobokan.

For two years she and Andrew were just friends, but early in 2014 they started a relationship. Before this she hadn't realised he was even interested in her. Then someone else pointed out to Feby that every time she visited the jail, Andrew, who had a kitchen set up at the jail, cooked for her.

When Andrew later asked why she had been blind to his attraction, she told him it was because he was always kind to everyone, and always cooked for everyone.

Feby began visiting Andrew regularly, and the couple shared their theological studies and backgrounds. An intensely private person, Feby revealed their relationship only to a small group. She was concerned for her family, who emanated from a Javanese family with links to the royal court in Yogyakarta. But the couple began planning a future, which included the establishment of a community centre and school on the remote Indonesian island of Sabu, west of Timor.

The couple had become engaged ten days ago, but those who were there for the small engagement party – a cake, red roses and a ring – had been sworn to secrecy. The couple wanted it kept private. There was so much else going on politically that they decided the happy news didn't need to be made public.

After the engagement party Andrew asked Veronica to come with him and Feby as he got his hair cut at the jail barber. He was excited to have his new fiancée with him to advise on how his hair should be cut. He loved Feby deeply, and now to be engaged to her left him beaming. He was also keen that Feby and Veronica become friends. It was as though he were thinking ahead to a time when he was gone: he wanted to make sure she was comforted and cared for by someone with whom he had been very close.

Now Andrew asked Veronica to investigate how he and Feby could marry in jail.

Veronica promised to do so.

Raji was having nightmares. She kept thinking about her son's dead body being handed to her. She couldn't stop thinking about the violent way he would be killed. Every night she got down on her knees to pray that the president, the attorney-general and all those who controlled the fate of Myuran and Andrew would look again at their cases and see how unique they were, and why they were deserving of mercy. She could not understand how the ending of a life could be authorised so quickly.

THE FIGHT INTENSIFIES

The family was falling apart. They sat together but couldn't look into each other's eyes: it was just too sad. Chinthu felt it was an awful punishment to inflict upon his mother, who did not deserve such searing pain. Sam was so sad but couldn't seem to find the words to express it. The whole family was heartbroken. They had no idea how much time they had left with Myuran, and couldn't bear to think about never seeing his smile again.

So desperate was Raji that, when she saw Bali's chief prosecutor, Momock Bambang Samiarso, inside the jail one day, she approached him, following him from room to room, trying to get him to listen. Momock was involved in organising the prisoners' move from Bali to Java in readiness for execution. Raji begged him not to move her son, not to kill him. Momock spoke no English, but one of his deputies, Olopan Nainggolan, translated. Olopan told Raji, 'You pray, you pray.' Like the Sukumaran and Chan families, Olopan was a Christian.

Helen Chan was also haunted. According to Andrew, she hadn't slept properly in the decade since he had been arrested. She suffered from insomnia and nightmares; Andrew was saddened that her pain would only get worse. She didn't speak to him about her nightmares but he knew they didn't end well.

In the midst of such dreadful news, Myuran was keen to tell me that he had almost raised enough money for the operation for Maria. After selling a portrait of Maria and a self-portrait of Myuran, they had raised $2750. He had two more to sell, and they only needed another $1000. I was amazed that he could remain so focused on raising the money for Maria's operation when he had just been told he would be dead within weeks.

That same day the paintings were sold. Two long-term Australian residents of Bali, Aki and Samantha Kotzamichalis, had bought them. Maria Lopez sobbed uncontrollably when she heard that the money had been raised. (She went on to have the operation, and remains in Kerobokan prison today.)

Aki had been associated with the renowned Bali restaurant Kudeta since it started, and now he called for suggestions on where to hang the paintings. He also added his voice to the calls for mercy for Myuran and Andrew. 'The Indonesian prison system has done a remarkable job rehabilitating these boys,' he told the media. 'They are not serial killers with no remorse whatsoever . . . their remorse is proven by their actions. They have tried to do the best for themselves and others after making a huge mistake in their younger years! We as humans are surely not that barbaric. Leave them there to help others for as long as is required.'

Andrew sauntered over to the governor of Kerobokan prison, Sudjonggo, and handed him a card. Written in Indonesian, it read: 'Get out of jail free!' It was from the local version of Monopoly. With a straight face, Andrew asked a puzzled Sudjonggo: 'Can I use it now?'

At first the governor looked serious – then he realised the joke. 'Sorry, it's not that easy,' he replied.

Quick as a flash, Andrew asked Sudjonggo if he wanted to buy the card instead.

Sudjonggo laughed. Despite the uncertainty and fear caused by his looming death sentence, Andrew was somehow maintaining his characteristic sense of humour.

Another time Andrew tried to convince some guards that he'd been a police officer in his former life. He pulled out his Police Credit Union ATM card and claimed that the numbers on it were his police ID. He was amazed when they believed him.

Andrew often joked with me that I would miss him being a smartarse when he was gone. He was always looking out for funny cartoons to show people. Like the four-panel cartoon about a prison escape. In the first panel we see a sad-looking prisoner in a cell with just a window and a door. Panel two shows the prisoner using a crayon to draw a ladder on the wall beneath the window. Next we see the guards coming into the cell, with question marks above their heads; they can't see their prisoner, who is hiding behind the door. In panel four the guards are climbing the ladder and looking out the window – while the prisoner escapes out the door. We joked that he'd better start drawing a ladder.

Earlier that day, BRIMOB, the paramilitary wing of the police, had conducted a dress rehearsal of how the two Australians would be moved from Kerobokan jail to the airport for their flight to Nusakambangan, where the executions would take place. It was 27 February. Two policemen played the role of Andrew and Myuran. Their hands were cuffed with cable ties. The officers wore helmets, their faces covered by black masks.

There were guns everywhere as the two actors were walked into Barracuda armoured personnel carriers. The 'prisoners' wore hats. At one stage a police officer pulled the hat of one of them down, covering his face. They were leaving nothing to chance in the simulation, which was a massive show of force.

Andrew was intrigued, and wanted to know all about it. 'Were they violent with them?' he asked me – and then joked that he might get a souvenir hat out of it. When I told him the police intended to use armoured vehicles to transport them from the jail to the airport, he was amazed. 'Terrorists don't even get this treatment,' he said. 'Just insane really.'

For his part, Myuran was in a grey mood. It should have been a day for celebration – Curtin University in Perth had awarded him an Associate Degree in Fine Arts. All his hard work had paid off. But he wasn't feeling good. It had been an emotionally draining period, and it was only getting worse. If dress rehearsals were being conducted, Myuran knew, a move away from Bali was nearer than ever. It was getting harder to remain positive.

Lizzie Love told Myuran how her first husband had died in a plane crash when she was 23. Myuran was again talking frequently and deeply with Lizzie, with whom he had now reconciled. Myuran suggested there was nothing after death. Lizzie told him she wasn't religious but she believed there was something.

The day of her husband's death Lizzie had been playing water volleyball and took her wedding ring off so she wouldn't lose it during the game. There had been nothing wrong with it. That night the plane crashed. Lizzie heard about it on the news and contacted authorities. They told her that her husband and his father had been at the front of the plane and were most likely dead but many bodies had not yet been recovered.

The next morning, as Lizzie sat looking at her husband's photo and watching the news, she was willing her husband for a sign of whether he was alive or dead. The phone rang. She grabbed it with her left hand and immediately spotted her wedding ring, gold with a layer of white gold over the top. The white gold was cracked right through. She knew then her husband was dead. The cracked ring was the sign.

She told Myuran how, in the months and years that followed, she would get a sense – like a smell – out of the blue and in the middle of a conversation. It was the smell of the trees in autumn in Grass Valley in the US where she had lived. Lizzie felt the presence of her husband and it gave her peace. She told Myuran not to be scared because it was an okay place that he would go, if the worst happened. Her husband Jim would be there to meet him. Life was not over. It was a new journey.

11.
MERCY, PLEASE

The letter was written by Kerobokan jail prisoner Francois Jacques Giuily and addressed to the Indonesian president. It read:

> I hereby confirm that Andrew Chan has changed my life since I have been here at LP Kerobokan. He has a strong spiritual power and he has helped me a lot through his teaching. His execution would be a disaster. If you finally decide to execute him, I ask to take his place. I write this in good health condition and without any pressure and with all my heart.

Jacques was not the only prisoner to write to President Widodo begging to take Andrew's place before the firing squad. Another, Rico Richardo, wrote: 'If the honorable Bapak [Mr] President insist to execute Andrew Chan, I Rico Richardo as an Indonesian citizen, am ready to replace Andrew Chan as death row convict that will [be] executed.' Rico went on to say how Andrew had helped save his life only the month before. After Rico had fallen ill, it was Andrew who insisted he be taken to hospital and who paid the balance of the fees for his medical treatment. 'So what I can convey to the Honorable Bapak President, then even though Andrew Chan has been sentenced to death, he is still aware of other people's fate, like me for example,' Rico continued. 'Andrew Chan is never thinking about himself.'

In fact, there were many letters from many prisoners whose lives had been saved or turned around by the work of Andrew and Myuran. In an outpouring of emotion, they had decided to write to President Widodo to beg for mercy. They were hurting, knowing that their mentors, friends and teachers were about to be killed.

It was extraordinary, a mark of the men Andrew and Myuran had become that fellow prisoners were not only supporting them, but were offering to take their places in front of the firing squad. For the writers, it was a risk to be penning such words, in defiance of authority, in letters that were copied to the media for publication. They didn't care about the repercussions; they were simply desperate to save the two men.

Manuel Junior said he was sad and shocked when he heard that Andrew was to be executed. He described Andrew as a 'father figure, mentor, lecturer and a warm teacher guiding his children'. Suyoto Iskan said he deplored what was happening:

> Andrew Chan has a compassionate soul. I was a desperate person. But then Andrew Chan strengthened my faith. I became a happy and hopeful person. Andrew Chan is remarkable. Andrew Chan is needed by Christians in the prison. Andrew Chan baptized me in the prison. Andrew Chan has turned desperate souls into hopeful and happy souls.

And those who had freed themselves from drugs and found peace in a safe environment while learning to paint under Myuran's tutelage were equally glowing in their references. Nopi Nicholas wrote about his own stupidity in using drugs, which had landed him in prison with a heavy sentence. He was depressed and stressed about his wife and six children. Someone suggested he go to the *bengker*, as the art workshop was known, to meet Myuran. The Australian mentored Nopi in his painting, and he became closer to God with Andrew's help. Nopi had learned how to be patient, he wrote, and how to respect others, love and forgive.

Wayan Sudiasa said that many painters would be born at Kerobokan prison every year with Myuran's help. Others, who had left prison having learned to paint, were drug-free and had become good and productive people. 'He is the convict that was sentenced to death by the judge,' Wayan wrote, 'who became a mentor, teacher and guide of painting activity in Kerobokan prison. Children who are mentored become successful and have a better life and benefit the nation.'

A former prisoner who signed his name with an X questioned the point of rehabilitation if there was no chance at all for clemency. He quoted the Indonesian Correctional Services' own goal: 'The correctional system is a series of law enforcement that is aimed at the inmate realising their wrongdoing, fixing themselves and not committing crime again so that they can be accepted by the community again and have an active role in their development and can live normally as a good and responsible person.' This prisoner urged the president to consider Myuran's and Andrew's rehabilitation, and how they had touched the lives of so many people. 'You can use these boys as an example to spearhead your campaign against drugs. They can be the positive for change in Indonesia. Don't shoot the messengers.' Andrew and Myuran were worth more to Indonesia alive than dead, he wrote. 'You have the power to harness all the good they can do and commute their sentence to life. Have you considered meeting them? Talking to the prison officials, family and friends?'

Former prisoner X touched on something that those in jail already knew, but which was often not spoken of publicly. 'I was given the opportunity to pay big $$$ for my freedom,' he claimed. And he went further: if the president wanted to arrest the real criminal people, X would be happy to pass on information. He claimed to have the names of police, judges, prosecutors, lawyers, gang members and officials who were profiting from what he said was a prolific drug trade inside and outside Indonesian prisons 'with absolute impunity'. These people were the real problem.

Prisoner X finished by noting that Indonesia held a seat on the United Nations Human Rights Council; it had recently been re-elected for a fourth term that would run until 2017. 'There are human rights abuses going on in your prisons,' X wrote. 'I saw it with my own eyes. Andrew and Myuran are a shining example of what men can achieve if they have a genuine desire to reform and become persons of great integrity. Please let these men LIVE!'

These letters to the president were moving. Andrew lamented that Widodo probably wouldn't read them. Still he was proud of the work he had done within the church community at the jail, telling me that not one of the prisoners he had counselled had returned to jail after their release – at least not as a prisoner. Many of the ex-inmates did return to visit Andrew when they could. He told me:

> We got a really good community at church now that I have led for the last ten years. A lot of these guys had nothing when they walked in – their families were broken. I'm just lucky that Jesus equipped me so that I started up foundations inside here so if prisoners get sick, or need assistance for their family outside, we have an agreement that funds are to be used for important factors like sending kids to school, helping buy food, milk and so forth, for their kids and wife outside. I helped build this network for the last five years, and it's helped place kids in school, hospitals and many other

things. But as I said, a man can talk himself up; you should ask around yourself what has been implemented.

Andrew was keen that the letters from the prisoners were given to the Indonesian press. He was only too aware that they needed to raise the profile of their good works in the Indonesian media.

It was around this time that a story published in the Fairfax press claimed that a mastermind of the Bali Nine syndicate had won more than $5 million in the lottery a few years earlier. The man, who was not identified, lived in Sydney and had never been prosecuted in relation to the Bali Nine heroin.

Myuran said he had no clue who the story referred to, but described him as 'amazingly lucky'. 'Some people are just so blessed,' he said. Both he and Andrew had always maintained they were just above the courier level in the operation, and well below that of the real bosses; they'd been paid to come to Bali like everyone else. They had never paid for the drugs, owned them or sold them.

Andrew wanted to know where the hell the information had come from – he had never heard of it before. 'This story just sounds crazy, LOL,' he messaged me. 'I really couldn't tell you if it's true or not.' He said he would pray for whoever it was. 'If that's the case then yeah, it's pretty messed up, but hey, that's him and I'll pray for the fella, whoever it is.' Andrew wasn't being generous, he said; over time he had learned to forgive those who had hurt him. 'You know why I never said anything in court about the others?' he asked me 'Coz I told them, if I was them, I would probably say exactly what they said about me.'

Andrew was referring to evidence given by other Bali Nine members, during their own trials in the Denpasar District Court: that Andrew had threatened them into carrying the drugs that fateful night. Andrew said he had forgiven them all a long time ago, and held no grudges. But what about the fact that some had now retracted their allegations of threats, admitting they had made them up? It was pointless to dwell on that now, Andrew said. It wouldn't change anything.

The legal team was now working on its latest legal challenge: an application to the State Administrative Court in Jakarta, where they planned to challenge the president's blanket refusal of their clemency requests. The lawyers said their challenge was not some half-baked last-minute measure but raised 'genuine substantive issues of fairness and justice'. It would be a grave miscarriage of justice, they warned, if the executions were to proceed before the court had determined whether the president's decision to refuse clemency accorded with the law.

The application argued that Andrew, Myuran and the others on the execution lists had not had an opportunity for their clemency applications to be properly and genuinely considered, thus denying them of natural justice.

> The present Indonesian Government has consistently stated that clemency has been and will be refused for drug offenders as a matter of policy. It is absolutely clear from the statements of numerous Government officials, including the President himself, that it is the blanket application of that policy that has resulted in clemency being denied. The merits of Andrew and Myuran's case simply have not been considered.

The lawyers highlighted the fact that the Indonesian attorney-general had pronounced that the clemency decisions were not reviewable by the State Administrative Court, and that the power to grant clemency was the prerogative of the president alone.

'It is not for the AG to announce before the court hearing,' the Australian legal team claimed. 'A fundamental aspect of the rule of law is that all of the legal questions raised on the application are for the court alone to determine.'

There were strong arguments, the team claimed, that in refusing clemency in the way he did, the president had failed to comply with or have sufficient regard for the clemency laws. There was no evidence that the president had considered the advice of the Supreme Court, despite the statute requiring him to do so.

The lawyers touched on another matter, which was now being aired in Indonesia and around the globe. The accuracy of the drug emergency statistics so passionately cited by the president and his ministers were now being questioned. The lawyers called them 'dubious statistics'.

A PhD candidate in social intervention at Oxford University, Claudia Stoicescu, had published a piece on The Conversation website disputing the figures, saying they were 'based on studies with questionable methods and vague measures'. Stoicescu dissected the figures. The claim that there were 4.5 million drug users in Indonesia needing rehabilitation was a projection of the number of people predicted to use drugs in 2013, from the University of Indonesia's Centre for Health Research and the National Narcotics Agency (or BNN) as part of a 2008 study. Stoicescu argued that the stats did not estimate the number of people unable to manage their drug use, and could not be generalised to show drug use across the population. Moreover, Stoicescu wrote, the claim that 40 to 50 people died each day from drug use was even more problematic. Indonesia did not collect reliable drug overdose statistics.

The leaders of the BNN made no secret of the fact that they wanted drug traffickers executed. Many wondered why they didn't use Myuran and Andrew as anti-drugs ambassadors, holding them up as poster boys who could teach about the dangers of drugs. A similar approach had been used by the counter-terrorism police back in 2003, in the aftermath of the first Bali bombing: Ali Imron had eschewed his radical past and, unlike his brothers, Amrozi and Mukhlas, admitted his guilt and turned police resource. While his brothers got the death penalty for their role in the killings of over 200 people in two Kuta nightclubs, Ali Imron got a life sentence after admitting his guilt and apologising. So too did another accused man, Mubarok. The sparing of their lives came with a rider: testify against the others and become a force for good, educating others about the evils of terrorism and about the true meaning of *jihad*. Imron and Mubarok remain anti-terrorism ambassadors today.

Myuran wondered if the lawyers could suggest them as anti-drugs ambassadors, although he was aware that it might be considered a last-minute stunt. His mind was going round and round now, and he felt that authorities were determined not to listen, no matter what. How could the team give them a reason to back down?

'I was in a bad mood yesterday,' he told me. 'I said something really stupid – I hope it doesn't get me into trouble. I asked how much would I have to pay for them to let me out.'

The pressure was getting to him. 'Before, I felt like I deserved it,' he said. 'Now I feel like they are not doing the right thing.' It was unfair and unjust. He felt like the whole saga was unfolding like a movie. 'I hope this movie has a happy ending.' Why were the Indonesians working so hard to save their own citizens on death row overseas, but wouldn't spare them?

Myuran was trying to think of new ways to show that he deserved to live. 'For a long time I was thinking about renting a shop somewhere in the outside,' he told me, 'and turning it into an art space for ex-prisoner artists to go to work after they are released. I'm thinking about whether I should try to push it through or not. I don't have enough money from the sales of paintings, but I could probably borrow it. But would it look bad if I borrowed it?'

He wanted to show the president that he and Andrew were not in the same league as other prisoners – those who continued operating their drug networks from inside jail, right under the nose of the authorities. 'How can we make him understand?' Myuran wanted to know.

By this time Myuran was in a cell by himself. Of the original Bali Nine, only five remained at Kerobokan prison. Renae Lawrence had been transferred to another Bali jail after authorities claimed she threatened to kill a guard (something she has always denied). Scott Rush was also sent to another prison in Bali; he requested a transfer, apparently to escape the temptations of drugs. Martin Stephens and Tan Duc Tanh Nguyen had been moved to a jail in Java. Andrew was sharing a cell with an Iranian drug trafficker on a life sentence. Michael Czugaj and Si Yi Chen were cellmates; Matthew Norman had his own cell.

Myuran had taken over the cell previously used by Martin Stephens and Tan Duc Thanh Nguyen, and a Nigerian who was also on death row. When they moved out Myuran painted the walls bright blue. In many ways it was not unlike any bedroom in an Indonesian home. He had a desk with a reading lamp, and an office chair. A shelf on the wall held some of his precious art textbooks. There was an easel, and on the desk sat lumps of clay. He'd been getting into moulding clay before the clemency denial came through.

The only things on the walls were a painting – Myuran's first Archibald Prize entry, from 2013 – and a drawing done by Ben Quilty. Myuran had never plastered his walls with images of his family; he didn't like the guards or other people poring over his photos. They were private.

12.
THE LAST FLIGHT

'Thank you for choosing Wings Air. Hope you have a pleasant flight. In front of you, you will see an exit door . . .'

The flight steward, in a short red skirt and black stockings, demonstrated the safety features of the plane. She pointed out a safety card in the seat pocket, which contained, among other things, prayers from various religions, should there be an on-board incident and passengers felt the need to pray.

And all this she said with a straight face. Perhaps the absurdity of it had not registered. Or perhaps she was, as Myuran thought, terrified of him and Andrew.

'Here are the exits, should you need to escape . . .'

There wasn't much chance of that, Myuran thought, since he and Andrew were in handcuffs and shackles, and surrounded by heavily armed paramilitary policemen in balaclavas. In fact, the plane was packed with police and prosecutors. Some took selfies with the now infamous Australians.

After weeks of speculation, Andrew and Myuran were finally on the plane to Nusakambangan. In the end, the government had decided to charter a commercial airliner for the flight. Escorting them from Bali to Cilacap, in Central Java, were the fighter jets they had seen several weeks before. For the two Australians, it was their first time on a plane in a decade. The last had been in 2005, when they travelled from Sydney to Bali in preparation for their ill-fated drug run.

As dawn broke on Wednesday, 4 March 2015, the sky above Bali turning a delicate shade of pink, the Wings Air plane sat at the end of the runway and waited, engines running, propellers turning. The hold-up was not explained. Someone said it was because one of the fighter jet escorts had had a mishap back at the hangar; apparently its parachute had deployed accidently. Two fighter jets had already taken off. Finally, the third fighter jet taxied around in front of the red and white Wings Air plane and hurtled down the runway. Wings Air took off after it.

Andrew and Myuran were on their last ever flight. But there was little chance to look out the windows and see the majestic scenery of Bali – the beaches, Mount Agung, Kintamani. It had been a long time since they saw any of that. The prisoners truly believed they were going to be executed soon after arriving at their destination. On the plane with them were 20 BRIMOB officers and another 30 or so prosecutors and officials.

Before they had taken off, senior Bali police officers – men who would not be making the journey with them but who had organised the transfer – took selfies with both Andrew and Myuran. 'Smile, smile,' one officer said to Andrew. Myuran felt like every person on the plane took a photo with him during the trip.

When these photos later found their way into the media, the Australian government was horrified. It was like some kind of ghoulish circus. Then there was the spectacle of the fighter jet escort. No other prisoner being taken to Nusakambangan had been accompanied by such a show of military might.

Such was the security that Andrew and Myuran were not even permitted to use the toilet during the flight. When one of them needed to pee he was told he would need to do so in a water bottle, sitting in his seat. A giggling guard held the bottle for him as he urinated. Then the policeman had to ask his boss to discard it in the toilet. Both Andrew and Myuran were held by the arm all the way.

Andrew dozed off for part of the journey. It was impossibly hot. Unable to take off his jacket because he was shackled, he was sweating profusely. The armed officer next to him gave him a hankie to wipe away the perspiration.

As they landed, the 'too cute stewardess', as Myuran called her, made another announcement. 'Welcome to Cilacap. I hope you enjoyed your flight. Please do not leave any of your possessions behind.' She reminded them that the time in Cilacap was one hour behind Bali.

Andrew adjusted his plastic wristwatch. He had left his good watch, of which he was incredibly proud, and his ring, with Veronica the day before, for her to pass to Feby. As they prepared to disembark, Andrew reminded his guard to get his hankie.

Cilacap airport was on high alert. The tiny airstrip and surrounds were swarming with armed police, who, at gunpoint, warned off reporters and photographers who were getting too close. Clearly, this was serious business: handcuffs and leg irons were essential for transporting two prisoners who had never tried to escape. These men were not terrorists, although the Barracuda tanks awaiting them at Cilicap suggested otherwise.

Andrew and Myuran were bundled down the steps of the plane and led into the waiting tanks – the same kind that had ferried them from Kerobokan jail to the airport. They were pushed to the ground, and guns were trained on them. One guard asked Andrew what his case was: was this his first time in jail?

Andrew couldn't believe it. There was nothing to do but see the funny side of it.

One of the guards looked at Myuran. 'This is the guy that said people can change,' he said to his fellow officers. The painting had, by now, been shown to the media.

Myuran and Andrew were made to keep their heads down during the drive from the airport to the port of Wijayapura, where the two tanks were driven onto the jail ferry. They saw nothing of the journey to Besi prison, one of several on the island of Nusakambangan.

After the easy-going pace of Kerobokan prison, Besi was like another world. The men were weighed and measured by a doctor. Their watches were removed. They were put into one cell. Unlike at Kerobokan, there were no beds, just thin mattresses on the floor. The cell was about five metres by six metres. It had a toilet, running water and thick walls; the front wall was a cage.

No one had said anything about when they would be executed. For the first time in a decade, they were completely shut off from the outside world. In Bali they had access to news, and visitors almost every day. Here they had nothing. Andrew and Myuran were terrified.

That same day, Julian and Veronica caught a flight from Bali to Yogyakarta, and then drove to Cilacap. They spent the entire day trying to find out where Andrew and Myuran were being held. They knew they were on Nusakambangan, but not which prison. No one would tell them. Meetings with various officials went on for hours, with no result. The Australian embassy couldn't find out either. It wasn't until the next day the lawyers discovered it was Besi.

Only two people – Majell Hind and Veronica – would be permitted to visit the prisoners. Eventually the officials agreed to allow Julian to go as well. But no family would be permitted. When Majell, Veronica and Julian first saw them, Andrew didn't look well at all. Myuran looked stunned.

As they walked in, Andrew stared at Veronica as if he didn't recognise her. Then she realised – he wasn't wearing his glasses or contact lenses. He couldn't see. He walked to Veronica and started hugging her, squeezing her tight. The hug went on and on. Knowing that security cameras were recording everything, Veronica started to feel uneasy: such a long hug wasn't normal in this culture.

Andrew whispered in her ear. 'I've got something for you – can you take it, please?' He passed her some pieces of paper – his goodbye letters for his family.

He and Myuran were angry and wanted to know where the lawyers had been. Raheem, a Nigerian prisoner in the same cell block, had been visited by his girlfriend yesterday but no one had come to see them.

'Why couldn't you come?' Andrew asked. 'If you guys didn't come, I was planning to do a hunger strike for two days because the other guy got a visitor.' Things were dire and no one knew what was going on.

Still, the Australians hadn't lost their sense of humour. At Kerobokan prison, Andrew had been diligent about replying to every letter he received. Myuran, always busy painting, hadn't – and now he felt bad about that. 'Can you redirect my mail so I can answer them now that I have time?' he joked. And he wanted to know why he didn't get lamingtons. 'I'm shocked I didn't get lamingtons,' he told the lawyers. 'Being on death row is a lot more fun in Bali.' This point was further illustrated when one of the guards had told them that sometimes cobra snakes found their way into the toilet. It was a frightening prospect they shared with their lawyers.

Myuran and Andrew had not known that day would be their last at Kerobokan until the sun was almost down. Their families had spent the day visiting. After they left, Julian and Veronica had remained behind; no one had hurried them out. As they sat and chatted at a table, some guards sauntered over to say goodbye as their shifts finished. But this wasn't a normal farewell: it was a genuine goodbye. Veronica sensed the guards' different mood. She had been visiting Kerobokan jail now for years and knew their characters. Some were hiding tears as they clocked off. Before long it was obvious that the Australians were being moved that night or the next day.

Outside, the chief prosecutor, Momock Bambang Samiarso, had made the announcement: Myuran and Andrew would be transferred to Nusakambangan in the morning. It ended weeks of speculation. Julian and Veronica were permitted to stay until 6 p.m. They tried to calm Myuran and Andrew, who were getting anxious.

'I promise you that we will find you,' Veronica said. 'Just go, and don't resist. When you return to your room, start packing – take only the things you need, just a small bag.' She emphasised again that they should not resist. 'Just go.'

Andrew and Myuran went back to their cells to pack and say their goodbyes. If they were going to be dead within days, they needed to talk to people. Both spent hours on their phones, talking and texting.

When I spoke to Myuran that night he was calm but despondent. His voice was flat, resigned. All he wanted was for his mum to be proud of him. He was upset that she was now so stressed and in such pain. He wished he could take it away. Most of his belongings had already been taken out of the prison by his family, he said, in anticipation of this day. He had already sorted out who would take over all the rehabilitation projects once he was gone, and how he hoped they would continue.

He lamented that all his work on the projects now meant little: 'They say it's all really good but it doesn't mean anything in the end.' Over the past few days he had painted portraits of some of the people in charge of his fate – the chief prosecutor, the minister of justice and human rights, the attorney-general. But he hadn't yet thought about what he would ask for when the time came for his last request. It was all too hard.

Myuran spoke of his life over the past ten years, joking that he could write a TV reality show about what went on inside Kerobokan jail. People would never believe it, he told me, but it would rate like crazy. Like the time a cake was brought in for the departing Schapelle Corby. Pictures of the cake – which only arrived after she had already left the jail, and which she therefore never actually saw – ended up in the women's magazines, which were desperate for any titbits about her last days at Kerobokan. The money earned from the sale of those pictures went into the prison kitty to help fund the rehabilitation programs. Myuran hadn't arranged any of it but was happy to get a funding windfall from what was essentially a fabricated story. The guards enjoyed the cake and everyone laughed themselves silly at how gullible the press could be.

Somehow, Myuran had managed to run the rehabilitation projects and navigate the prison bureaucracy at the same time, as well as keeping any drug merchants out of his art studio. He abhorred the dealers and the gangs who ran the jail. And he had a short fuse, as fellow Bali Nine member Renae Lawrence found out once when the pair argued.

Unlike other Bali Nine members, whose relationships were quickly publicised, Myuran kept his romantic attachments hidden. One early girlfriend was a prisoner in the women's block, but the relationship did not end well. He had another close friend, a former prisoner, but insisted it was not intimate. They needed each other, he said. 'She needed somebody to care for her and I needed somebody to help me,' he said. 'I filled the gaps for what she needed and she filled the gaps for me.' He asked her not to come to Cilacap, once he was moved. She didn't need that stress. He cared for her deeply.

Myuran had had many differences, over the years, with various Bali Nine members. But that was the past, and Myuran had moved on. There was no point harbouring old grudges when they had to live together.

That night, Myuran also told me that he had made his peace with his father, Sam. Their relationship had previously been fractious, and Myuran had found Sam's illness hard to cope with as a young boy. But over the past few months, with his father in Bali with the family, Myuran had decided the past was the past. There was no point digging up the pain of those days.

Myuran told me he and Andrew were sorry: they had stuffed up, but they didn't deserve this. 'We made a mistake, a lot of bad things have happened and we have changed,' he said. 'We made an effort and have done so much work inside here.'

No one he spoke to that night knew what to say to him. Most thought it could well be their final time with Myuran. It was 11.03 p.m. when my conversation with him ended. I didn't want to say the word 'goodbye' – I didn't know what to say. I made small talk as I tried to think of something. In the end, I said the only thing I could bring myself to say: 'You take care, Myu.'

That night, Andrew was trying to keep his humour up. 'I'm busy like Tiger Airways right now, so many calls an[d] text[s],' he joked. 'It's like the customer service line.'

He was busy writing, he said, wisecracking with me via text message about how he might finally write an article that would be published in the newspaper – it was a 'golden opportunity to put my own article up', he joked. 'UR gonna miss me being a complete smartarse now,' he told me, saying he would lose his phone when he got moved. He signed off, promising more dealings in the future.

The transfer was planned for the early hours of the next day, and no one had much sleep. Friends held a candlelit vigil at the front of the jail. Before 2 a.m. hundreds of police started massing around the complex. All the roads around it were blocked off, and police kitted out in riot gear were everywhere. Ominously, a water cannon parked in front of the building. It was unclear what the authorities were expecting, but clearly they were taking no chances.

Feby was not letting the love of her life go without saying goodbye. She wanted to see her fiancé one last time. Battling the noisy crowds, she and Michael made their way to the front door of the prison. Please, could they see Andrew before he left? It wasn't possible, they were told. Feby begged but eventually they left dejected, not commenting to anyone.

By now it was 3 a.m. Inside the prison, the time of departure was nearing.

'Andrew, what are you wearing?' Myuran shouted out to the next cell.

'Ask Veronica,' he replied. 'I don't know.'

Both men dressed, and Myuran began to eat some bread. When the guards came to get them, Myuran asked them to wait until he was finished.

At 3.22 a.m. Andrew, who still had his phone, asked me if I was out the front of the jail. He had heard the roads were blocked off. 'How long have they blocked it off for and how many police?' he wanted to know. He said he was good. When I told him there was a water cannon there too, he commented: 'That's not nice, who they gonna spray?' He wanted to know how many Barracuda armoured personnel carriers were there.

At 3.24 a.m. Myuran sent a message: 'I think we are going, they are here.' By this time the Barracudas had driven into the jail to collect their passengers.

Myuran gripped the hands of Si Yi Chen as he was led past his cell. They were like family. Caught together, they had now lived together for ten years, and two of them were leaving.

As they were led out of Kerobokan prison, the guards lined up to say goodbye. Andrew and Myuran shook each one by the hand, thanking them for their care and attention over the past decade. They thanked the prison governor for allowing them to rehabilitate and to run prison programs. There was no resistance. They went calmly and with grace. They were dignified. Some guards cried. The contrast between the military might that was on hand for their transfer and the two men's actions that morning could not have been starker.

They had arrived at Kerobokan back in 2005 as criminals. The police had dubbed them the Godfather and the Kingpin. They were leaving as reformed men. They were the Pastor and the Painter.

13.
NUSAKAMBANGAN

'You'd think being locked up 24 hours a day he can sit still. He doesn't even stay still in his sleep. He does a full 360 in his sleep.' Myuran was telling his lawyers what it was like sharing a cell with Andrew at Besi prison.

Clearly, the new living arrangements took a little getting used to. Andrew and Myuran were like two brothers made to share a bedroom for the first time. They bickered good-naturedly, but they had each other's backs and made all decisions together.

After the shock of the transfer and the initial visit from their lawyers, it seemed the suspicion that they were to be executed immediately was incorrect. The day after they arrived at Nusakambangan, the Bali prosecutors who had escorted them were ordered to return home. They had to be present for the executions; if they were going home, nothing would be happening immediately. Still, no one was taking anything for granted because nothing had been said officially.

Like Myuran and Andrew, drug convict Raheem Agbaje Salami believed he was about to die. In fact, that was not his real name, it was the name under which the Nigerian had been convicted; the name on the false passport he had been using at the time of his arrest. His real name was Jamiu Owolabi Abashin, a point which his lawyers had tried to make during their pleas to save him. How could you execute someone if you couldn't even get his name right?

On 2 March 2015 he wrote a heartbreaking final letter, telling of his love for his girlfriend, Angela Intan, and setting out his last requests:

> My clemency has been rejected so I have to be prepared for the execution at any time. About that I feel grateful to the God for what He has given in my life. I understand that all God's plan is beautiful and good for you because God knows what is the best for me . . . I also say sorry to Indonesia and all the people for my wrongdoing . . . Thank you to the prison governor and all the staff where I had been held, Madiun, Malang, Porong [prisons in East Java].

Since being convicted 17 years ago, Raheem wrote, he had obeyed prison rules and had become more active in his religion. He thanked his pastors and recorded his belief in Jesus.

I am sorry if I have [made] mistakes, deliberate or not deliberate. The last thing and most important that I want to say thank you and goodbye to my girlfriend who I love very much, Angela Intan, who has been very loyal to accompany me in happy and sad times . . . I pray for Angela to finish her study in senior high school and graduate with good results.

Raheem wanted Angela to be strong in facing the execution and leave her future in God's hands, telling her how much he loved her. He recorded his hopes for the future:

1. Let the execution of me become the last in Indonesia because life and death of humans is in God's hands, only God has the right to take away human life.
2. Execution is not the major way to eradicate drugs. The justice system needs to be fixed because drug dealers are mostly free because they have the ability to play the law. They are now free and can do transactions. That's why drug eradication is difficult to achieve. I know and went through the situation. Because of my poverty I cannot engage in that practice so I received a heavy punishment.

And he listed his final requests:

1. I plead to be allowed to call my family in Nigeria;
2. I plead to be allowed to donate my organs – cornea, kidney and others for humanity and for those who need it;

3. I sincerely plead to executioners to hand my body to the Pastor in St Cornelius Chuch, Madiun to treat and bury in the Catholic cemetery.

'That is my last request, I hope it can be done,' Raheem wrote, adding his thanks to the prosecutors, the Nigerian embassy and his lawyers. He asked to be accompanied during the execution by his priest.

In his powerful final letter, Raheem expressed something that all who had been caught up within Indonesia's criminal justice system knew: money talks. Money buys verdicts, acquittals and lower sentences. Money buys freedom. Those who have it can work the system. Those who don't get harsh sentences. As Raheem put it, the big-time drug dealers could 'play the law'. People like him, who lived in poverty, had no hope.

Myuran and Andrew and their families knew this only too well. Like Raheem, they would probably not be in this position, they were sure, if they'd had the resources to influence the right people.

It was now Friday, 6 March, two days after Andrew and Myuran had arrived on Nusakambangan. The lawyers and the consul-general were allowed to visit again, but not the families. It was not a general visiting day and the authorities were sticking strictly by the rules.

The Chan and Sukumaran families had travelled from Bali and were at a hotel in Cilacap, with little to do except wait, hope and pray. They were told they could not visit until Monday. It was like torture, knowing their boys were just across the water but they couldn't see them or hug them.

Michael Chan said his family just wanted to see Andrew physically. They were taking things day by day, as they had been for a long time now. He and Feby had returned to Kerobokan prison after Andrew was moved, to collect some of his belongings.

Raji Sukumaran was dreadfully upset. She was desperate to know how her son was. Was he okay after the transfer? What was he feeling? Did they even know the executions had been delayed? She had no idea. She just wanted to hold him close.

Raheem told his visitors that the trio were now giving each other strength. Myuran wanted to know when he could start painting again. All he was allowed was a book and pencils – no paints, canvases or easel. Having just arrived, he and Andrew were in a quarantine period, and would not yet be allowed privileges. The governor of the prison said he didn't know how long that phase would last.

A pastor who lived at Cilacap and ministered at the jail was a godsend for the Australians and Raheem. Ibu Yani brought them food and ensured they were being treated well. She had earned extraordinary trust from the jail authorities, and was well placed to help the two Australians adjust to their new lives at Nusakambangan. She was an angel, single-minded in her devotion to the inmates.

It was a full five days after the duo arrived at Nusakambangan before their families could see them. By now, Myuran and Andrew were adjusting to life inside one of Indonesia's highest-security prisons. 'Give me Kerobokan any time,' Myuran joked. 'It was like a resort.'

After the families' visit on 9 March, the lawyers were allowed back. Their presence gave vital strength to the boys, but also meant they could deal with various practical matters that needed attention – such as Myuran's wishes for his paintings. He wrote and signed a note:

> My brother chooses the paintings that he and Mum want – as many as they want. Give the ones you don't want to the exhibition and sell for lots of money to [pay for an art gallery] outside. Keep the good ones.

He and Andrew also compiled a list of items for their families to bring them. But the lawyers urged them to cut it back to what they really *needed*, not what they wanted. They wanted a fan – it was so hot and humid that the cell was like an oven. But the lawyers urged them to remember that other inmates had nothing; their families were dirt-poor. They needed to scale back their desires.

One thing Andrew and Myuran insisted on was that whatever they got, their fellow prisoner, Raheem, was to get the same. They asked for three of everything – three pillows, three portions of food. He was one of them, they told him; they were in this together.

They had known Raheem only a few days but already they were close. Their generosity of spirit inspired many around them.

They had also developed a close bond with Majell Hind, Australia's consul-general to Bali. On 10 March, in Veronica's notebook, they penned a joking letter to Foreign Minister Julie Bishop. 'Please open an Australian Consulate post in Cilacap,' they wrote, 'and make Majell the Australian Consul-General to Cilacap. Thank you.' Two stamps, of the type commonly used on Indonesian documentation, were stuck to the letter, and Myuran and Andrew signed over the top of them, like true government officials. 'PS. Majell is not allowed to leave Cilacap until we are off the death penalty and moved to Bali.'

The legal team was now working at fever pitch to save the lives of Myuran and Andrew. They challenged the February decision of the State Administrative Court, which had found that the Indonesian president had full authority to make a decision on clemency, and that such presidential decrees were beyond its jurisdiction. The Australians' lawyers argued that President Widodo's blanket rejection of clemency for all 64 inmates on death row showed a lack of justice and procedural fairness, and failed to take into account their rehabilitation. The president had not even read the clemency pleas of Myuran and Andrew, which outlined their rehabilitation and the programs they had set up, when he rejected them. On appeal, the court agreed to hear from legal experts from both sides in late March. The Australians' witness would argue that the court did have the power to challenge the president's clemency powers.

It might have seemed a long shot, given the court's initial ruling – not to mention the public statements of the attorney-general regarding the ongoing legal proceedings pursued by many of those on death row. But the lawyers were doing everything they could to halt the executions.

In Cilicap, Chinthu granted an interview to a local Indonesian television station, SCTV. His family had been shocked and ashamed when Myuran was arrested in Bali, he said. But since then his brother had worked hard to make up for his crime, to apologise to Indonesia. Chinthu described how the prison staff and guards had supported Myuran as he became a better person. 'Now we are very scared that he may die. He did something wrong, he committed a crime and he deserves to be punished. We accept that he must be punished, we just don't want him to be executed. We want him to stay in prison.'

This was the same point the legal team was arguing: not that Myuran and Andrew should be freed, but simply that they should not be put to death.

'We don't ask that he goes free,' Chinthu continued. 'We just ask that he be allowed to stay in prison and continue to help people. There are many prisoners that have talked about the things he has done to help them. He has learned to paint . . . we just ask the Indonesian people and the Indonesian government to show mercy.'

The fight to save Andrew and Myuran was garnering more and more support. The Virgin Group founder Sir Richard Branson, in his capacity as a commissioner of the Global Commission on Drug Policy, wrote to President Widodo, pleading for him to spare the Bali Nine and others on death row. Sir Richard, along with two other commission members, Fernando Henrique Cardoso and Ruth Dreifuss, said the death penalty was inhumane and failed as a deterrent:

> Countries that still carry out executions for drug offences have not seen any significant shifts in supply and demand. The drug trade remains remarkably unaffected by the threat of capital punishment. Furthermore the death penalty removes any chance of forgiveness for the remorseful. It is our understanding that several of the defendants, many still in early adulthood when convicted, have expressed enormous regret for their offences and resolved to live better, more purposeful lives . . . As advocates of evidence-based drug policy reform, we have studied different national approaches in great depth. We have learnt that treating drugs as a health issue and not as a criminal one, helps lower the number of drug deaths, limits the spread of infectious diseases like HIV/AIDS or hepatitis, reduces drug-related crime and allows people who struggle with addiction to become useful members of society again. If you were to find it helpful we would be happy to come to Indonesia to discuss the issue with you and your administration.

In Canberra, in a rare moment of solidarity, Australia's political leaders stood side by side at a candlelight vigil at Parliament House.

There had been missteps, however. In February Prime Minister Abbott had appeared to link Australia's aid funding – worth a billion dollars – to Indonesia in the wake of the devastating 2004 Boxing Day Tsunami with the bid to save the two Australians from the firing squad.

'I would say to the Indonesian people and the Indonesian government,' he said, 'we in Australia are always there to help you and we hope that you might reciprocate in this way at this time.'

Abbott recalled how 'Australians lost their lives in that campaign to help Indonesia'. A Sea King helicopter, while conducting humanitarian aid flights, crashed on Nias Island on 2 April 2005, just 15 days before the Bali Nine arrests. Nine service personnel had been killed in the crash – six Royal Australian Navy and three Royal Australian Air Force officers – and two survived. The military had been providing aid following a deadly earthquake a few days earlier, and just a few months after the tsunami had struck.

So incensed were some elements of Indonesian society by Mr Abbott's comments that a #CoinForAustralia campaign began, urging people to return Australia's money. In the end not much money was raised but the campaign epitomised the fervour surrounding the debate. There was, in Indonesian society, a widespread belief in the truth of government claims that drugs were ruining the nation. Not many, even those in senior positions, understood that the Bali Nine's drugs were in fact destined for Australia, not the streets of Indonesia.

The Coordinating Minister for Political, Legal and Security Affairs, Admiral Tedjo Edhy Purdijatno, was incensed at Abbott's linking of the executions and Australia's tsunami aid. He suggested that Indonesia release a 'human tsunami' of 10,000 asylum seekers to Australia. The minister was referring to Indonesia's cooperation over recent years in stopping boatloads of asylum seekers from leaving Indonesia bound for Australia. Speaking on Jakarta's Metro TV news channel, Tedjo said: 'If Canberra keeps doing things that displease Indonesia, Jakarta will surely let the illegal immigrants go to Australia.'

Also poorly received was Australia's offer, in early March, of a prisoner swap – whereby Andrew and Myuran would be returned to Australian custody, in exchange for Indonesian prisoners currently in Australian jails. The offer was made just after the dramatic transfer of Myuran and Andrew to Nusakambangan, Foreign Minister Julie Bishop raising the prospect with her Indonesian counterpart, Retno Marsudi, during a heated phone conversation. Bishop reiterated the offer by letter several days later, addressing her counterpart as 'my dear Retno'.

The 'one-off' offer was to swap the Bali Nine duo for three Indonesian prisoners convicted in New South Wales of attempting to import 390 kilograms of heroin into Australia in 1998. Bishop's letter highlighted the fact that Kristito Mandagi, Saud Siregar and Ismunandar were smuggling 47 times more heroin than the Bali Nine. Sentenced in the New South Wales District

Court, the three men received lengthy sentences – Mandagi was given life with a non-parole period of 25 years, while the others received 20-year sentences. On appeal, Mandagi had his sentence reduced by six years. While Myuran and Andrew were preparing themselves for execution, the Indonesians had just a couple of years left before they would be eligible for parole and flown home to their families.

(On 13 October 2017, two and a half years after Myuran and Andrew were executed, Mandagi was granted parole and left jail in New South Wales a free man. The original sentencing judge had described him as the 'pivotal figure' in the smuggling operation, saying it was a crime of massive proportions.)

Bishop had a second option for the Indonesians to consider. If a prisoner transfer were impossible, the Australian government would pay the costs of keeping Myuran and Andrew in jail for life in Indonesia. It was clear that Australia was pulling out all stops to save the lives of Myuran and Andrew.

Three days later, Marsudi replied. The offer was firmly rebuffed. President Widodo said such an exchange could not take place: there was no legal basis, under Indonesian law, for such a prisoner swap.

In fact, attempts to set up an official prisoner transfer between Australia and Indonesia had already been under discussion for years, with no result. It had first been mooted after Schapelle Corby was convicted and sentenced to 20 years' jail; talks were reinvigorated after the sentences given to the Bali Nine. But the years of meetings had come to nothing: there were simply too many sticking points for Indonesia. And any arrangement wouldn't have applied to those on death row anyway.

While Marsudi was diplomatic in her official language, Attorney-General Prasetyo was blunt. A prisoner swap was 'unthinkable', he said, not to mention irrelevant to the country's plan to execute drug traffickers. His colleague, Defence Minister Ryamizard Ryacudu, was even harsher, telling the media that the Indonesian criminals in Australia should also be executed.

The issue was now becoming very politically sensitive. An exhibition of artworks by prisoners at Kerobokan jail, including Myuran, was scheduled to open in Bali on 13 March; it was cancelled by the prison authorities hours before its launch. A silent auction of the art was to have raised money to set up an art studio outside the jail, so that ex-prisoners could continue their passion. Myuran's portrait of President Widodo, by then a well-known work, was to have been exhibited. Chinthu had travelled from Cilacap to Bali to attend.

The authorities claimed the organisers had breached an agreement that they would not mention anyone specifically. A flyer had emerged calling the exhibition a tribute to Myuran. The organisers said they had no idea who had printed and distributed it. It was all a bit odd; many wondered whether someone had made the flyer with the aim of shutting down the show.

It was 4.30 a.m. on 17 March. As Myuran lay on his mat in the cell at Besi prison, everything was silent. Suddenly, in the distance, he heard gunfire. He was startled – and frightened.

For months now, his sleep had been fitful, disturbed by thoughts of firing squads. Now it was so close. There was a police shooting range nearby; was he hearing a firing squad training? Were they practising shooting, in the darkness, at the hearts of him and Andrew and the others? It was terrifying.

The restrictions at Besi were now easing slightly. Myuran and Andrew were allowed to go to church inside the jail. No fewer than 15 guards escorted them, and no other prisoners were allowed to approach them or talk to them. They were still segregated. Apparently the guards didn't want them becoming too friendly with other prisoners, as it would cause unrest when the time came to execute them. Still, it was a treat to be allowed out of the prison block, and to see some new faces and recover some semblance of normality in their lives. During the service Andrew played a guitar with broken strings.

Myuran joked around with the lawyers about what he wanted. He wrote a list of instructions:

1. Majell can't leave the island, Veronica as well and Julian.
2. Veronica is allowed to go to Jakarta for our case but has to come back directly to Cilacap/the island.
3. Julian, Veronica and Majell have to be miserable until we get off this island.

4. Myu and Andrew aren't happy!
5. [Get us] Off the death penalty.

There was no good news on the judicial front. The State Administrative Court threw out their appeal: a panel of three judges ruled that presidential clemency was outside the court's jurisdiction. That legal avenue had now closed. The next step was to request the Constitutional Court to hear the argument that the president should consider each case individually when deciding clemency. It would be a way of having their rehabilitation considered. But there was an extra hurdle to jump: foreigners did not have standing in the Constitutional Court.

The attorney-general was not happy, accusing the Australians' lawyers of stalling and toying with the law. There would be no more delays, he declared, as others on the list of drug dealers to be executed scrambled to mount similar court actions.

Finally Myuran was granted permission to paint at Besi prison. The authorities said he would be allowed to have an easel and his brushes and paints, so he could get back to his true love – expressing himself on canvas. Chinthu set about getting him the art supplies he needed. Cilacap, a small port town that saw few foreigners, was not the place to find them.

Armed with a long list of the paints, colours, brushes and papers Myuran needed, Chinthu went to Yogyakarta, a five-hour drive on a good day, and much longer on a bad one. He bought most of what was on the list but could not find everything. Chinthu knew that most of what his brother needed was sold in an art supplies store in Bali; Myuran had regularly ordered materials from it over the past few years. So Chinthu caught a flight from Yogyakarta to Bali, and went straight to the art shop to get the rest. He stayed overnight in Bali, flew back to Yogyakarta, picked up the other supplies and packed them into the car for the long, bumpy journey back to Cilacap. Chinthu dropped the boxes of supplies at the port, to be sent over to the prison, hoping desperately they would be allowed into the jail.

When he next was able to visit, Chinthu eagerly asked his brother if he'd got everything.

'Yes, but where's the paper?' Myuran asked, referring to the one thing Chinthu couldn't find anywhere, a particular kind of art paper.

With the supplies he needed and a green light from authorities, Myuran wasted no time. At first it was hard to find people to paint, so he focused on Andrew a lot. He also painted guards and their cell. In order to paint self-portraits he needed a good-sized mirror, which wasn't easy to find in Cilacap. Finally Chinthu located a bathroom cabinet with a mirror – it was the best he could do.

Towards the end of March some family members returned to Australia. They could only visit on two days per week, and

Cilacap wasn't Bali. There was little to do on non-visit days, and Yogyakarta was a long and difficult drive away. Plus, they had jobs in Australia and responsibilities that needed attention.

Tina Bailey and Denise Payne made the trip from Bali to Cilacap to visit, bringing scores of messages and letters from inmates and friends at Kerobokan. The Kerobokan prisoners had given Tina money to buy some special treats for Andrew and Myuran, such as KFC. Tina soon found out she needed to buy three portions rather than two, because Myuran and Andrew insisted on Raheem getting everything they got. KFC was one treat you could get in Cilacap, such is the Indonesian liking for the fried chicken, generally accompanied by rice.

On 11 April, after five weeks at Besi prison, Myuran wrote me a heartbreaking letter in which he detailed the pain he was feeling:

> It's very good to hear from you! I'm okay at the moment. We have been kept in isolation since we arrived, in a bare cell – they watch us all the time. They read and photocopy everything coming in and out. It looks like we will be kept this way for some time to come.
>
> Yes, we are allowed to go to church once a week but they don't like us talking with the other prisoners. The church here is very small, with 17 Christians.
>
> The prison is similar to Kerobokan but much smaller and not as nice. The guards, I think, are the same anywhere you

go. But I have to say, if Kerobokan was a prison I'd give it six stars. Really never knew how good we had it over there.

The isolation is tough. It's maddening not knowing what's going on on the outside. Before I was so connected with what's going on – I felt a little in control whether the news was good, bad or ugly. Here I feel completely helpless.

I have been drawing since I got here but nothing good. It's actually quite [illegible] here so I have been a little stumped on what to draw – nobody willing to sit for me at the moment except for the guards, who like to ask me to draw them but then they take the drawings. Recently the warden has asked me to paint five portraits of his friend, which I have started. I have ordered some paint and canvases from my brother and hope to paint something soon.

I have also been pushing to start an art class as soon as possible. They like the idea but are not very eager for me to mix with the other prisoners. The guards seem sympathetic but I think there is pressure from Jakarta to keep us this way. Please don't say anything to anyone that I've been drawing or am going to start painting as I'm afraid they will stop me.

I am hoping that something good will happen soon. It's not fair for them to keep us like this – at least at Kerobokan, even with this hanging over our heads, it felt easier; we were allowed to live! They let us be with our family, work, play – basically enjoy life. Here everything feels harder, more tiring – isolation – limited visits. Here feels like some sort of limbo or purgatory before we are punished. Here for some reason they won't allow us to know the time, which is weird and can be a little disorienting.

I'm happy to hear the news that my paintings were well received in Amsterdam and I am looking forward to hearing how the London exhibition goes! I'm jealous that my international art career is starting without me!

I haven't read the story about Si Yi yet. I will ask my brother to try and get it to me. They don't like me getting news from the outside.

Tina [Bailey] visited me two weeks ago and I am happy to know that things over at Kerobokan are okay and running smoothly. I'm glad the projects can continue without me – means I did something right! I really do hope that I can start an art project here!

Hoping this letter finds you well.

Myu.

Six days after this letter was written, Myuran turned 34. It was 17 April, ten years to the day since the Bali Nine had been arrested. For ten years they had been allowed to live, but now they were being readied for death. Ibu Yani, the pastor who had been helping them, brought a cake in for Myuran's birthday. A banner read 'Happy 34th Birthday Myuran' and official photos were taken of the group – Myuran, Andrew, Raheem – standing together with two chocolate cakes. It was not an official visiting day, so Myuran spent his birthday with his cellmates and prison officials. But it was a bright spot in what was, by now, a dismal and wretched time. It seemed likely it would be Myuran's last birthday on Earth. But there was still no certainty about anything.

Myuran's wish to start an art class at Besi was finally granted, and the painter held his first class. His students were eight prisoners. He was thrilled. It felt like he was getting some of his old life back. Raji was so proud. It was also a testament to the extraordinary trust he had earned from his guards in a short space of time.

That class, however, would be his last.

14.

72 HOURS

We, from the Attorney-General's Office, will notify you, Myuran Sukumaran, that the execution will take place . . . within three x 24 hours. The court has sentenced you to death. Your clemency has been denied.

It was 2.50 p.m. on Anzac Day, 25 April 2015. Officials read out the history of his case, from the time of the arrest, back in 2005, to the denial of clemency. There was no mention of the more recent legal proceedings that had been lodged, some of which were still afoot. All that was left was for Myuran to sign his own death warrant – the warrant of execution.

He took a deep breath. He was calm. He was dignified and peaceful, watching those whose job it was to organise his death.

'I ask not to be executed because I have been rehabilitated, and both Andrew Chan and I have changed,' Myuran said in

Indonesian. 'I feel that it is unjust and over ten years I have tried and succeeded in changing myself. I have apologised.' He spoke of the good he had done during his years in prison, and why he should not be executed.

'I am not signing this because it is not correct,' he said of the execution warrant. Myuran eloquently listed all the good works he had been involved with at the jail, the people he had helped and saved, and the programs he had set up.

There was stunned silence as everyone looked at Myuran. No one had ever refused to sign an execution warrant before. The officials appeared flummoxed as to what to do. Some were sweating.

At 3.14 p.m. officials asked Myuran for his last requests. He wanted Julian to be his witness and be with him at the end; he wanted maximum time to spend with his family; he wanted to be allowed to continue painting to the end; and he wanted fresh air twice a day.

Someone started taking notes. He wanted the document to be retyped with his reasons included. There were spelling mistakes, substantial errors and minor ones.

Julian, Veronica and Majell were with him. Speaking in Indonesian, Veronica stated that the document was simply not acceptable. 'You are about to execute my client and you could not even get the warrant that is going to take his life correct,' she noted.

Officials rushed to retype the document and find somewhere to print it. Now the printer wouldn't work. The original warrant, with Veronica's handwriting on it, was put aside. She demanded it back, insisting that a document with her handwriting on it not be left lying around. Tension was building. Someone crumpled it up and tossed it in a bin. Veronica wanted it back. That document was going nowhere. Ever a meticulous lawyer, she could not allow her client to sign a document that was riddled with inaccuracies. In frustration, the senior Bali prosecutor, Olopan Nainggolan, struck a match and burned it.

It took an hour of back and forth before Myuran was satisfied the document was accurate and reflected his feelings. He signed it, having courageously said what he needed to say. Veronica, Julian and Majell embraced him, and he was handcuffed.

As the cuffs were put around his wrists, he winced as they cut his skin. Veronica was angry. 'You need to loosen them,' she protested. 'That's too tight and it's cut his skin. He's in pain!'

Throughout, Myuran was calm. There was no fear in his eyes. The Australians were in awe.

Andrew Chan came in next. It was now 3.45 p.m. Olopan Nainggolan read his warrant of execution.

'I refuse to sign,' Andrew began, 'and the reason why is because I have been in prison for ten years. I have rehabilitated myself. The nation of Indonesia helped rehabilitate me. I want a second chance. I helped other inmates and they have provided documents in relation to that.' Andrew listed all the projects and programs on which he had worked at the jail, also mentioning the church community he had established, which had helped so many prisoners. Like Myuran, he was calm and eloquent.

As his final requests, Andrew asked to spend as much time as possible with his family; that he be allowed to go to church every day; that David Soper and Feby act as witnesses at the execution; and that he be allowed fresh air twice a day. Like Myuran, Andrew insisted that the documents be retyped before he would sign.

After witnessing the events that day, Julian said: 'It was a quiet, slow collision between the dignified reformed prisoner and the power of the state.'

Julian knew he was watching a historic moment unfold. He thought of how many more famous people had been known for their sense of history and courage in similar circumstances. His clients had never heard of some of those people but that momentous day they grasped the moment, confronting the injustice of the state, the cruelty. 'They had prepared themselves for that moment and they were able to speak with quiet integrity and calm confidence about who they were and the injustice of the situation because for years they had known that this might come about and they had chosen to prepare themselves to be honourable at this moment,' Julian says. He was not at all surprised by what happened. He was proud. 'I felt privileged to be watching it. I felt that I must pay close attention because I was privileged to be a witness to something remarkable. But I was not surprised because I had been talking to them for nine years and I understood what they had become. They had outgrown all the people around them and they had certainly outgrown the machinery of death.' From time to time they had also fallen heavily, Julian says, but no one's perfect.

After the Australians were finished, the other eight prisoners to be executed were brought into the room, one by one. Some of them, following Andrew's and Myuran's example, refused to sign their death warrants.

The embassies of the foreigners on the execution list had only been notified a day earlier of what was to come. But the signs had been ominous. On Thursday 23 April, the original prosecutors of all nine on the execution list received a letter from the attorney-general's office in Jakarta, telling them to prepare the executions. The only thing missing in the letters was the actual date, but everyone in authority knew it was imminent.

The prosecutors in Bali, who were required to witness the executions of Andrew and Myuran, prepared to fly from Bali to Yogyakarta the next day. It was a task none of them wanted. At least one, a devout Hindu, had already told his superiors he would not attend the executions; he wanted no part of it. But as prosecutors, it was their sworn duty as officers of the state. They didn't have a choice.

For another prosecutor it was the second time he had been called upon to witness an execution. Back in 2008 he was there in the same place when the three Bali bombers were executed by firing squad. Now his job demanded he do it again. Also a

Hindu, he had been deeply affected the first time, and afterwards had spent time praying at his family temple, holding a Hindu cleansing ceremony. He didn't want to do it again.

One of the senior prosecutors asked the veteran court and police translator Wayan Ana to accompany them to Cilacap to help with translations. The energetic, ever-smiling and friendly Balinese man didn't even have to think about it. No way. He wasn't doing that job. He liked Andrew and Myuran a great deal. 'Pak [Mr], I don't want to take my friends to hell,' he said in answer.

By now Myuran was painting madly, desperate to document everything. On 24 April he completed two self-portraits – 'A Strange Day' and 'After the New Arrival'. Both showed a dark shadow looming around his head.

Mary Jane Fiesta Veloso was transferred to Besi on the Thursday night from her women's prison at nearby Yogyakarta, arriving in the early morning. It was a men's jail; there could be only one reason she had been brought to Nusakambangan.

Indonesian man Zainal Abidin was transferred from Pasir Putih, one of the six other prisons on Nusakambangan, to the Besi isolation cells. His lawyer, Ade Yuliawan, complained that Abidin still had a judicial review before the Supreme Court in Jakarta. Rodrigo Gulerte, a Brazilian, was also transferred from Pasir Putih. Three Nigerians – Sylvester Nwaolise,

Okwudili Oyatanze and Martin Anderson – were brought from Batu prison.

The authorities had previously said the executions would not take place while the Asian–African Summit was taking place in Indonesia. It had finished on the Thursday, 23 April, and the international dignitaries were now departing. Julian and Veronica were in Australia when the embassy notified them that the execution warrants would be issued on the Saturday. They rushed to the airport.

Lex Lasry, now a judge, tweeted:

> So the executions delayed 'til after conference in Indonesia – avoids bad look. Now notice to kill 2 Australians to happen 2morrow, Anzac Day.

The journey to Cilacap is not quick. You fly from Bali or Jakarta into Yogyakarta, in Central Java, and then drive for five to six hours on crowded and bumpy roads to the town of Cilacap, on the southern coast. The lawyers made it just 15 minutes before the meeting started.

Bizarrely, they were told there was a limit of one lawyer per country. Veronica was angry. 'I am Andrew's lawyer,' she said, 'Julian is Myuran's lawyer, and we need to be there for our clients.' She pleaded with an official from the Indonesian Foreign Ministry, who eventually agreed they could both attend.

There were about 20 people in the room: embassy officials from the various nations involved, lawyers, prosecutors and other government officials. The assembly was informed that the prisoners would be asked for their last wishes; the officials would inform them which were possible and which were not.

Representatives for Rodrigo Gularte said they wished to apply for a second judicial review and seek a medical evaluation of his mental condition, and asked that the rule of law be respected. They were told that this was not the forum to discuss legal issues. Everyone in the room looked at each other grimly. The Australians argued that Myuran and Andrew had a Constitutional Court hearing pending, but again, no one would discuss legal matters.

The group boarded a bus headed for the port, and then a ferry to Besi jail. Even now, no one was certain that the warrants would in fact be read out that day. It was like waiting beneath a slow-moving avalanche.

The wife of a staffer at the Australian embassy had baked some Anzac biscuits for Andrew and Myuran; her husband asked Veronica to give them to the boys. The officials were not so sure, and only relented when Veronica explained the significance of Anzac Day.

Myuran was led into the room. 'Oh my God, it's so good to see you,' he said, hugging the lawyers and Majell. He sat down between Veronica and Majell; Julian stood behind him for the reading of the warrant.

When the warrants for all nine had been read, the group of lawyers and officials was taken back to the mainland.

That day, 25 April, Myuran painted several more artworks. 'After Our New Arrivals, a Bad Sleep Last Night' depicted him in almost a foetal position, while 'Time is Ticking' was a self-portrait with a gaping hole in place of his heart. Another work featured just his face and head; it was titled '72 Hours Just Started'. The countdown had begun.

The families of the condemned would be allowed to visit for the next three days. Raji was already in Cilacap, and had been visiting Myuran on the two days each week he was allowed to have visitors. When news came though of the meetings and the official 72 hours' notice, Raji had just returned from Yogyakarta, where she had bought more art supplies for Myuran. He had been excited about getting new paints, and Raji had wondered how she would get it all into the prison.

Chinthu had been in Cilacap only the week before. When he left, he believed he and Myuran would have a lot more time – that the executions were still a long way off. On hearing about the lawyers and embassies being called to meet, he was shocked. Wasn't the judicial review process still incomplete? When I spoke to him in Sydney he was wondering if this was it, or if it was just another furphy. He wanted to know if he should go or wait for further confirmation. Drop everything and get on the plane, I urged him, they are serious this time. You all need to get there. It's going to happen. My Bali-based assistant Komang Erviani, had been told the same thing in Bali. All the Bali prosecutors had been ordered to Cilacap. The caravan of death had begun.

As Mary Jane had been transferred to Nusakambangan the night before, Chinthu thought, Myuran and Andrew must have had a sense of what was going on. As he booked his flights to Indonesia, Chinthu had no clue how the next few days would play out.

Feby had been visiting Andrew regularly before the announcement and was already in Cilacap. Michael flew with his mother from Sydney, and the family's closest friends all travelled to Indonesia. Everyone knew time was now precious.

The first of the last visits was on Sunday, 26 April. The families of all nine condemned prisoners on the list were now in Cilacap, along with lawyers, priests, pastors and imams, and embassy representatives.

Mary Jane Veloso's two young sons, her parents and her siblings arrived from Yogyakarta. They had been in Indonesia and due to visit her in prison there on the Friday. But she was moved to Nusakambangan the night before. Her sons, Mark Daniel and Mark Darren, had made a video plea to the son of President Jokowi, 19-year-old Kaesang Pangarep.

'Kaesang, please help my mother. Please tell your father not to execute her. We beg you to lift our mother's sentence and not to execute her.'

Filipino lawyer Edre Olalia had arrived in Indonesia and, at Cilacap, reminded the Indonesian government that Mary Jane still had legal remedies on foot, having requested a second judicial review; her application was still before the courts.

Olalia, the secretary-general of the National Union of People's Lawyers – Philippines, had taken up Mary Jane's plight personally. Migrante International, a vocal alliance representing overseas migrant workers, was also campaigning furiously on her behalf. People displayed banners and posters at the port reading 'Save Mary Jane'. In Manila, too, their campaign was in full swing.

The lawyer vowed never to give up the fight to save the young mother's life: 'We will never give up until the last breath of somebody like Mary Jane Veloso . . . a mother of two little boys coming from a very poor family forced out of her country because there are no economic opportunities to live a decent life like a human being, whose father worked in the large former estate of the Philippine president. We are not giving up.'

Olalia urged the Indonesian government to allow Mary Jane to tell the world her story of being set up. 'We don't want any more Mary Jane Velosos,' he said. Serious questions needed to be answered about the chain of custody of Mary Jane's luggage on the day she was arrested.

The young Manila mother had been arrested on 25 April 2010 at Yogyakarta airport, allegedly with a quantity of heroin in her luggage. At her trial, held in the Sleman District Court in Yogyakarta, she barely understood what was going on. She was provided with an Indonesian–English translator – but at the time she spoke only Tagalog, her native language.

Mary Jane had consistently maintained her innocence, claiming she was set up by Maria Kristina Sergio, the daughter of a godparent, who was to help her get domestic work in Malaysia. The family was dirt-poor and she needed a job. But when Mary Jane arrived in Malaysia, the job was no longer on offer. In April 2010 she was told she would go to Indonesia to work. She was given a suitcase and told to pack.

When she arrived at Yogyakarta airport her luggage was searched and 2.6 kilograms of heroin was found secreted inside the lining. At her trial, where she had a court-appointed lawyer, prosecutors sought a life sentence. The court gave her death. According to Olalia, Mary Jane was, first and foremost, a victim of human trafficking.

The campaign to save her was high-profile and vocal, both in the Philippines and in Indonesia. Migrante International was holding rallies on her behalf. Execution 'is not the solution', Olalia said.

Like Myuran and Andrew, Mary Jane had refused to sign her death warrant. It was 5 p.m. by the time she was called into the office by the prosecutors. She was allowed to call her sister, who passed the phone to Edre Olalia. He apologised for being so passionate. She was dirt-poor, he said, and her story tragic.

Raheem Agbaje Salami's Indonesian girlfriend, Angela Intan, was also there. His lawyers held up a photograph of the pair, smiling and happy, taken before the executions appeared imminent. She was now broken.

At 8.25 a.m. on Sunday, 26 April, the Chan and Sukumaran families and friends left Cilacap port for the first of their final three visits on Nusakambangan. Forty-five minutes later, a truck laden with plastic chairs and corrugated iron sheeting went across to the island on the ferry. The logistics of the execution were now in full swing. The chairs were for officials, family members, lawyers and embassy staff. The iron sheeting was to construct a temporary roof over the area where the nine prisoners would be shot. Chairs and tenting had been delivered the previous day. Things were now moving quickly.

At Besi prison, Myuran and Andrew were waiting when their families arrived. Raji's heart was palpitating. Andrew came out first, then Myuran. He's okay, she thought. He was holding a book, trying to disguise what was around his wrists. He didn't want to increase his family's distress. It was the first time they had seen him handcuffed, and it was a shock, especially after they'd spent so much carefree time with him at Kerobokan jail.

Raji was particularly upset by the handcuffs. Myuran clumsily tried to hug her but a proper embrace wasn't possible. Eventually, the guards agreed to remove the handcuffs for the time they were with their families, to reduce the stress and emotion. It was another sign of the trust and respect Myuran had earned at the jail in only a short time.

Since the 72 hours' notice had been given, the duo had not seen their families. Now, the tears flowed. The family hugged Myuran, all of them weeping. Everyone who hugged him cried – parents, siblings, aunts and uncles.

He wanted to know what was happening in the outside world. Being locked up and in isolation, without even a watch to tell the time, he had no idea what was going on elsewhere. It was like living in a bubble.

He told his family how stupid the authorities were, pushing ahead with the executions. He told them about Mary Jane. He thought it was beyond belief that they would execute her. He told them what he had learned about each of the eight to be executed with him. He wanted his family to know the story of each one, so it could be told to the world. He felt terrible that no one was advocating for them.

Even though Myuran had been in prison for a decade, he felt like he had had a good life. Some of the others had gone through dreadful times – being beaten, tortured. He related some of those stories. The family watched as the guards brought Martin Anderson out in a wheelchair for his visit with his wife. What was the point of executing a man who couldn't even walk, Myuran asked.

Anderson had been sentenced to death in 2003, found guilty of possessing a mere 50 grams of heroin. According to his lawyers, he had been shot in the leg by police at the time of his arrest.

He had been carrying a false Ghanaian passport, and for the entirety of his trial and sentence he'd been classified as Ghanaian. He wasn't – he was Nigerian. And he appeared never to have had any consular assistance. Anderson had married an Indonesian woman and had asked her to bury him according to the traditions of Islam, his religion. And he asked his wife to remain a Muslim. They would meet again after death.

Myuran said that Anderson had told him some guy cut a deal with the police, leading to his arrest. 'Look at him now – all these years later, he is an old man in a wheelchair.'

Raheem, he said, had been in prison for 17 years. He was a changed man, and a good person. 'He doesn't deserve this,' he told them. Myuran tried to keep talking to his family about other prisoners so they wouldn't dwell too long on what was about to happen to him.

He told them how, once all nine had arrived at Besi prison, they had been scared. He and Andrew had talked the guards into unlocking the cells so the condemned people could come together to pray. Everyone prayed together, except the Indonesian, Zainal Abidin. They talked and prayed.

Myuran also spoke with Veronica and Julian. He was thoughtful and introspective. 'This is really wrong,' he told them. 'I understand there is a big problem in Indonesia with drugs, but just to execute a few people won't make a difference.' He had been thinking deeply about this, and spoke to his lawyers with clarity. He and Andrew had been in prison for a full ten years.

I know how much he has done and he knows what I have done. We have done as much as possible to change . . . Other people don't do the same thing. Prison is where you go to become a better criminal, a school to become a better criminal. We are the few who have stood out, pushed for change, been there for good. This is just completely ridiculous.

I have prepared myself to be killed, but I don't agree with this and I don't understand it. It is wrong, not just for me but for the others too. These five people are good people – me, Andrew, Raheem, Okwudili, Mary Jane. Raheem, since I have known him, he is a good person. He knows as much as Andrew about the Bible – he knows it inside out, and prays from it. Raheem talks softy, politely. Just like us, you can feel he is a good person. Mary Jane is a poor little girl. I feel so sad to see her – she is poor, she doesn't have money, her family just came from the Philippines. She said she was set up. I believe her too, but even if she did it she doesn't deserve the death penalty. She is small, not a drug kingpin. This is making me really upset.

They said they want to fight drugs, but they are not. Why kill the prisoners who are rehabilitated? Makes me think whether they really want to fight drugs or they want to get rid of people who speak out about it. The Brazilian guy doesn't look stable – he doesn't talk to anyone, doesn't look healthy.

I don't know what they are gaining by killing these people, killing us. I don't understand why Jokowi and the attorney-general would refuse to even look to see how good people are becoming in prison. They only want to see the bad things inside prisons. They turn a blind eye on the good things. We have become good people. At the start we were bad but now we are good.

The problem of drugs in Indonesia isn't just our fault. I have been in prison and it's very rare for drug kingpins to face the firing squad. The only people killed are the pawns and the little people. They are the ones whose blood is spilt. In Kerobokan I saw shabu [methamphetamine], huge amounts . . . People can use 200 to 300 grams in prison of different substances. Drugs on drones come in. The people who don't change, they buy off people and they will never ever face justice.

Myuran spoke of his hopes that, one day, he would have been allowed to go home, to teach people in Australian prisons, to see his family and make sure the Australian people were proud of him.

In addition to spending as much time as possible with their families that day, Myuran and Andrew also had to address some practicalities of their impending deaths. A list of the people they wanted to make final phone calls to before they died had to be prepared and submitted to the authorities for approval. The pair also needed to provide their funeral instructions.

Andrew had spent time that day praying with his family and friends. They prayed, reading Matthew 10:28. '*Do not be afraid of those who kill the body but cannot kill the soul. Rather, be afraid of the One who can destroy both soul and body in hell.*'

He and Feby were planning to get married the next day. They were keeping this quiet, except for a small group, for fear that the authorities might find some reason to stop them. A list was compiled of those invited to the jail's chapel for the ceremony. The couple didn't want a big deal made of it.

Chinthu and Michael left Besi early that day, in order to make a plea. They needed to beg the president – they had to do whatever they could to reach the authorities in Jakarta. Their message was one of mercy. They looked exhausted as they fronted the cameras again.

Chinthu went first. 'My brother has asked for his last request – to be able to paint as long and as much as possible. He has found peace with what may happen. But he [feels], as we all feel, this is a grave injustice and that this did not have to be this way, and it still doesn't have to be this way . . . We ask the president to please use his powers to show the same mercy that I know that he has asked for Indonesian citizens. We ask the president, please, please show mercy. There are nine people with families that love them – that's mothers, fathers, sons, daughters, brothers and sisters. We please ask the president to use his powers and intervene and save their lives.'

Michael followed. 'Andrew's last wish, one of his wishes, would be to go to church with his family in his last few days. The two boys are still holding up pretty well, considering they feel this isn't just, what has happened over the last ten years with their whole case. Somewhere in the legal system for Indonesia there has got to be mercy, and the president has to show that now, and he's the only one that can stop it. And it's not too late to do so, so I please ask the president to please show mercy.'

That night at Besi, the eight men and one woman – now the walking dead – had Kentucky Fried Chicken for dinner. Andrew and Myuran had asked their families to have it sent from the mainland, enough for all nine. They were now as one.

15.

DEATH ROW WEDDING

The groom wore bright blue crocs. The bride wore jeans and a bright floral blouse. Andrew, a beaming smile on his face, watched Feby intently as he slipped a ring onto her finger. He was the happiest man alive.

The small chapel was decorated beautifully. Someone had gone to a lot of trouble to make it nice, putting flowers around. It might have been a death row wedding, but everyone wanted it to be a special, sacred moment. Feby held a bunch of bougainvilleas.

Many of those closest to Andrew were there. Helen and Michael. But his father Ken had not been well enough to make yet another arduous journey. It was heartbreaking for both Andrew and Ken. Andrew's two sisters and their families also remained in Sydney to comfort and care for Ken. Julian, Veronica and Mulya were there as well as Christie Buckingham, Majell, Andrew's close friends Alan and Ann Wilkins from Melbourne and friend Miranda Ridington and other close friends. They had all been visiting him in jail for years and supported him and the family.

David Soper, a Sydney Salvation Army major, conducted the ceremony. He was a long-time Chan family friend from Sydney and had known Andrew since he was three. It was actually David's wedding ring, from his marriage to wife Shelley, also a Salvation Army major, which Feby slipped onto Andrew's finger. Her own engagement ring also served as her wedding ring. Communion was celebrated, complete with the host and small sachets of non-alcoholic communion wine.

The wedding had been approved by Attorney-General Muhammad Prasetyo. He spoke about it to local media. 'There was a wish from Andrew Chan, which I thought wasn't serious and wasn't the last wish, but it turned out to be serious,' he said. 'He wanted to be tied in matrimony with his girlfriend. He's been in isolation so I thought he wasn't serious.'

Andrew was very serious and had been for a while. In mid-2014 he wrote about Feby and their plans:

> In May 2012 I was acquainted by a personal friend with an Indonesian pastor by the name of Febyanti Herewila, who for the last 15 years has experience in running prayer departments and also youth ministry in various places such as Yogyakarta Indonesia and also in Singapore. Over the years our friendship has flourished and God gave us visions in doing certain things for God's kingdom. Earlier this year God also placed us in

contact with a pastor by the name of Josie Freer, who has had 20-plus years' experience in ministry, such as . . . counselling and also skills in teaching ESL. Through this we had a huge confirmation that this is exactly what God wanted and where he wanted to take us and use us. Which brings me into this vision of ours, which will guide what and why we are trying to reach where we are, and what we are hoping to achieve. To give you a better understanding, bear with me as I share the culture, agriculture and also the vision and mission within our hearts.

In the document, which he sent me to read, to give me an insight into the project, he wrote about Sabu. It was as if he had been there. In a way, he had – in his head, while locked up in Kerobokan, as he planned what he would do upon his release.

Sabu is the largest of the three islands situated midway between Sumba and Rote, west of Timor in Indonesia's eastern province. Seba, the capital of the tiny island of Sabu, is one of the most isolated of all Indonesia's scattered islands in the archipelago. Approximately 92,000–100,000 (according to the census of 2012) currently live on the island, with a majority of the islanders having traditional ties with traditional roots of the Jingi Tui religion that still lingers on the island. These beliefs practise a lot of black magic stuff – not exactly the stuff you would see in *Harry Potter*, rather a very dark occult that still has a huge impact as you enter onto the island. With an exceptional handful of Muslim Sabunese Arab families, there are also only a handful of Protestant Christians, who still hold very strong traditional ties. South of Seba, the village of Namata holds the original ties of Jingi Tiu, and during the ceremonies that are held for Jingi Tui people from all over Sabu descend on Namata.

The descendants of the Sabunese originated in India, but Sabu was aligned to the Dutch colony in the 1600. The neighbouring island of Flores, ruled by a Portuguese colony, was also present in Sabu, as more people spoke Portuguese than they did Dutch. Today you will find that the Sabunese have a number of dialects that distinguish which tribe they are from. They are very simple people who live in houses having long thatched roofs by using lontar palm leaves to shelter them. Approximately 95% of the Sabunese people live in simple homes like these, as the island lacks most resources such as education, health and an understanding of most things that we in the West would gasp at. There is a huge lack in the education of relational building, career guidance for youth, impartation of life skills, financial planning as none of these things exist. As youth with nothing to partake in, things such as alcohol abuse come at a young age – also drugs. Indonesia has one of the biggest increases of drug and alcohol related problems growing in the past ten years, In fact it has grown roughly 8% in the last ten years. Children as young as three are smoking their first cigarette and by age ten they're already drinking.

The document went on, setting out mission, vision and goal.

> Our mission is to help build stronger families and work with the youth in the community of Sabu and to help give them an understanding of breaking away their traditional ties so that they may understand how to serve God. We are hoping to build a community centre for the youth so that they will be able to have a place to hang out and also to have extra educational studies to help build the community. Through the management of a team we are hoping to educate these disadvantaged teenagers and also low-income families throughout Sabu. This community centre will contain a place so that missionaries will be able to stay and help to volunteer their time and efforts to help. It will contain hopefully a greenhouse, basketball court, soccer pitch, computer room, library, music room and also a class for teaching ESL. We are also hoping to also build leaders to help assist more in the local church. We will be working with the local church hoping to build a bigger kingdom for God.
>
> Our vision is to see lives transformed in families, resulting in a brighter future and also a brighter understanding of working in synergy.
>
> Our goal is that this year itself we are hoping to build a community centre on a piece of land that we have recently just been approved for. The community centre will have at least two things by the next year, we are hoping, which is a music class and a place where the youth can come to commune in

sports activities such as soccer or basketball. We are hoping that mission teams will be prepared to help this community grow and also educate the youth in educational understanding and studies.

Andrew and Feby hoped to put their plan into action in early 2015. But the early January news of his clemency being denied put that on hold.

Feby's love for Andrew was not borne out of any sense of pity. She loved him for who he was. 'Andrew is one of the strongest, kindest people I have ever met,' she said. 'I have never seen him as just a prisoner or someone who is on death row. If you ask me why do I love him, because he also has weaknesses as well, but he also has a lot of good things about him. But I accept him the way he is. I am also very proud of him. I love him for who he is.' Seeing everything Andrew did for others made her love him even more.

The day of the wedding, 27 April, didn't start well. When the families got to Cilacap port to take the ferry across to the prison island, they were informed they needed new visitor paperwork. That would have to be done at the prosecutor's office, back in town. There had been no suggestion of this the previous day.

With so few hours left with their boys, every minute lost was one too many. As the bureaucratic wheels at the prosecutor's office slowly turned, new forms were filled in and photographs taken, everyone was getting anxious – Feby especially so. All worried that Andrew and Myuran would be fretting, wondering what had happened to them.

The families and friends finally left the port at 11.30 a.m., several hours late. When they arrived, Andrew and Myuran didn't want to dwell on the inexplicable delay; they simply embraced their families.

Myuran asked Christie Buckingham and Tina Bailey to lead communion with his family as they prayed together. Some of the other prisoners joined in. All up, about 20 people gathered. After Myuran led them in prayer, he started singing 'Bless the Lord', a song also known as '10,000 Reasons', and one they all knew and loved.

There was still some time for jokes amid the sad pall that hung over the Besi prison visiting area. As Myuran got stuck into some more junk food, someone told him it wasn't good for him.

He smiled. 'There are worse ways to die.'

While the Chan and Sukumaran families were treasuring every moment of their visiting time, the legal team was working desperately, often late into the night. Once Veronica fell asleep at the desk, her head on a notebook.

There was some brief and short-lived good news late on 27 April when the Indonesian Constitutional Court agreed to hear their challenge to the country's clemency laws. The lawyers wanted clarity on the Indonesian president's obligations when considering clemency pleas, amid claims that Jokowi had failed to even look at the two Australians' extraordinary rehabilitation. He had, it was claimed, simply refused all clemencies for drug traffickers, regardless of individual circumstances.

But the date given for the hearing was 12 May – two weeks after the Australians were scheduled to be shot. Attorney-General Prasetyo was forthright in his comments: the Constitutional Court hearing was not part of the normal appeals process, which they had already exhausted, so it would not affect the executions, which would go ahead regardless. In the future, he said, the government would impose time limits for these types of appeals.

It was also troubling that the attorney-general was making pronouncements that the various appeals lodged by the nine condemned prisoners would be thrown out by the courts, before they had even been considered by a judge. Did the rule of law have any sway here?

Mulya was trying everything. He was clearly frustrated. He called on the attorney-general to see common sense, to act with regard to justice, and to do his job as attorney-general and uphold the law. The legal teams were now counting the hours, having exhausted every legal avenue and done everything possible under the legal system to save their clients.

There had been only silence concerning the Judicial Commission's investigation into Muhammad Rifan's allegations of bribery and corruption during Andrew and Myuran's initial trial in the Denpasar District Court. On 26 April Rifan had outlined to Fairfax Media and the former host of SBS's *Dateline* program, Mark Davis, what he claimed had happened as the trial came to a close. Rifan, a Bali lawyer who defended many foreigners, claimed that the judges involved had sought a Rp 1 billion bribe (at the time about A$130,000), in order to give Andrew and Myuran sentences of less than 20 years.

But several weeks before the verdicts were due to be handed down, Rifan said, the judges told him they had been directed by Jakarta to give both men the death penalty. They were feeling the heat, he alleged, and asked for even more money. Rifan believed they were bluffing and would relent. But they didn't, and in February 2006 the accused were given the death sentence. The first time Rifan had mentioned this to anyone was in February 2015, when he visited Andrew and Myuran at Kerobokan prison.

A complaint had immediately been lodged with the Judicial Commission, but no witnesses had yet been interviewed. Mulya said the lawyers and families were deeply disturbed by the allegations, and that they had to be investigated fully before the men were executed. Any attempt at bribery or corruption was a defect in the whole legal process, he said.

'This is a matter of upholding the law, upholding the due process of law, and seeking the truth and justice,' Mulya said. 'Until they have finished the investigations they should not be executed. We appeal to the attorney-general, we appeal to the president, in the name of due process of law, in the name of fairness and justice, not to do the executions. This is not an act of desperado here. This is a demand for justice, a demand for justice. And [the] Judicial Commission has an obligation to commence a complete investigation, and it is not too late to save the legal system.

'The attorney-general keeps saying there is no more legal avenue[s] for appeal, but I think he forgot to mention there is a report filed at the Judicial Commission, and that is extremely fundamentally important . . . If it is proven [that the trial was] a defective process, then the whole decision, the whole judgement must be annulled.'

Just because this was the first case of its kind, the lawyer emphasised, doesn't mean it isn't legitimate.

Mulya had met with the chief of the Judicial Commission, who had promised to proceed with the case. The lawyer didn't know why the case had not even been started, or why witnesses were yet to be interviewed, given that his clients were to be shot within days.

Remarkably, even the judges from the Denpasar trial had not yet been interviewed by the Judicial Commission. It wasn't because they were hard to track down – after all, the media was speaking to them.

Just that day, one of the judges, Wayan Yasa Abadhi, said he had never been contacted by the Judicial Commission with any questions. He denied any contact with the lawyers during the trial, and said he knew nothing about any money being demanded or offered for a favourable sentence. 'Why didn't [Rifan] report [it] at that time?' the judge asked. 'They can report it as extortion. It is better if they report it. What is the data? Who is it? What is the evidence? Just report it. So it can be processed. Do not give statements in media like this, so that we who were not doing that, become contaminated. For me, personally, during the process there was no pressure. We gave the verdict based on the facts revealed in the trial, based on the law. I didn't know the lawyer personally and I never contacted or was contacted by him.'

Asked if he thought it was possible the other judges could have requested bribes, Abadhi said: 'I cannot comment about it.'

Mulya attended Andrew and Feby's wedding that day, briefed them on the legal avenues still being pursued, and left the prison with yet another of Myuran's paintings, given to him by the artist. The last thing Myuran had said to him was a request: 'Please make sure they abolish the death penalty in Indonesia.'

According to the lawyer, both men were still optimistic. They were not giving up hope. Mulya again called on Jokowi to take action in response to the bribery allegations.

As the exhausted legal team furiously typed letters and workshopped strategy, they also had to deal with the practical matters of death. An official from Indonesia's Foreign Ministry had been dispatched to Cilacap, and needed the details of the funeral home in Jakarta to which the Australians' bodies were to be taken. He also requested an official letter detailing the names of all Australian officials and lawyers who would be on Nusakambangan the next night. Everyone would need a special ID.

There would be a special waiting area for them on the island, the lawyers were told. The whole process of the executions would take two to three hours. When it was done, a convoy of vehicles would depart: police cars, and two ambulances carrying the bodies of Andrew and Myuran. Myuran would be in ambulance number one and Andrew would be in number two. Details of the route from Cilacap to Jakarta were outlined.

When it was time to identify the bodies, the Australian lawyers and Consul-General should open part of the coffin, look at the face and check the name on the coffin. No names would appear on the ambulances. There must be no phones and no cameras.

That afternoon, back at Cilicap's port, Michael Chan confirmed his brother's marriage to Feby. 'Andrew had a special day today,' he said; he and Feby had held a bit of a celebration with family and close friends. He was coy about using the word 'wedding', but confirmed the pair had married, saying it had been an enjoyable time for all.

'Hopefully the president will show some compassion, some mercy, so that these two young people can carry on with their lives,' he continued. 'It is in the president's hands – please show mercy. It is tough but it is a happy time at the same time, and we just hope that the president, somewhere, will find some compassion and mercy for these two . . . that they can carry on with their lives.'

Chinthu, too, wanted to say something. The two men had become eloquent spokespeople for their families. 'All I wanted to do is ask the president again,' he began. 'I spent the last five hours watching young children playing with their parents, and I ask the president to not make orphans out of children . . . There are family members just crying inside the prison as we count down the hours. Please step up and show mercy.'

The strain was showing. Everyone looked tired and worn down. Like the Australian officials, the Chans were staying at the Hotel Dafam in Cilicap. Many Indonesian officials, including those in charge of the death squad, were at the Dafam hotel as well. It was an uncomfortable mix. The Sukumaran family was staying out of town, in Purwokerto, a 50-kilometre drive away, because the Dafam was booked out.

The lawyers asked the Chan and Sukumaran family members to do some interviews with Indonesian television. Raji seemed numb, almost defeated. Her eyes were dull. Looking across the hotel lobby, she spotted a woman with long hair. 'The French lady is lucky, isn't she,' she said softly to me.

The woman, Sabine Ataloui, approached Raji and embraced her. They said nothing as the embrace lingered – there were no words for what Raji was going through.

Until this moment the two women had barely met. Sabine's husband, Serge Ataloui, had been slated to die alongside Myuran and Andrew. But he had been removed from the list due to ongoing legal appeals before the 72 hours' notice was given. Raji's heart ached.

In another part of the hotel, Catholic priest Father Charlie Burrows met with the lawyers and family of Brazilian man Rodrigo Gularte. Rodrigo's cousin Angelita Muxfeldt looked exhausted and defeated. They too were trying to work on last-minute strategies. How could a man who had been diagnosed with a mental illness be executed? It just wasn't right.

As family members went in and out of media interviews, begging for mercy, telling the story again and again of the rehabilitation of Andrew and Myuran, the exhausted Raji rested on a mattress in one of the hotel's meeting rooms. She still faced a 90-minute drive that night before she would even see her bed.

In his cell at Besi prison, Myuran was painting madly, producing some of his last works. 'The Last Chapter' and 'The Second Last Day' were both self-portraits. Then came 'Falling Apart' and 'Beneath the Shadow' – further self-portraits, the artist's face streaked.

16.

THE LAST DAY

Chinthu looked up to see an incredible sadness pouring from Myuran's eyes. He could feel it. He was only five or ten metres from his brother but it felt like such a long way. As they looked at each other, they felt a sorrow that needed no words.

'There's only half an hour left,' Chinthu said quietly.

'Let's talk, let's talk,' Myuran said, urgency in his voice.

It was almost time to say goodbye – forever. And there was so much more to say.

It was the last day, 28 April, and Myuran had asked Chinthu to go to the jail office to check the time. No one on this death island was allowed to wear a watch – not the prisoners, for whom time was ticking, and not their visitors and loved ones. The reason was never explained but Andrew suspected it was for security reasons – so the prisoners could not anticipate guard changes, for instance.

THE LAST DAY

Myuran talked about Chinthu's future. 'I want you to do big things,' he said. 'Don't worry about me – I'll be okay. Make sure you take care of Mum and Dad and Brintha. You need to get past this. You need to make the most of every opportunity. Don't be sad for me. You will move past this.'

There were nine families there – mothers, fathers, siblings, wives, children, girlfriends. It was surreal, almost like a Sunday afternoon picnic in the park. Mary Jane's children, two boys, played around as their bubbly and likeable mother flittered here and there. Each family was in its own space; some were talking, some holding hands and praying. All were savouring every single minute.

Visitors were limited on this last day. Raji's family had already been. She had asked them to come to the prison, but to give her and her immediate family – Sam, Chinthu and Brintha – their final hours with Myuran. It was 10.30 a.m. by the time they left, taking with them some of Myuran's final paintings, as well as his wooden easel. The painter had completed his final works.

Mulya said his goodbyes at the same time. Such a politically sensitive case had been difficult for Mulya, and had earned him some critics and even enemies. Disembarking the ferry at Cilacap, he proudly displayed Myuran's still-wet art, with the extended Sukumaran family behind him, clutching the last works he would ever paint – two profound images and two self-portraits.

'Satu Hati, Satu Rasa di Dalam Cinta' – or 'One Heart, One Feeling in Love' – was the name Myuran gave to his painting of a heart, dripping with blood, which he had completed not long before. On the back of the canvas were the signatures of some of the nine who would be killed with him. 'God Bless Indonesia,' wrote Okwudili Oyatanze, a gospel singer who had written and released CDs from jail. Sylvester Obiekwe Nwolise, a fellow Nigerian, wrote: 'Am covered with the blood of Jesus Christ.' Mary Jane Veloso: 'Jesus always love us until the eternal life. Mary Jane. Keep smile.' Raheem Agbaje Salami wrote the words 'One Love'. Zainal Abidin, the only Indonesian in the group and a Muslim, simply signed his name. So too did Andrew Chan. Myuran himself wrote his name alongside a simple inscription: 'Besi Prison, Nusakambangan, 28/04/2015'. It was their last day alive. The messages and signatures symbolised the bond that had developed between the nine prisoners, the love that had formed.

Myuran had thought deeply as he painted his final works, the pieces he knew would be remembered long after he took his final breath. He stayed up late into the night painting, surviving on little sleep, desperate to complete as many works as possible before his brushes and paints were taken away. Sometimes Andrew helped him name the paintings.

His last painting was a haunting image of the Indonesian flag, the red and white – the red dripping onto the white, blood being spilled. The death row prisoners had also signed it on the back and dipped their fingers in the red and then stamped their signatures with a fingerprint.

One of Mulya's staff held it up at the port, the paint still drying. It was titled simply '28/04/2015'. On the reverse, the words 'Pasal 340 KUHP' were in the top left-hand corner – a reference to Article 340 of the Indonesian Criminal Code, which concerned 'premeditated murder'. It was poignant and powerful.

This time, Mary Jane wrote part of her message in Indonesian: 'Bersuka citalah karena tuhan sudah menanggil kita. Mary Jane. Keep Smile.'

Sylvester: 'Am covered with blood of Jesus Christ.'

Steven (Raheem): 'God will is the Best.'

Okwudili: 'God bless Indonesia.'

Again, Zainal Abidin and Andrew had signed the canvas.

The evident bond between the eight men and one woman was extraordinary. Until the last 72 hours was about to be declared, only Myuran, Andrew and Raheem were in the isolation cells of Besi prison. Mary Jane was transferred from her Yogyakarta prison just one day before they were given their 72 hours' notice. The others were also then moved in, and very soon the group was eating together, praying together and planning their deaths together.

Mulya said the paintings were marvellous. When he left Besi prison, he revealed, both Andrew and Myuran were still upbeat. Andrew was leading prayers with his family and close friends. As Mulya prepared to go, Myuran had told him: 'Thank you for believing in us, and please fight for the abolition of the death penalty.' It was the last thing his clients said to him, the lawyer noted; it was something they wanted everyone to do.

Some of Andrew's friends, former Kerobokan prison inmates, were among those visiting. Gede Arthanya didn't say the word 'goodbye' to his friend, a man who meant everything to him. He had first met Andrew one month after he was jailed. In October 2013 Gede converted to Christianity: Andrew had brought him to Jesus, turning his life around. 'I love you,' Gede told his friend as he left. He hadn't meant to cry but he did.

'I love you too, Gede,' said Andrew. 'Just pray for one thing, that we will never die.' He was still hoping to make people laugh.

According to another former prisoner, when Andrew's friends and family started to cry at one point, Andrew had suggested they all pray to the Lord.

That morning, at the HOM Premiere hotel in Cilacap, Julian and Veronica tried to get some breakfast to fortify themselves. News had come through that the Judicial Commission in Jakarta had dismissed Muhammad Rifan's allegations of bribery during the initial trial at the Denpasar District Court.

Julian almost choked as he read the statement that had been released overnight. It said, among other things, that the Judicial Commission had handled the investigation professionally, carefully and without intervention from any parties. 'The Judicial Commission does not have the authority to change the Judge's decision,' it read, 'including cancelling the execution and the implementation of the death penalty of Andrew Chan and Myuran Sukumaran.'

Further, the Judicial Commission hoped the Supreme Court would actively investigate the alleged bribe to the judges handling the two cases. It asked both parties to respect the legal process of Indonesia.

President Widodo had also had something to say on the matter, questioning why the bribery allegations had been brought up at the eleventh hour, given that Rifan alleged the offence had occurred way back in 2005.

Julian was fuming and the day had barely begun. As far as he knew, the commission had not spoken to any witnesses – certainly they had never contacted Andrew or Myuran. How could there have been a careful and professional investigation if nobody was interviewed? And there had been no communication with the lawyers either. It was extraordinary.

Around him, the Indonesian officials tasked with organising the executions ate breakfast. So too did the family and lawyers of Zainal Abidin, the sole Indonesian among the condemned. The breakfast room was crowded. There were not enough tables and chairs as parties from all sides of the execution business sat crammed together – police officers with guns on their hips, Justice Ministry officials, prosecutors, lawyers and the media.

The day only got worse. Rumours circulated that Andrew and Myuran would not be allowed to be accompanied that night by the spiritual advisers of their choice from Australia; they would be forced to spend their final three minutes (the allotted time for last rites) with Indonesian pastors they didn't know. It seemed that the Indonesians were unhappy about who Andrew and Myuran had chosen. Myuran, at one stage, had wanted Julian to be with him. Andrew had asked that he be with Feby. The

Australians believed that, under the execution legislation, it was lawful for a pastor or a lawyer to be present.

Andrew's request was denied on the grounds that he and Feby were husband and wife. Meanwhile, the Indonesian prosecutors had busily googled the name 'Julian McMahon'. He was their lawyer, and clearly in press photographs with them. He wouldn't be allowed either. So a decision was made that two Indonesians would be with the men.

Matius Arif, the former prisoner from Kerobokan, had studied law before his jail convictions; he'd been in the same class as at least one of the Bali prosecutors. When he got wind of the plans to assign Andrew and Myuran Indonesian pastors they did not know, he met the prosecutors. He said he would report them to the Human Rights Commission if Andrew and Myuran were denied their own spiritual advisers. The issue was then sorted: David Soper could be with Andrew and Christie Buckingham could be with Myuran. Both were pastors and had their credentials with them.

Still there was more trauma to come. When the families arrived at the Cilacap port for their last trip to the island, new barricades had been set up; their vans were forced to stop way back from the entrance. Police and military were everywhere. It seemed the families would not be able to drive right up to the port building, as they had done previously.

Anxious not to lose any precious last moments with the boys, and distraught at the Indonesians' unthinking bureaucracy, the families and lawyers got out of the vans and started walking. It seemed the only thing to do. They walked straight into a throng of waiting media, police and snarling police dogs.

Struggling to get through, and with Australian officials and supporters trying to clear a path, a guttural howl pierced the air, drowning out the shouts of police and their barking dogs. Brintha could hold it in no longer. Screaming, she was half-carried through the crowd by family members.

Long after the family was safely inside the port building, the screams continued, echoing through the building and outside, as family members tried to calm Brintha. But the months of pent-up anguish, held deep inside, could not be contained any longer. Rattled officials appeared and asked Veronica to calm things down.

After the families departed for the island on the small ferries, the execution preparations intensified. The local police chief crossed to Nusakambangan to check preparations. Nine ambulances drove through, numbers on their windshields. Inside each vehicle was a coffin shrouded in decorative white material. Wooden crosses, engraved with the names of the nine and their dates of birth and death, had already been made.

At Besi prison, Sam Sukumaran was not at all well and spent time lying in a room at the jail. Myuran was worried about him and kept asking Chinthu to go and check on him. The family had brought lunch but Myuran couldn't eat. Raji urged him to have something, offering him food with her hand. He was her baby. She couldn't help herself.

Raji wanted Myuran to do the talking, not her. All she wanted to say was that she loved him. They held hands and touched. At one stage, Myuran patted the bench beside him. 'Come and sit here, Ma.' She had been standing behind him, holding him.

Out of the corner of his eye, Chinthu noticed guards moving closer. It startled him. Raji saw it too and her heart started beating faster. Why were they standing there? Were they going to drag him away already? Her mind was racing. They held Myuran's hand. He had seen it too.

'Don't worry – focus on me,' Myuran told them. 'Don't worry, don't worry.'

No one actually said their time was up. But it seemed inevitable. Julian too saw the guards quietly moving around.

Mary Jane was wearing a T-shirt with the words 'Jesus I trust in you' and a picture depicting Jesus. She started screaming. 'Some people were told 2 p.m. and some people told 4 p.m.' She had thought the families could stay longer. 'I was told four o'clock, four o'clock,' she cried. 'I haven't spent time properly with my children.' She started howling. 'Need some more, need some more!' She screamed that she had wasted her time doing procedural things. Someone should have told her it was 2 p.m.

Her elder child wrapped his arms around her. The younger one leaned on her. Mary Jane showered her children with kisses. Julian watched silently, struck by the poverty etched into the face of Mary Jane's mother. She had only one tooth, and the lines on her face were those that only sustained poverty can bring. She wept helplessly, the weeping of the powerless. The anguish of the Philippino family was unbearable. Little children and a mother saying goodbye. Their pain was unconstrained and unquenchable to Julian. Gradually they were eased apart. Everyone seemed to be watching. Julian kept thinking it was unimaginable to take this woman and kill her and leave those two little children.

Sylvester leant against a wall, bereft. His family were weeping uncontrollably. Female prison guards were in tears. Male guards stood in shock.

Martin Anderson was alone. His poverty-stricken wife had already left to make the journey to Jakarta to collect his body. They were too poor to arrange someone else to do it.

Now Raji and Brintha were moaning, guttural howls.

Helen draped herself around Andrew, sobbing and sobbing. Michael stood quietly behind, holding plastic bags of empty food containers. Everybody was frozen. The nine families howled and cried. Veronica went to the gate where Andrew's close friends were waiting, having already said farewell.

The prisoners had been allowed to make a series of approved phone calls, and Andrew called Ken and the family in Sydney. He said what he needed to say, when he could finally get a proper line. There was little phone credit on the mobiles that had been provided, and it was quickly chewed up by calling Australia. It was yet another frustration for the families.

Andrew had been desperate not to put either of his parents through the ordeal of this last day. But Helen would not stay away. She needed him and he needed her while Ken and Andrew's sisters remained in Sydney.

Veronica had convinced the guard to let Chan family friend Alan Wilkins back inside. 'Grab those bags from Michael,' she told him, 'because he needs to look after his mother.' Alan took the bags and silently, sadly retreated. Veronica saw the look in Andrew's eyes as Helen clung to him. He was going to break. She knew him and she knew that look. How were they ever going to get the mothers to let go of their sons? It was heartbreaking chaos and everyone was traumatised.

Feby comforted Helen. 'It's okay, Mum, he's okay.' Feby was incredibly strong that day – she gave Andrew strength.

The Sukumarans hugged Myuran. Each one clung to him for 20 or 30 seconds. Raji was last, hugging him as tightly as she could. Eventually, Myuran and Chinthu locked eyes, big brother urging little brother to do what no one wanted to do – take the mother away from the son she had nurtured in her womb.

Chinthu felt the weight of expectation: everyone was looking to him to care for his mother. He gently prised Raji away.

Veronica had hugged Myuran and told him she was proud of him. Andrew asked her to look after Feby. She would. Veronica kissed him on the cheek too. 'I'm so proud of you.' He beamed.

The prisoners went into the office area. There was one small window, up high, open to allow air in. Andrew, Myuran and the other seven crowded at the window. Their families on the other side thrust their hands up, seeking one last touch through the bars of the window. No one wanted the goodbye to end. Hands everywhere, tears, love. A decade of heartbreak poured out. Time stood still. Myuran asked Brintha to look after Raheem's girlfriend, Angela. Seconds were precious now.

The prisoners walked away. It had to happen. As he moved away, Myuran turned his head one final time to look at his family. It was the last thing they saw.

It was a magical second for Julian. Myuran turning around and looking over his shoulder in the midst of everything that was happening. That second that he was saying, we part forever, I am undefeated. Julian watched him intently. He wanted to burn that casual, over the shoulder glance into his mind because it felt like one of those extraordinary moments that many people never see in a lifetime.

As the legal team left, the guards apologised. 'I am so sorry, I am so sorry,' one said. 'It wasn't my decision.'

Julian was overwhelmed by the sense of absurdity – that good, young men who had made mistakes and committed serious crimes were having their innocent families put through this. He was brutally aware that they were being killed for reasons that were inadequate and unjust.

Everyone sat in shocked silence as the bus drove them away from the jail to the port. Raji had her head down. The misery didn't need words. The silence shattered only once, when Helen poured out her grief: 'Andrew!' Her guttural scream startled them all. Her heart was broken. All their hearts were broken.

The silent families caught the jail boat from Nusakambangan to Cilacap. There, Michael and Chinthu walked slowly towards the media throng. The awful business of an execution was now in full swing. Media satellite trucks were set up, generators were humming, police were everywhere. The dogs, so menacing earlier in the day, were in their cages. About 1200 police and military personnel had been brought in for the executions.

Michael went first. 'I'd like to say that our brothers were dignified at our last visit and we are very upset as a family to have to go through this,' he said. 'No human being should ever have to go through this. It's torture. Anyone with a heart –' he paused and shook his head – 'would forgive these guys for what they have done and show them mercy. I call on the president to exercise that, that he still has a chance to stop this cruel, undignified way of torture.'

Clutching one of Myuran's recent paintings, Chinthu took a breath. 'Mr President, I ask you please to show mercy,' he said. 'You're ordering the murder of nine people, and those people have families that love them and they don't need to die. I ask you to please show mercy. Myu is at peace with what may happen. He knows that he has to be strong and take care of the other eight people with him, and that's his focus. But I ask the president, please, the Indonesian people, please show mercy. Please, President Jokowi, please exercise your powers, intervene and save the lives of these nine people. Thank you.'

As they walked away, Michael patted Chinthu's back. These two men, from different backgrounds, were shouldering an enormous burden, and had been for ten years now. Both had just had to separate their mothers from their brothers. Their lives would never be the same again.

The buses pulled into a hotel parking lot and the saddest procession of people got out in silence. Helen was helped to a room. She looked frail, hunched over, clutching a tissue. Further down, the Sukumarans went into another room. There was little left to do but wait and pray.

Building work was going on at the hotel. Makeshift bamboo scaffolding was everywhere. A second floor appeared to be under construction. It was basic but it was the only hotel in town the Australian officials could find that would accommodate them all as they waited for the executions to be done. Everywhere else was booked out – by Indonesian officials, family members, the media.

The Chans and Sukumarans did not want their grief to be private. They wanted the world to know the heartbreak and the senselessness of this madness. Slowly, they emerged from their rooms and walked towards the microphones and cameras. The waiting media was in shock too. None of us had covered anything like this before.

Michael came forward. Behind him stood Andrew's staunchest supporters, those who had spent his final hours with him: Helen, Alan and Ann Wilkins, David Soper, Miranda Ridington. Ann held Helen's left arm as Helen clutched a tissue. The Sukumaran family was there too.

'Today was probably one of the hardest days I think we will face as a family,' Michael started. 'To see Andrew hold up the way he did, being dignified, courageous . . .'

As his voice broke, Alan put his hand on Michael's shoulder, comforting and giving him strength.

'. . . in these tough and dark hours. I saw today something that no other family should ever have to go through. Nine families inside a prison saying goodbye to their loved ones. Kids, mothers, cousins, brothers, sisters – you name it, they were all there. And to walk out of there and say goodbye for the last time, it's torture. No family should go through that.

'There has to be a moratorium on the death penalty. No family should endure it because now the family is going to have a grieving process for the rest of their life, not only to lose a loved one but to grieve for the rest of their life. I just hope the president in some . . . somewhere in his heart, that he can find some courage to show mercy to these nine individuals and call this off because it's not too late. It's up to him.'

Chinthu came forward, with Brintha clutching his arm. She was sobbing, and Michael moved forward to console her. 'We spent the last few hours with my brother,' Chinthu said. 'We didn't have much time. There were so many things to talk about. We did talk about the death penalty and he knows this is just a waste. He knows this is not going to solve anything with drugs. He knows drug trafficking is still going to be there. If these nine people die today, tomorrow, next week, next month, it's still not going to stop anything. I ask the president to please show mercy, please don't let my mum and my sister have to bury my brother. Please, please, I ask the Indonesian people to show mercy.'

Brintha, a portrait of grief, started talking through her tears. 'Please don't do this to my brother, please, please, Mr President Joko Widodo, I'm begging, please don't take my brother from me. Please. Please.' She closed her eyes, gripping Chinthu's arm. Calm and patient, Chinthu waited for her to finish. He had more to say.

'He told us that he is going to be strong,' he said, 'that him and Andrew are going to take care of the other seven people, and he is worried for Mary Jane and for her family as well. He just knows this is a waste. And we still have hope, right up until the last second, that the president will see each of these people as individuals, as people with families that love them, and show mercy.'

Raji was distraught but she wanted to tell the world what it felt like to say goodbye to her healthy and vibrant son. Sam was with her. 'I just had to say goodbye to my son,' she wept. 'I won't see him again, and they are going to take him at midnight and shoot him. He is healthy and he is beautiful and he has a lot of compassion for other people. I'm asking the government not to kill him. Mr President, please don't kill him today. Please don't, call off the execution. Please don't take my son. Please don't.' She sobbed, burying her head in Sam's shoulder.

Chinthu helped her move away and the families retreated to their rooms. To pray. To cry. To hope for a miracle. Chinthu couldn't stay still. He walked from one room to another. He sipped stale coffee. He constantly watched his multiple mobile phones for any news; months earlier, he had set up Google Alerts to monitor any news about the executions. No one was giving up hope that the president would call off the executions. The attorney-general in Jakarta had still not yet formerly announced that the executions would take place that night. Until he did, surely there was hope.

Chinthu talked to the media who were at the hotel, filing their stories. Was there any news? Was there any word from Jakarta yet? Surely, until that happened this was not a certainty. Surely there was some hope, in the absence of an announcement.

At 9.30 p.m. Attorney-General Muhammad Prasetyo ended the wait. The executions of nine people would take place after midnight.

17.
PREPARING THE SPIRIT

Christie Buckingham went to David Soper's hotel room door. She was wearing her pastor's collar. Myuran had initially told her he wanted the 'full robes', but she didn't have them with her. She knocked the secret knock she and David had devised so he would know it was her. It was almost time to go.

They had one last thing they needed to do. Their heads bowed, they prayed – for strength, for guidance, for wisdom, that they would be everything the boys needed them to be that night. Christie prayed for David, and then he prayed for her. They agreed to stick together. It was a simple and poignant prayer for the pastor and the chaplain.

Christie went to the room where the Sukumaran family was waiting. Raji called them all together to pray. They prayed for Myuran, that he would be strong. They prayed for a last-minute reprieve and for Christie, to give her strength for the night ahead. They prayed for the Chan family. Some of the family had notes and letters they wanted Myuran to have. They sang a few songs and told a few stories. It was intimate and thoughtful. The tears were gentle.

Tina Bailey and Denise Payne had both come to Cilacap. Myuran had considered asking Tina to be his spiritual adviser that night, but he wanted his spiritual adviser to speak out against the death penalty after he was gone, and believed that asking this of Tina might jeopardise her work at the prison.

Now Christie spent some moments with the two women. 'I can't do this alone,' she told them. 'I know you guys will be praying for me but is there some way that I can take you with me?'

Tina offered her gold-coloured religious stole, which Christie hung around her neck. Denise gave Christie her treasured butterfly pendant. It symbolised how people can change, just as caterpillars turn into butterflies. Significantly, 'People Can Change' was the name Myuran had given to his painting of President Joko Widodo. It was a simple yet powerful statement, and both Myuran and Andrew had changed so much.

Christie had spent the whole day in her hotel room, praying and seeking guidance. She had not gone to the island for the final visits and the dreadful goodbye, as visitor numbers were limited. She wanted to fully prepare herself. She wrote in her journal that she had 'a desire to be fully present to assist in whatever way I can to whomever I can'. She would withhold any feelings for herself, she noted, or recognition of her own

PREPARING THE SPIRIT

needs in order to fully stand with and be completely present for Myuran.

She had a list of the things Myuran wanted to do on the field during the time he was tied up before the execution, and the songs he wanted to sing. Christie and Myuran had been through it all the day before, and Christie had agreed to bring the list in case they needed prompting when the time came. She went through the list now, in her head, making sure nothing had been overlooked.

Myuran had thought deeply about his final moments, when he would be strapped down and facing the firing squad. He had told Christie he wanted everything that night – the works. 'What do you normally do when someone is dying?'

She had explained that, usually, she would go through some scriptures, ask for forgiveness, have a period of consecration, and anoint them with oil.

Privately, though, she recognised that this was not something she had trained for in any way – ministering at the death of a healthy young man, in his prime, who had years of life ahead of him. Christie and her husband, Rob, both pastors at the Bayside Church in Melbourne, had assisted at about 200 deaths, but these had always been of people whose bodies were weak or who had been in accidents. Never like this.

'The most important thing I want to say,' Myuran had told her, 'is that I forgive people, and I want to declare a blessing on Indonesia; it is really important that's among the last things I want to say. Can you just remind me that there are things I want to say?'

Christie, David, Julian, Veronica and Majell drove together from the hotel to the port, where they would take the ferry to Nusakambangan. It was about 7 p.m. No one knew exactly what was going to happen. An Australian embassy official briefed them. 'We are not sure what is going to happen, or how far you will get, or how long you will have. One thing for you to know is the Indonesian word for please: *tolong*.'

It was an intense journey and there was no talking. Christie and David were to be taken to the cells where Andrew and Myuran were waiting. Julian, Veronica and Majell were to go to a marquee set up near the dock.

As the lawyers and spiritual advisers separated, Julian put his hand on Christie's shoulder. 'Just make sure the boys get what they need,' he said. 'They won't shoot you.'

'If I get shot,' Christie replied, 'tell my husband and family I love them and I will see them on the other side.'

Julian said the same thing to Father Charlie Burrows, who was ministering to Rodrigo Gularte, the mentally ill Brazilian man.

Security was incredibly tight as the spiritual advisers were driven to the jail cells. The driver wore a black mask over his face and head. Every hundred metres or so they were stopped so guards could check for mobile phones and other banned articles. At one point, to break the tension, Christie said, '*Saya tidak gila*,' or 'I'm not crazy' – of course she didn't have a mobile phone.

PREPARING THE SPIRIT

At the jail, Christie was searched by female guards. Her mouth, nose, ears – everything was checked.

'What are you looking for?' she asked.

'Razor blades or tablets, to pass to the prisoners.'

Nothing was being left to chance or overlooked.

'We are so sorry,' one guard told her. 'Myuran is such an inspiration to us. We have seen his painting. We are so sorry that this is happening.' Myuran was looking forward to seeing her, the guard said, and had showered and was waiting for her with his Bible.

Christie saw Rodrigo Gularte. 'Sister, they are singing,' he said to her. 'Am I going to church?'

'No, Rodrigo, I think you are going to heaven,' she replied.

He wanted to know if there were snipers in heaven.

Christie assured him that Father Charlie was on his way and would look after him.

By now it was about 10 p.m. A guard told Christie and David that they had about an hour with Andrew and Myuran, who were sharing a cell. The Australians greeted them as they arrived. Andrew hugged Christie warmly.

'Welcome to my place,' Myuran said. 'Have you eaten? Would you like some chocolate?'

Myuran took Christie to a mat on the cell floor, which was actually his bed. He was showered and ready. 'Make sure you tell Mum that,' he said, wanting her to know that he had done exactly as she had asked.

Christie recounted how Raji had called everyone together for prayer that evening. Myuran beamed: his mother was strong and amazing. 'You remind me of her,' he told Christie.

David and Andrew sat together on Andrew's sleeping mat, but it was obvious the two parties needed their own space so they could prepare in privacy for what was to come. David asked if he and Andrew could go outside. The guards agreed.

Christie gave Myuran the letters from his family. He read through them. So much love. Then he tapped the Bible and told Christie, 'This is what I want to talk about.' He said he wanted to make sure he had all the 'brownie points' he could muster for later that night.

Myuran had been brought up in a Christian family but had frequently questioned his faith. As a young man he had been ambivalent, then lapsed. He didn't really know what he believed. Back in January, when his clemency request was denied, he had said he was angry with God but didn't know why, because he didn't know if he even believed in him.

Christie had her small, well-thumbed travel Bible with her; Myuran had his. They started reading Genesis, then moved to Exodus 14:14, about God fighting our battles. Christie and Myuran had first spoken of this back in February.

They moved on to one of Myuran's favourite verses, Micah 6:8: *'And what does the Lord require of you? To act justly and to love mercy and to walk humbly with your God.'* Myuran told

Christie he liked the simplicity of the verse. She talked about providing shelter and clothing, and feeding the hungry. Myuran had been doing this, through his work with other prisoners back at Kerobokan.

He asked after a baby boy in Africa whom Christie's church had adopted. Julian had chosen his Christian name: Myu Mpilo Michael. Myuran wanted to know if the baby's AIDS test had come back clear, and what would happen to him next. He asked what the name Mpilo meant – it was the Zulu word for 'life', Christie said. Smiling, Myuran hoped the boy would have a long and good life.

They moved to the Book of Psalms. Myuran read out a scripture which one of his aunts had sent over for him. He talked about his love for his family, for his aunts and uncles. Flicking through the two Bibles at once, they next went to the 'Roman Road', a selection of verses from St Paul's Epistle to the Romans. Christie had a copy of it stuck in the front her Bible. 'You're making me do Bible gymnastics,' she joked to him.

'This matters most right now,' he told her.

Myuran looked up each verse of the Roman Road, reading it aloud and following the text with his finger. As they read, Myuran noticed that Christie had in her Bible the song sheet for later that night. He smiled, pleased she had remembered. They were organised and ready.

He read Psalm 121 at least four times. *'The Lord will keep you from all harm, he will watch over your life; the Lord will watch over your coming and going both now and forevermore.'* He pondered the word 'forevermore'.

Myuran liked the fact that God would protect his steps. He didn't want to make a fool of himself that night, he told Christie; he didn't want to fall down or stumble as he was being led out for execution. They discussed that he would be walking in shackles. Myuran knew what it felt like, and how hard it was to walk. 'Just take small steps,' Christie told him.

Their discussion ranged in this way from the spiritual to the practical. Myuran asked Christie to take his asthma inhaler in case he needed it later; he didn't want to be coughing or struggling to breathe at the end. He wanted to be calm and in control. He asked her to give the inhaler to his mum when it was over, and to give a hoodie of his to Brintha.

The end was nearing, and Myuran was thinking about how he would be remembered forevermore. He spoke about surrendering himself to God. They read Psalm 23: *'In the presence of my enemies you have prepared a table before me . . .'* He loved that part and they read the psalm three times.

Christie asked him what table God was preparing for him, and what the table meant to him.

Myuran answered by talking about his family, about love and nurturing. He said that for him to die with courage, honour and dignity would be God preparing a table for him. He was calm. Often when Myuran was stressed his eyes twitched, but tonight it was like a switch had been turned off. Christie was struck by the fact his eyes did not twitch at all during those final hours.

He wanted to be brave. 'At this moment I feel calm and brave,' he said, 'and I just want to be like that on the field. I feel like God is preparing the table for me to do that . . . does that make sense?'

Yes, she told him, it made perfect sense. 'It's about one step at a time,' she reminded him. 'And the closer it gets, it's about one breath at a time.'

They talked about the seven deadly sins: envy, gluttony, greed or avarice, lust, pride, sloth and wrath. 'I have done all of those,' Myuran said.

Christie assured him that everyone had.

Myuran was grateful for the ten years he had spent in jail, which had helped him to alleviate his own shame and that of his family. 'Had I died ten years ago, I would have died a criminal,' he said, 'but now I can honestly say I have done everything I can, not only to change me but to change other people's lives and to change them.'

Until this moment, he said, he had never really understood love. He came from a loving family but had never understood true love. He cared about other people and realised how much love came his way when he turned outward and looked at and helped other people.

Christie was struck by his honesty.

'I always thought I would get married and have children, and that would show me what love is,' he told her. 'But I actually now know what true love is.'

Myuran wanted to write a note for his mentor, Ben Quilty. He started scribbling madly on some post-it notes that Christie had inside her Bible. He wanted Ben to know that in some of the last paintings there was a darkness over his head, a black hole over his heart. But the next day, he didn't feel like that anymore – he didn't feel like he needed to focus on that but on the light as he looked to it. 'Ben should see,' he wrote.

At the beginning, when he was painting his final works, he was focused on how they would kill him. He had painted a single bullet. The wooden cross to which he would be tied. In those paintings, darkness was over his head. But in his last paintings he had looked beyond this. When he did the last paintings, he said, it was like something falling off him.

'I came in here as a criminal and I leave as a successful artist,' he told Christie. 'Now I know that my mum and dad and family will be proud of me.' He finally knew love, an everlasting love. He loved his lawyers too, Julian and Veronica, and spoke fondly of them to Christie.

Myuran pointed to the wall of his cell, just above his mat on the floor. A page of dates was stuck there. There was also a note in his handwriting:

> Every day above ground is a good day
> 10 a day practice started 16-04-2015
> The journey is the reward it's not the
> accomplishment of something incredible
> it's the doing of something incredible, day

in day out, getting the chance to
participate in something really incredible.

The first date on the wall was 4 March 2015 – the day he and Andrew were transferred from Kerobokan to Nusakambangan. The last was 28 April 2015 – today, the last day of his life.

Since 16 April he had been focusing every day on ten things he could be grateful for. Christie and her husband, Rob, had suggested this practice to Myuran some time ago, but it wasn't until this moment that Christie realised he had been doing it. She was amazed by his dedication: most people, even outside prison, could think of only three things a day.

Myuran spoke about how much this had helped him. He didn't have to think much further than his family and friends to come up with ten. Some of the guards were even on the list. Ten seemed like a good number, he told Christie.

He was now so attentive to everything. Grateful when he ate something that tasted good; grateful for the breeze; grateful when he saw new things as he painted. Myuran told Christie how angry he had been when his clemency was rejected. Rob had been visiting him at the jail that day, and explained that it was okay to be angry with God, who had big shoulders. This had surprised Myuran. He started to realise that if he was talking to God and being angry with him, then he must believe that he existed.

He told Christie he had highlighted a 16-day period, from his arrival at Nusakambangan, when he had started to explore his anger and had been saying short, simple prayers. He had circled 27 March, which related to a time when he had felt God's love come over him, like he was standing in a shower. He had felt things falling from him. Everything had started to make sense, he said – even sharing the cell with Andrew.

Christie took Myuran's hand. Was he scared? she asked.

'Of being shot? No, I am not scared of being shot at all. I just want to make sure that my life is right before God.'

Christie put her hand on his chest to see if there was any anxiety. There was none. Myuran had less than two hours to live but he was calm and at peace. Relaxed. Christie felt like time was standing still.

They moved on to confession. Myuran prayed and asked for forgiveness. He forgave those who had in any way sought his forgiveness. He asked Christie to continue to speak out against the death penalty, and to take care of his mother and sister. The only thing he hated was the death penalty. He apologised to Christie for not painting her the image of the cross that he had promised. Time had run out.

'Let's do it now,' Christie said, urging him to close his eyes. 'If you can imagine God in this room now, where would he be?'

Myuran reached out his arm, pointing in front of him.

Christie asked if he was seeing God the Father, God the Son or God the Holy Spirit.

'God the Son. I see Jesus.' He told Christie he had bronze-coloured eyes.

'What is he saying to you?'

Myuran sat quietly, contemplating, then smiled, his body relaxing. He said Jesus had a cross in his hand. 'It's gold, it's beautiful . . . it's beautiful. I have never seen that before, it's beautiful.' Myuran told Christie he felt a warmth come over him: he felt comfortable, safe, at peace.

Christie said it was the spiritual presence of God, there in that jail cell on this death island.

The pastor was amazed. She had expected both Myuran and Andrew to be anxious, especially as the appointed time of their death grew closer. But Myuran's smile was more radiant than ever. Christie was struck by his eyes, which were alive, fiery and compassionate at the same time.

Christie told him that no question was off-limits: she didn't want him to feel inadequate or unprepared in any way. 'If you are frightened, you tell me,' she said. 'If you are angry, you tell me, so I can guide you for how you need to be when you walk out onto that field.'

As they prayed, the songs of Myuran's childhood were coming back to him. He was surprised. He started remembering 'Jesus Loves the Little Children', a hymn he'd sung as a child.

He took communion, insisting on opening the little cups of wine. Christie prayed for him and anointed him with the oil she had brought with her. He commented on the nice smell, saying it was better than the oil in Indonesia, which reminded him of fish and chips. 'Would you take it and anoint me in Australia?' he asked. 'And please do a communion with my family and anoint them with the same oil. Would there be enough for that? Please keep it safe.'

After Christie anointed Myuran on his forehead and hands, a silence descended on the cell. He smiled. They prayed a prayer of consecration and Christie committed Myuran to the Lord.

She sensed time was almost up. As Myuran was praying, a guard moved towards the cell and held up a finger. They had just one more minute.

Prayers and confessions were happening along the row of cells, for all nine of those to be executed, Christians and Muslims alike.

Father Charlie was with Rodrigo. Arrested in August 2004, he had been convicted of attempting to smuggle 6 kilograms of cocaine into Indonesia, hidden in surfboards. He had also been diagnosed as suffering from paranoid schizophrenia and bipolar disorder. He'd experienced mental disorders since he was a young child, and had been treated in psychiatric institutions before his arrest in Indonesia.

His lawyers had fought hard for a stay of execution because of his mental illness. But Attorney-General Prasetyo said the government's own psychiatrists – two police doctors – had examined the Brazilian and declared him mentally fit for execution. Their reports were never provided to his lawyers or family. Only pregnant women and children under 18 years were exempt from execution, Prasetyo claimed.

The lawyers disagreed, arguing that the law specified that a mentally ill person could not be punished in this way.

Charlie tried to explain to Rodrigo that he was being executed that night. He'd been attempting to tell him this for the past three days, but Rodrigo was paranoid and hearing voices. Charlie had a hard time convincing Rodrigo that he had to leave his cell that night. He was afraid that snipers in the trees would get him, or that he would be shot in the car.

Andrew walked back into the cell. 'I'm up first, mate,' he said. The guards had come to take him. He hugged Christie, asking her to give his glasses case to Feby. 'I'm going to wear my glasses because I'm as blind as a bat without them,' he said.

He was wearing the wedding ring Feby had placed so lovingly on his finger the day before. It was actually David's ring, of course, but Andrew intended to wear it at his death. 'Make sure they get this on the other side,' he said to Christie.

Andrew and Myuran wanted to go into Raheem's cell to pray with him as he was anointed with oil. The guards initially wouldn't allow it but then relented, letting the men hug and pray together. Andrew prayed a simple blessing; Myuran said, 'Yes, amen.'

Myuran, now handcuffed, motioned for Christie to walk ahead of him. But it wasn't allowed; the guard told Myuran he must go in front. This was the walk of the condemned, past all the cells. Myuran told Christie to help him if he started singing and forgot the words.

'Amazing grace, how sweet the sound that saved a wretch like me . . .' But for the singing of the dead men walking, there was silence.

Mary Jane was in the final cell. She was dressed in white and getting ready to leave.

'I'll see you down there,' Myuran called to her.

The wardens formed a guard of honour to say goodbye. Myuran and Andrew threw their handcuffed arms over their heads and around them in one final goodbye. No one stopped them, despite the obvious security risk this could have posed. These two men were no risk, the guards knew. Some had tears in their eyes. They apologised: 'We are so sorry . . .'

The prisoners kept singing. As they reached the door of the cell block, the shackles were put on – a chain running down from the waist, and attached to chains around each leg. 'Small steps,' Christie reminded Myuran. He nodded back. Now his hands were cable-tied behind his back. She walked beside him, her hand on his elbow. 'Small steps, small steps . . .'

Just outside the door, Myuran stopped. He craned his neck back and looked up at the sky. No one hurried him – they let him be. He looked at the sky, the stars, shaking his head and smiling. He drank it in. 'God, you're magnificent.' It was the first time in a long time he had actually seen the beauty of the night sky. When you're locked in a cell, there is no night sky to see.

Time was suspended. Quietly, Christie urged him to take his time. It was his night. When he was ready, he was told to get into a car. He sat down on the seat but, with his legs shackled and his hands tied behind his back, he was unable to get his feet in. Myuran rocked backwards and forwards but couldn't do it.

No one moved to help him. Every policeman had his job, and no one had been assigned this duty.

Christie tried to help. At first she was stopped but then the guards allowed her to move in. 'Respect,' she had begged. First she grabbed the chains from the top, but he was too heavy. Then she put her arms underneath, lifting with all her strength. 'When I lift, you rock back,' she told him, heaving his legs in.

Christie didn't want Myuran to get out of the calm space he was in, and she knew he was desperate not to look silly. She wanted him to have his dignity. The end was very near.

18.
THE END

A tiny tear trickled over Christie's hand. She had reached up to Myuran's face, cupping his cheek protectively with her right hand. 'You are a good man,' she said softly. 'You are a courageous man. You are a reformed man.'

'Thank you, thank you,' Myuran mouthed back.

His tear ran delicately down the outside of her hand, a feeling that instantly embedded itself in her memory. Her three minutes with Myuran were almost up.

The guard's instructions to Christie had been clear: 'You talk to the prisoner, you calm him for three minutes, and then we will touch you on the shoulder and you must go.' She knew she couldn't stay with Myuran but there was no way she was leaving until she was sure he was ready.

When Christie was escorted to Myuran a few minutes earlier, he was already strapped to a wooden cross that was mounted on a platform. His arms were bound to the cross at the elbows; he could move his hands up and down. His feet were tied.

The night was still and dark. Aside from the small lanterns carried by guards, it was pitch-black. Andrew was strapped to the cross next to Myuran. Raheem was next.

Each of the condemned prisoners wore a white T-shirt. That was mandatory – so that their chests, and specifically their hearts, were visible in the darkness. The sky was beautiful. Stars twinkled delicately, as if in defiance at the scene below them.

Christie sensed what Myuran needed. 'Let's close your eyes,' she said to him. Her voice was gentle, ministering. A police officer tapped her on the shoulder: the three minutes were up. She would have to leave soon.

She made every second count. They were all singing now – Myuran, Christie, and the other prisoners and their advisers.

The policeman moved forward and took Christie's elbow, urging her to leave.

Christie put her hand on Myuran's heart. 'Myu, remember what we did back in the cells. What did Jesus say to you, and what did you say to him?'

'I trust you, I trust you,' he replied.

Through his white T-shirt she felt Myuran's heart beating rhythmically. There was no panic or angst, just the pump, pump, pump of the heart of a young man in his prime. There was no fear.

'Myu, I am just going to take a step back,' Christie said, easing backwards, ever so slowly. 'Can you still hear me?'

'Yes,' Myuran called.

'I am going to take a few more steps back but I am still here,' she continued. Singing pierced the air. 'I am still here,' Christie called out. 'I'm going to the side but I will still be here.'

'I'm great, I'm great,' Myuran called back to her.

When Christie had first been escorted to Myuran, and saw him strapped to the wooden cross, she almost gasped. He was big, both in stature and in spirit. And he had the most beautiful smile she had ever seen. He'd always had a beautiful smile, she knew, which lit up his whole face, but now it was more radiant than ever. It's like a bit of heaven touching a bit of hell, she thought. She could barely comprehend it but he seemed at complete peace.

Earlier, as Christie, David and the other spiritual advisers waited solemnly out of sight in the marquee, the silence was pierced by a loud *clunk, clunk, clunk*. None of them immediately registered what it was. Then they realised: it was the sound of the prisoners walking with their legs shackled at the waist by chains.

Christie was startled. In the darkness there was no other sound. No one spoke. She couldn't describe the haunting sound. 'I have no words for it. No words for it,' she wrote later in her journal of the events of that night.

Then Andrew's nasal voice bellowed out. He wasn't much of a singer but that had never stopped him before. 'My saviour, He can move the mountains. My God is mighty to save, He is mighty to save . . . Forever, author of salvation, He rose and conquered the grave . . . Jesus conquered the grave.' Soon all the prisoners were singing as they were strapped to the wooden crosses.

The Christian advisers started singing too. They got stuck on the second part of the verse, but Christie had the song sheet with her. Myuran had been very impressed, back in the cells earlier in the night, that she had remembered these.

Aware that there were Muslims among the prisoners, Christie asked the imams who were there to comfort them if they were okay with the singing of Christian songs. They nodded. But, concerned not to upset anyone, Christie asked one of the Indonesian pastors, Ibu Yani, to check with them in Indonesian. 'Yes, yes, yes, please,' they said, motioning for the Christians to go ahead.

'Mighty to Save' ended, and Christie began singing 'Hallelujah'. But it wasn't the original – it was the version from the movie *Shrek*. Through the darkness, Andrew realised it was the wrong version and got them all back on track. Amazed, Christie pictured Andrew's cheeky face puzzling at her choice of song and guiding them to the version they had decided they would sing. She couldn't believe he was able to do so at that moment.

As 'Hallelujah' came to an end, there was a lull. Then came the haunting strains of 'Amazing Grace'. It was at this moment that the guards came for Christie, David and the other advisers. They now had three minutes.

'Hello, Big Dave! Hello, Mrs B,' Andrew said as the spiritual advisers were escorted to their prisoners. Christie saw Andrew and Myuran next to each other, almost within touching distance.

Myuran smiled at Christie. 'I just want to say that I am truly sorry that I have asked you to do this,' he said, 'but I am really thankful that you are here and I know that you will speak out,' he said. Now he needed a favour. 'I've been bitten by a mosquito – can you scratch my feet?' he asked.

Christie moved quickly to scratch his feet – too quickly. A guard, sensing her sudden movement, and on alert for any trouble or departure from the rules, came up behind her. It was not menacing but officious.

As she scratched Myuran's foot, he looked directly at the guard. 'I forgive you for what you are going to do. Please, bless Indonesia, please.' He asked Christie to make sure she looked after his mother. She promised him she would. They talked about his family.

Beside them, David ministered to Andrew. The Salvation Army minister had known Andrew since he was a little boy. He was like family.

'Sing up! We can do better than that,' Andrew called as the singing lulled.

Time was precious. 'What did God show you back in the cell?' Christie asked Myuran. 'Get that picture back in your mind again,' she urged him. His face broke into a big smile. Christie felt humbled. Myuran and Andrew led prayers. 'Lord, we pray for Mary Jane. She is here as a woman by herself. Lord, let her not be frightened, and give her peace and protect her family,' Myuran prayed.

'Amen,' Andrew finished.

'Lord, we pray for Rodrigo, that he will have peace and he will be calm,' Andrew prayed. He called to Okwudili, 'Are you okay?' He called out to Mary Jane too, but there was no answer.

Myuran prayed for his killers. 'Father, forgive them because they don't know what they do. God bless Indonesia!'

As Ibu Yani, the pastor who had been looking after them since their arrival at Besi prison, walked past, having left her prisoner, Myuran shouted to her: 'I believe, Ibu Yani, I believe!' She came to him and anointed his forehead with oil.

As Christie eased backwards and away from Myuran, behind her the firing squads were preparing. Each of the prisoners had a firing squad of 12. They lay on their stomachs on the ground, their rifles on small tripods. Christie had seen their red laser beams piercing the black night, seeking out their victims' chests. At one stage, she had raised her arm to ensure that Myuran did not see this. Now the laser beams were turning from red to green.

As Christie passed Andrew, he called out to her. She knew her time on the field that night was up, but the spiritual advisers had been told that if another prisoner called them they could respond. She approached Andrew and put her hand on his heart. 'I love you and I'll see you on the other side,' she said.

'I will be on the other side,' Andrew replied.

Rodrigo was five down from the Australians. He was upset, and Father Charlie was trying to calm him. The prisoner kept asking why this was happening, and telling Charlie it was not right. A polite and sensitive soul, he hated being manhandled. 'We made a small mistake once,' he moaned. 'Why is this happening?'

'I am 72 – it won't be too long and I'll be meeting you up there,' Father Charlie told him. 'You must work in that garden and grow flowers and trees. That's your job.'

The priest had refused to wear a traditional Indonesian Batik shirt that night, in protest at the executions. He had also eschewed the vestments of a priest. Rodrigo didn't need a sermon; he just wanted to talk, like friends. He knew Rodrigo didn't mind praying, as long it wasn't too holy.

As the spiritual advisers moved away, the prisoners continued singing. Now they started singing 'Bless the Lord'. They had made a pact that this was the song they would sing as they were executed. They'd sung it many times in the previous days, like a choir rehearsing. Now their voices were passionate and strong.

As Christie retreated, the song in her ears, she hoped the firing squad's dreadful task would be completed quickly.

19.
EXECUTION

'Bless the Lord, o my soul, o my soul! Worship His holy name! Sing like never before, o my soul! I'll worship Your holy name . . .'

The prisoners sang. The spiritual advisers sang. They completed the first verse and chorus and were halfway through the second verse. 'You're rich in love and You're slow to anger. Your name is great and your heart is kind. For all your goodness I will keep on singing—'

Bang!

A shocking boom ripped through the air. It was like nothing any of the witnesses had ever heard before. The sound of a hundred high-powered rifles firing simultaneously.

The shockwaves reverberated up Christie's legs and jolted her backwards. David, on her right, threw his arm out to protect her. They looked at each other, bereft. Nearby, Father Charlie and Ibu Yani also looked shocked. The sound had been deafening.

Then, complete silence. They looked at each, stunned, unable to speak or move.

Christie leaned back in her chair, registering what had happened. *That is it. It's over.* Then she bent forward and started praying.

Ibu Yani urged them all to pray. 'They could still be alive,' she said.

An enormous rumble jolted them again. For a brief, awful moment Christie wondered if the bodies had fallen from their crosses. Or was it an earthquake?

An official told them it was the firing squads leaving – the sound of 96 men running from the scene. They had to be gone within a minute. Their job was done and they were to witness nothing further. It was for their own psychological wellbeing.

In fact, the firing squads had been fully vetted, their psychological state assessed. Could they handle this? Were they personally and emotionally able to take the lives of fellow human beings? Those who were not were spared the duty.

Christie and the others said the Lord's Prayer. At the same time, Christie desperately listened for any noises – any groaning, any moaning, any sounds at all. She prayed that death had come quickly to the victims.

If the bullets had gone astray and someone had not died immediately, she knew, she and the other advisers would need to witness the unfortunate prisoner being shot in the head with a revolver. This was the law. Earlier that night an official had briefed them on this: 'When they shoot, if one not dead, all must see.' Christie had initially understood that she would only need to witness this horror if Myuran did not die immediately.

Now she was desperate. When an official appeared, she spoke quickly. 'Do we need to see?' she asked.

'No, no need,' he replied.

The shots to the heart had all been clean. No one was left moaning and dying slowly. No one would have to be shot in the head.

Christie felt a weight lift from her body. She and Myuran had talked about this, and he'd been clear: if it happened, he urged, make sure he was dispatched quickly. 'Don't pray for me for 27 minutes – just make the call, don't muck around.'

Nothing had been off-limits in their preparatory discussions the night before. She had explained to him about anatomy, and what would happen when the bullet pierced his chest and then his pericardial sac. She assured him he wouldn't even know it, it would happen so quickly. But if he did feel something, in the twilight zone between the bullet entering his body and his brain shutting down, she advised him to call upon the Lord.

Ibu Yani gathered the spiritual advisers for communion. Christie blessed the body of Christ, Father Charlie blessed the wine, and Ibu Yani read a blessing. Then Father Charlie launched into a thoughtful and poignant homily about grief and the way Indonesians face the grieving process. As he talked, Christie was struck by the powerful and thoughtful words of a man who had spent some 42 years in Indonesia.

Father Charlie explained how, three days after death, then seven days, then 40 days and then 100 days, people in the Javanese culture remember the dead. After this, it is done every year, until the last ceremony, 1000 days after death. The church, he said, followed this system with prayer vigils and celebrations of the Eucharist. It was a strategy to help them process their grief, psychologically necessary for those affected.

This was not the Catholic priest's first execution. He'd been present in June 2008, when two Nigerian drug traffickers, Samuel Iwuchukwu Okoye and Hansen Antonious Nwaolisa, were executed. He had ministered to them during their time in jail at Nusakambangan. They hadn't died immediately: for up to seven minutes they had moaned in agony, strapped to the crosses. Charlie sang 'Amazing Grace' as the men suffered, the life slowly leaving their bodies.

Describing that scene brought Father Charlie to tears every time. 'It was torture,' he said, 'simple as that.' So incensed was he by the injustice of the death penalty, and so keen was he to fight it, he even agreed to testify at a Constitutional Court hearing brought in 2008 by the Bali bombers. Their lawyers were arguing that death by firing squad was cruel. Father Charlie had no hesitation in giving his first-hand account of what he saw as wanton, horrifying cruelty; it did not matter that it was a challenge being brought by three men who had murdered more than 200 innocent people in the 2002 Bali bombings. The challenge was ultimately thrown out and they were executed by firing squad in late 2008.

As Father Charlie finished his homily, silence descended upon the group. Everyone was deep in their own personal reflections, prayers and grief. One by one, the advisers were called out to sign the paperwork of death. Christie went first, then David.

Nearby, in a makeshift tent set up near the killing field, the bodies had been removed from the crosses and washed and dressed. Christie needed to use the toilet. As she walked in the darkness, she caught sight of the bodies. There was no mistaking Myuran and Andrew. Only minutes ago they had been alive and singing 'Bless the Lord'; now they were laid out on tables, their ugly deaths exposed.

A wave of sadness overwhelmed her.

At the hotel, the families waited and prayed. The Sukumarans prayed, read scripture and sang songs – 'Bless the Lord' and 'Amazing Grace'. Tina Bailey and Denise Payne were with them. Everyone was praying for a miracle.

Chinthu phoned me, wanting to know if the executions were done yet. He had to tell his parents and sister.

I told him it was over. We knew already.

He pleaded with me, his voice cracking, wanting more details. There was a rumour that Mary Jane had not been killed. If she was still alive, perhaps Myuran and Andrew were as well?

'No,' I told him. 'They are gone. It's over. I'm sorry.'

There was nothing else I could say. I felt bereft and incredibly sad.

Chinthu hung up and went back to his family. 'It's done,' he said.

Brintha collapsed to the floor. They cried and cried.

Over on the island, the group of advisers waited for hours for the bodies to be cleaned, dressed and placed in the wooden coffins that had been specially built for each victim.

Bali-based prosecutor Olopan Nainggolan approached Christie. He was shaken, and wanted her to pray for him. Having been the lead prosecutor in Andrew's trial, Olopan had been required to attend. Earlier that evening, before the executions, he had told Christie he hoped God would forgive him.

Christie took his hand. Olopan, a Christian, closed his eyes. Christie asked God to forgive him. 'Only God can take and give life, and this will change you as a man,' she told him.

'Thank you, thank you,' Olopan said.

Later, Christie was stopped by some policemen. '*Maaf, maaf,*' they told her – meaning 'sorry, sorry'. 'Please don't hold this against Indonesia,' they begged.

At last, the spiritual advisers were brought down to the port area, from where the coffins, each in a separate ambulance, were to be transported to the mainland.

Suddenly a rumour swept through the group: 'Mary Jane's not dead!'

What?

'A reprieve – she got a reprieve!'

The words swirled around in Christie's head. She couldn't work it out. Slowly the pieces fell into place. In the witnesses' tent, the chair reserved for Mary Jane's spiritual adviser had been vacant. On the killing field it had been dark; Christie had not actually seen Mary Jane strapped to her cross. Nor had Mary Jane answered Andrew's and Myuran's calls to her. Christie suddenly realised that Myuran and Andrew had no idea that she hadn't died with them.

Mary Jane had been ready, dressed in all white, which she had chosen to wear that evening as a symbol of her innocence. All the prisoners would be wearing white T-shirts at the end but Mary Jane had chosen to wear all white clothes. Before their spiritual advisers arrived that evening, the nine condemned prisoners had prayed together in one cell.

Mary Jane's pastor, Romo Kieser from Yogyakarta, urged her to be strong. 'Whatever happens is God's will,' he told her.

As her fellow prisoners were led past her cell that night, each one urged her to be strong. She prayed one last time with Romo Kieser, who blessed her, before the guards came to take her too. They walked her slowly towards the gate and the security checking area.

A group of officials approached. 'Mary Jane, get back to your room,' a female prosecutor ordered. 'Sleep and take a rest, because tonight you will not be executed.'

Mary Jane was speechless. All she could do was hug the prosecutor.

She had been ready to die. Like the others, she had prepared herself. She had no fear. She told one of her lawyers, Agus Salim, that she had already eaten. She cried and cried in her cell as she heard the shots.

Christie and David were finally driven back to the port, after what seemed like an eternity waiting with their own thoughts. There, they met Julian and Veronica. The two lawyers who had fought so hard had been waiting with Majell Hind in another marquee at the port area. They had heard the shots.

Julian looked bereft. He wanted to know if Andrew and Myuran had been treated decently.

'The boys were magnificent,' Christie told him. 'You would have been so proud of them.'

Next she hugged Veronica. 'I can't believe that this has actually happened,' she cried.

It was at this marquee that the national representatives were to identify and take possession of the bodies.

Plastic chairs had been adorned with white satin covers. Red bunting was wound around the corner poles, and draped ceremoniously around the marquee roof. Boxes of KFC and water had been brought in. It felt surreal. Waiting by the water – for people to be killed.

A massive explosion. That's what it sounded like from the tent. Loud. Shocking. Dreadful. Veronica had not contemplated that she would hear the shots, and was left stunned.

Mary Jane's two sisters, Darling Veloso and Maritess Veloso-Laurente, had chosen to be at the tent with their lawyers. They howled hysterically, calling out her name, feeling their hearts were being torn from their chests. Their screams pierced the air. They gave voice to everyone's feelings. It was torture. They slumped face-down on the tables.

Almost immediately, Mary Jane's lawyer, Ismail Muhammad, started hearing rumours that Mary Jane had not been taken to the firing range. But there was nothing official. Finally, at 2 a.m., a prosecutor approached him. 'Congratulations, I think this is a miracle,' he said. 'Mary Jane's execution was cancelled.'

The two hysterical women were ushered away. Within minutes they were screaming again, this time with joy and elation. Mary Jane was alive and in her cell. She had been spared.

Everyone else, hearing the joy in their voices, guessed the miracle. The family and lawyers emerged, suppressing their delight. Mary Jane was alive but eight others were dead: this was no time for celebrations. Ismail urged them to keep hold of their feelings, in deference to the other families.

Mary Jane's other family members and the officials from the Philippine embassy were already on a bus, travelling to Jakarta to claim her body. They could barely believe the news as a series of frantic phone calls were made. The bus pulled over.

At the St Stephen's Catholic Church, where Father Charlie worked, Father Harold Toledano, a priest from Bandung, was lying in bed. He jumped up when he heard the news. Three hours earlier he had farewelled Mary Jane's parents and children as they boarded their bus for Jakarta. As they left that night, he'd told them never to lose hope – that miracles could happen. Mary Jane had told her family the same thing as they left the prison earlier that day.

Maybe Andrew and Myuran were saved too ... In the back of her mind, amid the pain, Veronica couldn't help but wonder. Climbing into the back of the ambulance, she delicately lifted the coffin lid. Myuran lay there, dressed in an ill-fitting tuxedo, his white-gloved hands crossed in front of him. Tenderly, Veronica touched his chest and whispered good-bye. Julian, too, said goodbye. They closed the lid and put an Australian seal on it.

They did the same in the ambulance bearing Andrew's coffin. He was also dressed in a tuxedo. A surge of anger rose in Veronica when she saw the comical way both had been dressed. Myu wouldn't have wanted to wear that, she thought. Perhaps Andrew would have been amused, such was his quirky nature, but certainly not Myu. They looked like waiters from a 1970s comedy.

The lawyers were careful not to open the coffins too wide, to ensure that no one took any photos. Majell kept at bay the crowds who were clambering with their mobile phones, trying to sneak a photo of the two Australians.

When they reached Cilacap, the ambulances carrying Myuran and Andrew's coffins were driven onto the dock. Myuran's vehicle went first; Christie, Julian and Majell walked ahead of it. Andrew's came next, with David and Veronica leading it. Spotting a KFC packet in the front of one ambulance, Christie asked the driver, out of respect, to get rid of it. She and David had decided earlier they would lead the coffins with a Salvation Army salute, pointing to heaven. It was a solemn and private gesture, recognition of the men they had become.

Christie smiled about the fact that Myuran was in ambulance number one, and Andrew was in number two. There had always been competition between the two. Back at the cells, Andrew had said, 'I'm up first, mate,' but now Myuran was in the lead.

The drive back to the hotel and the waiting families was silent. Christie, David, Julian, Veronica and Majell sat stunned and wounded.

At the hotel, Veronica hugged Michael Chan. The tears flowed. Helen was sitting alone. She looked lost, as if she wasn't there. Veronica knelt in front of her and hugged her. Veronica cried and cried, sobbing, broken. She let it all out. She couldn't stop weeping. Helen, too, was broken.

Then Veronica went to Feby, Andrew's wife for just a day but the love of his life. He looked handsome, she told her as they embraced.

Christie and Julian went to the room where the Sukumaran family was waiting. 'Myu was incredible,' she announced. 'He forgave Indonesia. He prayed for those killing him.'

She embraced Raji, the mother who had lost her beautiful son. When Veronica embraced Chinthu she could barely speak, such was her grief. She shared a group hug with Chinthu, his wife and his sister, Brintha. They were moved to learn that Myuran had gone peacefully and with courage, and that it was quick. There was deep sadness but also an incredible sense of pride.

Soon after the executions, in Jakarta, Todung Mulya Lubis tweeted his despair:

> I failed. I lost.

Michael Chan, too, took to Twitter:

> I have just lost a Courageous brother to a flawed Indonesian legal system. I miss you already RIP my Little Brother.

The bodies, in two ambulances, had already left for the 381-kilometre drive to Jakarta, escorted by Australian embassy staff. The Chan and Sukumaran families followed in two buses. Julian and Veronica drove in a separate car. It was 5.55 a.m.

as they pulled out of Cilacap, the Central Javanese town now synonymous with death, a place none of them ever wanted to visit again.

In the Sukumaran bus were eight of Myuran's final paintings. Seven were on seats, carefully packed by Tina Bailey to keep them from being ruined. Myuran's final painting, of the Indonesian flag, was in the bus's luggage compartment. Eight other paintings had been left behind in Cilacap; they were still too wet to be transported.

On the bus, a Foreign Affairs staffer urged everyone to try to get some rest. Christie felt wounded, like she had been thumped. But there were questions to answer, and messages to pass on. When she felt ready, Raji sat beside Christie. Christie had important things to tell her, things that she would tell no other soul. She had promised Myu.

Raji wanted to know that her beloved eldest son wasn't frightened at the end, and that they had treated him well. The things a mother would want for a dying child. She could not bear the thought of him being afraid and manhandled.

Christie assured her that Myu had died well. She recounted how she felt that Myuran had reached down and put courage inside her. It was as if Myuran and Andrew had given her a gift of bravery and courage and compassion – and she knew she would carry it with her forever.

Christie described how Myuran had sung so well as death stalked him. There was even a little laugh when she recounted how, early in the night, when she had first gone to his cell,

Myuran had told her to make sure Raji knew he was showered and ready.

Other family members talked with Christie during the bus ride, telling stories about Myuran as a little boy.

When they stopped at lunchtime for a break, Chinthu asked for everyone's attention. 'I'd like to make an announcement: this is courtesy of Myu,' he said. Myuran had given him his spare money before the end, and Chinthu used it to shout everyone's lunch.

20.

GOODBYE

Some letters are just too hard to read. So it was with the two written on 27 April 2015. The day before they died. Myuran and Andrew knew that by the time I got their letters they would be dead. It was a goodbye from the two young men I had first met a decade earlier, the day after their arrest.

Andrew had long promised he would deliver me an award-winning piece of writing. Like Myuran, he wanted the world to know not just about them, but also about the others dying with them. About the pure senselessness of all their deaths. Both men wanted those left behind to fight against the death penalty. The words of Myuran and Andrew speak for themselves.

Dear Cindy,
How are you? I hope you're going alright. I'm sorry I didn't get the chance to do the portrait of your son that I wanted to do,

everything happened so fast. I couldn't really believe it. This prison is a world away from Kerobokan, but I did get to start an art class with one lesson in drawing before all this started again. I can't really remember how many times we prepared to die in the last few months – I think we got used to it, actually. The thing that is really unbearable is each time watching my mum, brother and sister get torn up, my whole family and friends – they never get used to it, and each time they tear our families I can see the pain in their eyes, the helplessness for our families. This has got to be one of the cruellest things this president has done. I want to say so much about this president but am afraid of putting the words on paper, but I'm sure you know what I think of him and the AG. It's probably the same as you times infinity.

I've been here for almost two months and got to know Raheem well. I've got to say he is a good man and a strong Christian who knows the Bible inside and out. He's spent 17 years of his life behind bars – he's no kingpin – his faith just as strong as Andrew's. He was a worship leader in his previous prison. After 17 years in jail for his crime, I can say he does not deserve this.

I got to meet Mary Jane a few days [ago] and it gutted me. I can't believe how dumb these people are. She's so small, has two children. We've prayed together and talked and joked – she is like a child. Honestly, she has got the mind of a child – she's not mature or educated for her age. And she is strong and trying to be happy as she can.

I also met Okwadilie, the other Nigerian, and know he has become a reformed man. He is a worship leader as well in his previous prison and his faith is strong. I know what most Nigerians do in jail but these two guys are not like that. They were couriers and haven't played while inside. The guards know who does what here; as you know, nothing is a secret inside prison walls.

I have had few conversations with the Brazilian man – there's something not right with him – it's obvious! There's another old Nigerian man in a wheelchair who has been in jail for a long time. I don't know much about him and wonder if they will shoot him in the wheelchair or stand him up. The other two guys of the nine I won't talk about, so you know what that means. It's weird, again I am a part of nine. I've heard somewhere nine is a special number.

Please note that this must be one of the dumbest executions in the 21st century. I guess you can see dumb stuff happening in undeveloped places, warzones and third-world countries but happening in Indonesia, a developing country trying for leadership in South-East Asia I honestly don't know how reason and compassion are lost in an [illegible] democracy in the 21st century in Asia. It's weird – it feels like they are so hyped up and [illegible] enjoy killing foreigners that they stuck an Indonesian in there so they cannot get blamed for only foreigners.

One thing you learn in prison is about strength and weakness – and they look so weak, all of them. I feel great pity for them, they so much want to show the world how good and strong they are. In prison terms it reminds me when a young gangster comes inside and joins a gang – he wants to prove himself. You know in Hotel K there were so many – he puts his head up and back when he walks, pushes his shoulders up and chest spread wide, his arms as far out as it goes to the side. He's the man, juiced up on as much [illegible] as he can get, shouting around, showing his strength, but over ten years I've seen that the only people they prey on are the weak ones, the small ones, the ones who can't fight back and embarrass them.

I've written so many letters to so many people, more than I've ever written before. I have so much I want to say to you but don't know if I have the time. I was telling Julian that it was weird that they chose Anzac Day to deliver the news – or is it that they didn't think? I had just finished reading a book, *Gallipoli* . . . and it really opened my eyes. I know what those guys went through . . . but wow, the comparisons, leaders, great leaders making ridiculously stupid decisions for dumb reasons, pride, etc., sending people to die without a care in the world. Then I read 'Gallipoli Letter' from Keith Murdoch in 1915, . . . and say he [illegible] it in the last line you know, 'to be an Australian is the greatest privilege the world has to offer'.

And we put up a great fight. We fought to the very end with dignity and honour! We will not die with shame, fear, hate or anger but with our honour, knowing that we regained our redemption and only the kingdom of heaven awaits. I was telling everyone that in the last two months I was cramming hard for my final exam, the most important one of my life. All the previous times I was prepared to die but I hadn't made peace with God. This time I have and it feels different.

I passed on a message to the boys in Kerobokan. I will be waiting for them in heaven but if I'm not there when they arrive that they should wait for me because I'm still kicking JW and AG's ass in hell, putting my ten-year prison experience to good use . . . then will wait at the gates of hell and will make their time in eternity miserable – prison humour.

I also want to ask you one last request: that you help fight them for what they do so that they never do this to another person again, and also bring attention to the others – Matt, Si Yi, Mike, Scott, Renae, Martin, Tan. They shouldn't have to spend the rest of their lives in jail; ten years is already more than enough time. They shouldn't get extra punishment time just because they're Aussies. Please help – at least that way I can rest easy.

Your friend,

Myu

Andrew wrote:

Dear Cindy,

How are you? I hope you are well. I promised I would write a golden Pulitzer – I'm a man of my word, so here goes.

My name is Andrew Chan. Most of you would have heard my name or even feel as though you have known me. For the last four months I have had the privilege to share (some) of my story in your living rooms, offices, workplaces and even in your car. You have heard the story of how I'm a changed man, that my life and Myu's life should be spared. We have been labelled 'The Pastor and the Painter'.

The support that has been generated through this has absolutely been overwhelming, however since [arriving] here I have come to know seven other lives apart from me and Myu.

Mary Jane from the Philippines, age 30, was sentenced to death trying to import heroin from Malaysia to Yogyakarta. Most of us won't know Mary Jane's story as she's a maid from a third-world country that hasn't been bothered to be noticed until now. Her story is remarkable as she was a maid that was abused and raped. Trying to support her family, she went to another country to work as a maid, however [she] was tricked into thinking she landed a job. The man that set her up managed to get away. How he got away is a question authorities in this country should answer.

Rodrigo, Brazil. I don't know much of his story, however [he] was caught trafficking cocaine. Though I have only known him for two days I can see that he is mentally unstable, constantly wearing a cap thinking that aliens want to take his brain. His mental state shows he's not trying to pull something off the crazy card table. Take one look and you'll say the same.

Okwadilie, Nigeria. A man fully rehabilitated who loves the nation of Indonesia and has dedicated [himself] to helping other prisoners. A gospel singer and a man that has dedicated himself to serving God.

Steve, aka Raheem. Nigeria (however, his passport, which was fake, says Costa Rica). In 1998 he was caught, sentenced to death in 2000, has served 17 years in prison. In my two months getting to know Steve, he's a man that has truly changed and also wants to be a pastor.

Martin, Ghana (however, once again fake passport and from Nigeria). In a wheelchair and pretty much disabled. How they condemned a man to death after 50 grams – well more than half of Indonesia should be on death row then.

Zainal, Indonesia. Don't exactly know him as he won't speak, however he is a human being, someone's son, brother and father.

Sylvester, Nigeria. A man that now has plenty of time to contemplate his previous actions. I could tell you now that he was most likely still dealing inside, but to sentence him to death, I don't know if that really fits the punishment.

Steve the Nigerian wanted to have his real name used, however they refused – said it would delay the executions.

Now I only wrote points, Cindy, I didn't write properly as I have to write more letters and can't just [spend] all my time on one letter, however this gives you the idea of who is here, who the other guys are.

The warden here is nowhere to be seen. I was led out in handcuffs for a visit until Myu's mother broke down seeing him in cuffs.

Mary Jane is seriously like a little child, talkative to calm her nerves, makes me feel introverted.

The Old Testament teaches us an eye for an eye, a tooth for a tooth. In other words, you get what you give and give what you get. A murderer that takes the life of someone else for money or for pure violence is actually considered much better than a drug trafficker, according to the Indonesian president – he seems to justify his reasons only on statistics that he couldn't even get right in the first place. It seems to me that he has forgotten the difference between a drug trafficker and drug dealer.

What most don't know is that, 90% of the time, those who get caught are usually mules and those who use it personally. Very rarely will you ever catch a boss with two kilograms or one kilogram strapped onto them or even swallowed. The ones sentenced to die, we will take a closer look into seeing are they the kingpins that President Jokowi says they are? Has he made the right choice? Let's study the facts ourselves as we put this together.

Filipino maid (Mary Jane) – kingpin or mule?

Brazilian (Rodrigo) – kingpin or mule?

Nigerian (Odwadili) – kingpin or mule?

Nigerian (Steve, aka Raheem) – kingpin or mule?

Australian (Andrew) – kingpin or mule?

Australian (Myuran) – kingpin or mule?

Ghana (Martin) – kingpin or mule?

Indonesian (Zainal) – kingpin or mule?

Nigerian (Sylvester) – kingpin or mule?

As you follow the facts yourself, can you identify the mule and the kingpin? Each one has a unique story; most done it on the sense of more money and greed as they were young. Don't we all make some silly choices in life?

Just recently President Jokowi granted clemency for three murderers . . . the reasons in doing so are his own. It seems as though it's better to give clemency to those who deliberately threaten society and have not proven any source of rehabilitation. How President Jokowi makes these decisions we will never understand, however instead of moving the nation forward he's actually brought back the country. What he has done is actually classed him as a murderer himself, though he might not agree on that, saying he's helping his nation. He has not helped the nation, rather he has helped those drug dealers (bigger ones) get off lightly while those below will always suffer the effects. President Jokowi can only hope that others can show him grace when he's needing it most.

First day of countdown 72 hours was allowed to pray in one room together, which was really good. The guard was nice enough to allow it.

Myu rushing painting, painting his most inspired pieces in the last three days.

About 20 to 25 guards patrol our area constantly, and our area has been covered up with Perspex, sort of plastic (it has been like that since day one). We have been in solitary confinement for two months almost . . .

> Thank you, Cindy. Before I sign off I'll tell you a funny story. I locked a guard in the cell as he was using one of the empty cell toilets. I had just been unlocked briefly for our 30 minutes exercise when I saw him inside. So I locked him inside for about ten or 15 minutes. I told him it wasn't time for him to be let out – that he must wait.

It was classic Andrew – a larrikin to the end. He wrote his own eulogy, which was read at his Sydney funeral. In it he paid heartfelt tribute to his brother, promising not to steal his birth certificate and present as Michael in heaven. Andrew also paid tribute to Feby, the love of his life.

He concluded: 'My last moments here on Earth I sang out "Hallelujah". I ran the good race, fought the fight and came out as a winner in God's eyes.'

Hundreds and hundreds of people turned out for the funerals of Andrew and Myuran. Two days before Myuran's funeral, Raji wrote a lengthy letter to President Joko Widodo. She wanted him to know just how much his decision to kill her son and the others had torn the hearts out of so many people.

Raji was grieving deeply, and angry that Jokowi had signed the death warrants without even looking at the personal stories of those he was killing, at their rehabilitation and reformation, at the details of their cases. She told the president that she hoped that his children, grandchildren, nephews and nieces never made a mistake in their lives. And she reminded him that one of the last things Myuran had done on the night of his death was to seek forgiveness for Indonesia and for those killing him.

Raji was not sure, she wrote, that she could ever find forgiveness for the president; the pain in her heart would be there forever.

One year later, Raji sat down and penned another letter to President Widodo, this time pleading with him not to proceed with the next planned round of executions. It was July 2016 and Indonesia had announced it would execute 16 death row prisoners – the first executions since Myuran and Andrew and six others in April 2015. Raji was struck again by the same feelings of helplessness and despair she had felt one year ago when she was forced to say goodbye to Myuran.

> You are the only person who has the power to prevent another execution. I can't believe you would want to see mothers, fathers, sisters, brothers, children and grandparents grieving for their loved ones. Please don't let these families go through what we have gone through ... I pray you find the courage to show mercy, as one day you will no longer have the power and will be looking back at your choices and your mistakes and the decisions you have taken.

Raji's plea fell on deaf ears. On 29 July 2016 four men – an Indonesian, two Nigerians and a man from Senegal – were executed amid torrential rain. For reasons that remain unexplained, ten others who were to have been executed that night – they had said their goodbyes to their families – were spared.

Andrew Chan and Myuran Sukumaran, the Pastor and the Painter, died shortly after 12.30 a.m. on 29 April 2015 in Cilacap, Indonesia, singing praises to their last breaths. But before they took those last breaths, they forgave those who ordered their deaths and those who fired the shots. They had made their families proud. They were rehabilitated. They were reformed. They had redeemed themselves, and had saved and transformed the lives of countless others along the way. They did not deserve those bullets to the heart.

Their deaths are a powerful portrait of why the death penalty is wrong and can never be justified under any circumstance. They knew it, their families knew it, their lawyers knew it. It was wrong. So very wrong. And for it to be carried out in a country with such a questionable justice system, so lacking in transparency and where justice is for sale to the highest bidder, makes it even worse, if that is possible.

Andrew and Myuran should not have been executed and I hope that by telling their story we will be one step closer to the abolition of the death penalty. Theirs is a cautionary tale and a poignant reminder of what we all lose when we ignore the power of mercy.

AMNESTY AND REPRIEVE

If you are opposed to the death penalty you can help make a difference.

For 40 years, **Amnesty International** has been working to end executions. When they began this work in 1977 only 16 countries had totally abolished the death penalty. Today, that number has risen to 104 – more than half the world's countries. **Contact Amnesty via www.amnesty.org.au**

Reprieve Australia is also working hard to see a world without the death penalty. Reprieve work with volunteers, interns and their board to develop legal and policy solutions that will help save lives. **Contact Reprieve Australia via www.reprieve.org.au**

ACKNOWLEDGEMENTS

This book spans a decade in the lives of Andrew Chan and Myuran Sukumaran. It covers a myriad emotions, happy and sad times, hope and anguish. It could not have been written without the generous assistance of a large group of dedicated people who loved Andrew and Myuran and fought so hard to save them.

To everyone who talked with me over the years, I cannot thank you enough.

To Andrew and Myuran, the Pastor and the Painter, thank you for trusting me with your story. We must all fight to stop the death penalty.

Thank you, from the bottom of my heart, to the Sukumaran and Chan families, for trusting me and allowing me into your lives at such a devastating time. Your sons will not be forgotten.

Heartfelt thanks to the legal team – Julian McMahon and Veronica Haccou in particular, who treated this reporter with

ACKNOWLEDGEMENTS

the utmost respect for so many years. Your professionalism, your humanity, your generosity and your kindness are extraordinary. Thank you for sharing the story and for looking after me.

To Christie Buckingham, I cannot thank you enough for sharing such intimate details of the story. Reliving the events of that awful execution evening came at a personal cost to you. I know it was not easy. You are an inspirational woman.

To Lizzie Love and Tina Bailey and to the fellow prisoners, many of whom are not named, thank you for your insights and your kindness.

To my own wonderful family, my husband, Chris, and son, Tom, who supported me, cared for me and helped me throughout one of the most difficult stories I have ever covered.

Thank you to my second family in Bali. Photographer Lukman Bintoro, you were there with me on the day Andrew and Myuran were arrested in 2005, and you were there on the night they died. You are not just a colleague but a dear friend. Komang Erviani, the best fixer any reporter could ever work with, you were by my side for the last years of the story and in Cilacap at the end. Your wisdom and professionalism are unmatched, as is your loyalty. I am proud to call you my colleague.

To my journalist colleagues, with whom I spent many years covering this story and who all comforted and supported me at some stage on this journey – Mark Burrows, Tom Allard, Paul Toohey, Michael Bachelard, Jewel Topsfield, Kelvin Healey, Adam Taylor and so many others – thank you. To my colleagues and editors at News Corporation, thank you for believing in the story.

Last but not least, thanks to the amazing team at Hachette Australia, who nursed and believed in this book long before I sat down at the computer to finally write it. To Vanessa Radnidge, thanks does not even begin to express how grateful I am to you for encouraging me, over such a long period of time, to tell the story. Thanks for your support, encouragement, compassion, patience and for being such a thoroughly lovely human being. Without you, this book would never have been written. You are amazing.

To the editors, Julian Welch and Tom Bailey-Smith, I can't thank you enough for your wisdom and sage advice. You saved me, massaged the manuscript and made it so much better. And thanks to everyone at Hachette for believing in the value of telling this story.

INDEX

Abadhi, Wayan Yasa 229–30
Abbott, Rupert 109–10, 133
Abbott, Tony 78, 103, 133, 190
   aid to Indonesia comments 190
ABC Triple J *Hack* program 132–3
Abidin, Zainal 206, 215, 236, 237, 239
Agus, Lukman 41–2, 44
Allard, Tom xiv
Amnesty International 109
Ana, Wayan 206
Anam, Choirul 107
Anderson, Martin 207, 214–15, 243
Andriani, Rani (alias Melisa Aprilia) 102, 105, 106
Archibald Prize 90, 167
Arif, Matius 31, 32–3, 57–8, 59, 61–2, 240
Arms of Love foundation 63–4
Arthanya, Gede 237–8
Asshiddiqie, Chief Judge Jimly 38–9
Ataloui, Sabine 232
Ataloui, Serge 232–3
Australian Federal Police (AFP) 4–5
   knowledge of Bali Nine 4–6
   letters to Bali police 4, 5–6, 14, 81
Australian government
   efforts for clemency 131–4, 190
   prisoner swap offer 191–3
Australian public support xv, 116–17, 122, 133

Bachelard, Michael 135
Bailey, Tina 60, 197, 226, 252, 279, 287
Bali ix–x
   Adi Dharma Hotel 7
   Aneka Beach Hotel 6
   Australian Consul-General's office 3
   Hard Rock Hotel 6–7, 18
   Kudeta restaurant 152
   Kuta 6, 7, 8, 165
   Melasti Beach Bungalows 8, 13
   Plamboyan hotel 7
   police surveillance of Bali Nine 6–8, 14
   White Rose Hotel 6
Bali bombers 29, 126, 164–5, 205, 278

Bali International Women's Association 33
Bali Nine xii, 4–8, 86–7, 161–2, 166, 199
  appeals against verdicts 27–8, 36–9
  arrest 2–4, 9
  Australian public opinion 96
  interception of 8–9
  judges and corruption allegations 135–6, 227–30, 238
  Kerobokan prison *see* Kerobokan prison
  legal teams 13–14
  police surveillance 6–8
  relationships 15, 18, 29, 162, 176–7
  sentences 21–2
  separation of 12
  trials 14–18
Bali police 6
  case investigation and preparation 12–13
Bannakorn, Cherry Likit 7
Besi prison 172–3, 181–233
  art classes 200
  handcuffs 213
  visits 184, 196–7, 209, 213–17, 225–6, 234–5, 237, 240–5
Bishop, Julie 131–4, 187, 191, 192
Blackwell, Joel 37–8
Boyolali 102, 108
Branson, Sir Richard 189
BRIMOB 153–4, 169
Buckingham, Christie 63, 65, 122, 220, 226, 240, 251–67, 268–72, 275–80, 282, 285–8
Buckingham, Rob 63, 253, 261
Burrows, Father Charlie 108–9, 233, 254, 255, 264–5, 273–4, 275, 277–9

Cardoso, Fernando Henrique 189
Chan, Andrew ix–xiii, 13, 29–30, 236, 237
  anti-drugs work 57–9, 87–9
  appeals/judicial reviews 27–8, 36–9, 51–6, 123–4
  Bali Nine involvement 5–10
  Besi prison 172–3, 181–233
  childhood 25
  Christian faith 24, 43, 57–9, 63–4, 73, 74, 84–5, 112, 148, 218, 238
  Christian ministry xi, 42–3, 89–90, 143, 160–1
  church cell groups 59
  clemency pleas 66–7, 92–3, 101, 111, 187–8
  cooking classes 59, 113–14
  counselling by 74, 80, 84, 143
  death penalty 20–2, 102, 104
  duck breeding 65
  execution ix–x, xiii–xv, 269, 270–3, 275–9
  execution arrangements 230–1
  execution warrant 203–4, 207–8
  funeral 298
  'godfather' 47
  guilt, admission of 51–2, 124
  hate mail 82
  humour/personality 25, 114, 115, 117, 143, 148, 152–3, 154, 173–4, 177–8
  innocence plea 14, 18–20, 50, 51, 127
  instructions for post-execution 144, 186
  last day 237–40, 243–5
  legal teams 13, 30, 35–9, 111–12, 129, 162–3, 187, 226–30
  letter to author 293–8
  marriage 149, 218, 220–6, 230, 231

INDEX

mood 80, 110, 112–15, 121, 134–5, 137, 148, 177–8, 237
ordainment 122
police detention 12
preparation for death 256, 265, 266
prisoner support for 156–60
reform and rehabilitation xi, 39–40, 42–3, 51–3, 61–3, 73–5, 81–3, 112, 156–8, 252
refusal to testify 15, 16
responsibility, taking 80–1
rugby league and 137–9
Sabu plans 222–5
theology study 42, 52, 63, 74
transfer to Nusakambangan 145–6, 153–4, 168–72, 174, 178–9
trial 14, 15, 17, 20
verandah conversations 117
writing 115, 137–9, 177–8, 289, 293–8
Chan, Helen 4, 11, 24–5, 72, 114, 122, 124–5, 128–9, 139–40, 151, 210, 220, 243, 244, 245, 247, 285
conversion to Christianity 24
Chan, Ken 4, 11, 24–5, 72, 114, 125, 139–40, 220, 243, 244
conversion to Christianity 24
Chan, Michael 4, 11, 21, 67, 125, 128, 185, 210, 218, 219, 220, 231–2, 243, 244, 246–8, 285, 286, 298
clemency appeal letter 72–5
Chen, Si Yi 5, 6, 8–10, 15, 22, 28, 39, 86–7, 166, 179
Cilacap x, xiii, 108, 169, 170, 176, 185, 197, 207, 211, 230, 246, 285
Constitutional Court 36–7, 106, 123, 195, 208, 226–7
Criminal Code revision 39, 55
death penalty decision 38–9

Corby, Schapelle x, 9, 13, 29, 66, 96, 175–6, 192
Crosslink Christian Network 122
Czugaj, Michael 5–10, 19, 22, 28, 166

Davis, Mark 228
Dear Me: The Dangers of Drugs 87
death penalty xi, xv, 30, 55–6
appeal to Indonesian Constitutional Court 36–9
Australian public attitudes 132
Denis, Namaona 102, 106–7
Denpasar District Court 22, 55–6, 93, 112, 228
judicial review 112, 116, 123
Denpasar High Court 27–8
appeals and sentences 28
Denpasar police headquarters x, 9
Detik.com 108
Dreifuss, Ruth 189
Dwije, Gail 63

East Timor 32
Elliott, Sandy 43–6
Enemuo, Daniel 102
Erviani, Komang xiv, 210

Farrow, Mary 76
Franola, Meirika (alias Ola) '*Ratu Narkoba*' 105
Franola, Tajudin 105

Giuily, Francois Jacques 156
Global Commission on Drug Policy 189
Gulerte, Rodrigo 206, 208, 233, 254, 255, 264–5, 273–4

Haccou, Veronica xiii–xiv, 37, 111, 117, 118, 121, 144, 148, 150, 171,

307

Haccou, Veronica (*continued*)
  172–3, 174–5, 179, 187, 202–3, 207, 208, 215, 220, 226, 238, 241, 243, 244, 254, 260, 282–6
Hanh, Tran Thi Bich 102, 108
Harahap, Yahya 54–5
Herawati, Kristiani (Ibu Ani) 77
Herewila, Febyanti 149–50, 171, 178, 185, 204, 210, 218, 220–1, 225, 230, 231, 239, 240, 244, 265, 295, 298
heroin trafficking x, 81–2
  Bali Nine 3–9
Hind, Majell 124, 135, 172, 187, 202, 203, 208, 220, 254, 284, 285
Homebush Boys High School 10, 25

Indonesia
  #CoinForAustralia 190
  Australian intelligence phone tapping 77–8
  citizens facing death penalty abroad 133–4
  drug offence sentencing anomalies 105–8
  drugs statistics 164
  executions January 2015 102, 108–10
  executions 2016 299–300
  justice system 86–7, 184
  Widodo's stance on drugs 92, 190–1
Indonesian Correctional Services 159
Indonesian National Human Rights Commission (Komnas HAM) 107, 129, 240
Intan, Angela 182–3, 212–13, 245
International Covenant on Civil and Political Rights (ICCPR) 36, 55–6
Interpol Jakarta 4
Iskan, Suyoto 157–8
Ismunandar 191

John Q. 140
Johns, Scott 38
Johnson, Peter 13
Judicial Commission 227–30, 238–9
Junior, Manuel 157

Kerobokan prison 12, 13, 21, 29, 35–6, 166
  art exhibition cancellation 193
  computer course 40–1
  'death tower' 29
  drugs 31, 32–3, 48–9
  duck breeding 65
  female prisoners 60
  gangs 58, 61–3, 84
  Hermanus (prison guard) 85
  Jason (prisoner) 59
  medical services 97–8
  Moshen (prisoner) 61
  riots 61–3
  Siswanto (governor) 40–2, 44, 53–4
  Sudjonggo (governor) 152–3
Kesser, Romo 281
Kompas 107–8
Kotzamichalis, Aki and Samantha 152

Lasry, Lex 30, 38, 207
Lawrence, Renae 4, 5–10, 14, 15–17, 19, 22, 28, 29, 33–4, 166, 176
Lewis, C. S. 114
  The Four Loves 114–15
Lopez, Maria Cecilia 97–9, 126, 151–2
Love, Lizzie 33–4, 44, 46–7, 62–3, 91, 98–9, 154–5
Lubis, Todung Mulya 30, 53, 103, 112, 220, 227, 228–30, 235, 236, 237, 286
Lucado, Max 148
  Traveling Light 148

McKenzie, Nick 135
McMahon, Julian xiii–xiv, 30, 35, 37–8, 39, 53, 76, 84, 94, 111–13, 117, 119–21, 172–3, 174, 202–5, 207, 215, 220, 238–9, 240, 245, 254, 260, 282, 284, 285–6
Mandagi, Kristito 191–2
Marhawan, Deni Setia 105
Marsudi, Retno 191, 192–3
Medway, Brian 122
Migrant Care 134
Migrante International 211
Mirdjaja, Matius Arif 31–3, 57–9, 62, 63
Moreira, Marco Archer Cardoso 102, 108–9
Morrissey, Peter 38
Muhammad, Ismail 283
Muxfeldt, Angelita 233

Nainggolan, Olopan 151, 203, 280
National Narcotics Agency (BNN) 164
National Narcotics Board of Indonesia 36
National Union of People's Lawyers – Philippines 211
Nguyen, Tan Duc Thanh 5–10, 15, 22, 28, 39, 166
Nguyen, Van 30
Nicholas, Nopi 158
Norman, Matthew 5–10, 15, 22, 28, 39, 41, 86–7, 166
Nusakambangan prison island 29, 101, 102, 106–7, 108, 126, 135, 141–3, 145 *see also* Besi prison
Nwaolisa, Hansen Antonious 278
Nwaolise, Sylvester 206, 236, 237, 243

O'Connell, Michael 38
Okoye, Samuel Iwuchukwu 278

Olalia, Edre 211, 212
Oyatanze, Okwudili 207, 236, 237, 273

Pangarep, Kaesang 210
Pastika, I Made Mangku 4
Payne, Denise 61, 197, 252, 279
Penrith Panthers 137–9
Plibersek, Tanya 134
Ponto, Harry 107–8
Prasetyo, Attorney-General Muhammad 102, 104, 108, 123, 132, 193, 221, 227, 250, 264
Purdijatno, Admiral Tedjo Edhy 191

Quilty, Ben 76–7, 86, 90, 115, 116, 134, 167, 260

Richardo, Rico 156–7
Ridington, Miranda 221, 247
Rifan, Muhammad 13, 127–8, 227–30, 238, 239
Roy Morgan Research poll 132–3
Rush, Scott 5–10, 19, 22, 28, 36, 39, 166
Ryacudu, Ryamizard 193

Salami, Raheem Agbaje (Jamiu Owolabi Abashin) 173, 182–7, 197, 199, 212–13, 215, 236, 237, 245, 265, 269
Salim, Agus 282
Samiarso, Momock Bambang 151, 174
Sandiford, Lindsay 80
SBS *Dateline* 228
Sergio, Maria Kristina 212
Sianturi, Edith Yunita 106
Siregar, Saud 191
Soei, Ang Kiem 96, 102, 107–8
Soper, David 25, 204, 221, 240, 247, 251, 254, 256, 265, 272, 279, 282

Soper, Shelley 25, 221
Sri Lanka 26
State Administrative Court, Jakarta 162–3, 187–8, 195
Stephens, Martin 5–10, 17–18, 19, 22, 28, 166
Stoicescu, Claudia 164
Strain, Peter 38
Subianto, Prabowo 93
Sudiasa, Wayan 158
Suharto, President 31
Suika, Putu 136
Sukhoi fighter jets 145–6, 169
Sukumaran, Brintha xiv, 1–3, 21, 34, 39–40, 75, 94, 100, 125–6, 235, 241, 243, 245, 248–9, 258, 280, 286
Sukumaran, Chinthu xv, 3, 21, 23, 64, 67, 75, 94, 100, 128, 146, 151, 188, 193, 195–6, 209–10, 218, 232, 234–5, 241–2, 244, 246–7, 248–50, 279–80, 286, 288
  clemency appeal letter 75–6
Sukumaran, Myuran ix–xiii, 27
  appeals/judicial reviews 27–8, 36–9, 50–6, 123–4
  arrest 3
  art classes 44–7, 60, 117
  art workshop as sanctuary 85
  Associate Degree in Fine Arts 154
  Bali Nine involvement 1–2, 5, 6–11
  Besi prison 172–3, 181–233
  childhood 26
  Christian faith 256–64
  clemency pleas 66–72, 75–6, 92–4, 101, 187–8
  death penalty 20–3
  depression 29, 45, 79, 86
  drug trade involvement 27
  execution ix–x, xiii–xv, 268–79
  execution arrangements 230–1
  execution warrant 201–3, 207–8
  first artwork 45–6
  fund raising for Lopez 98–9, 151–2
  funeral 298
  guilt, admission of 50–1
  hate mail 82
  humour 194–5
  Indonesian language skills 48
  instructions for post-execution 144, 186, 217
  'kingpin' 47
  last day 234–50
  legal teams 13, 30, 35–40, 111–12, 129, 162–3, 187, 226–30
  letters to author 94–6, 289–93
  mood and emotions 79–80, 93–6, 101, 102–5, 110, 112–13, 115, 121–2, 126, 134–7, 141–2, 146–7, 154–5, 165, 175–6, 197–9
  painting xi, 41–2, 43–7, 76–7, 90–1, 97–9, 115–16, 119–20, 126–7, 141, 185, 195–6, 206, 209, 233, 235–7, 260, 287
  police detention 12
  portrait of Widodo 119–20, 193, 252
  preparation for death 256–67
  prisoner support for 157–60
  reform and rehabilitation 39–42, 61–3, 69–71, 75–6, 83–4, 94–5, 124, 129–30, 158, 299, 300
  refusal to testify 14–15, 16, 20
  romantic attachments 176
  trial 14–15, 20
  T-shirt printing plan 47–8, 64
  transfer to Nusakambangan 145–6, 153–4, 168–72, 174, 178–9
  verandah conversations 117
  yoga 61

INDEX

Sukumaran, Raji 1–3, 10–11, 21, 23–4, 26, 46, 64, 67–8, 94, 99–100, 124–5, 128–9, 141, 145, 150–1, 185, 200, 209, 213, 232–3, 235, 241–4, 249, 251, 256, 286, 287, 298–9
   clemency appeal letter 67–72
Sukumaran, Sam 26, 151, 177, 235, 241, 249
Supreme Court of Indonesia 28, 107, 163, 206, 238
   Bali Nine appeals 28, 30
   judicial review 28, 39, 50–6, 123
Sydney concert 'Music for Mercy' 116–17, 122

Tangerang District Court 105
Time 30
Tittensor, Megan 38
Toledano, Father Harold 284
Trood, Tony 38

United Nations Human Rights Commission 109
United Nations Human Rights Council 160
University of Indonesia's Centre for Health Research 164

Veloso, Darling 283
Veloso, Mark Daniel 210
Veloso, Mark Darren 210

Veloso, Mary Jane Fiesta xiv–xv, 206, 210–12, 214, 235, 236, 237, 242–3, 266, 272, 279, 281–4
Veloso-Laurente, Maritess 283
Vrielink, Nico 47

Ward, Christopher 38
Washington, Denzel 140
Wenham, David 116–17
Widodo, Joko (Jokowi) 78, 92–3, 99, 132, 239, 249
   clemency pleas 92–3, 96–7, 101, 111, 113, 120–1, 187
   drugs emergency speech 113, 164
   families' plea to 128–9
   letters to 123–4, 129–30, 156–8, 189, 298–9
   'Midline Letter' 129–30
   portrait by Sukumaran 119–20
Wilkins, Alan 220, 244, 247–8
Wilkins, Ann 220, 247
Wilson, Alex 38
Witt, Joanna 86

Yamanie, Achmad 135–6
Yani, Ibu 185, 199, 271, 273, 275, 276, 277
Yogyakarta 149, 196, 197, 205, 207, 209
Yudhoyono, President Susilo Bambang 56, 66, 105
   clemency appeal to 66–76, 78, 92
   phone tapping 77–8
Yuliawan, Ade 206

**MOJGAN SHAMSALIPOOR
AND MILAD JAFARI**
WITH JAMES KNIGHT

Under the Same Sky

From Iran to Australia, an unforgettable story of seeking refuge, being torn apart by government detention and freed by love

An unforgettable story of love, hope and a fight for freedom.

At seventeen, Mojgan Shamsalipoor wanted to be safe from abuse, go to school and eventually marry for love. In Iran, she was denied all of this.

Milad Jafari was a shy teenage boy who found his voice as a musician. But the music he loved was illegal in his country. Milad's father – a key-maker, builder and shopkeeper – wanted his family to live free from the fear of arrest, imprisonment or execution. To do that, they all had to flee Iran.

Mojgan and Milad met in Australia. But in the months between their separate sea voyages, the Australian government changed the way asylum seekers were treated. Though Milad is recognised as a refugee and will soon become a proud Australian citizen, Mojgan has been told she cannot stay here, even though the threat of imprisonment and further abuse, or worse, means she can't return to Iran. This is their story.

Under the Same Sky is a powerful insight into the human face of asylum seekers and the way history has shaped the lives of these two young people. It also shows the compassion found in our suburbs. For Mojgan and Milad, love keeps their hopes alive.

adele dumont

NO MAN IS AN ISLAND

One teacher's story of
how humanity and hope
flourished behind barbed wire

This is the book on immigration detention
all Australians need to read.

Twenty-four-year-old Adele Dumont lived in two worlds, her hometown Sydney and the Curtin detention centre near Derby in Western Australia. As an English teacher, she did not think the fly-in fly-out lifestyle was for her, but what kept her going back were her students: men from many lands who had sacrificed all they knew for a chance to live in Australia; men who were looking for an opportunity for a better life.

Tracing Adele's journey from volunteering on Christmas Island in 2010 through to her work in Western Australia, *No Man is an Island* is an insightful exploration of an important issue. Spending time inside this world opened her eyes – and it will open yours too.

A vividly told story of unexpected warmth, *No Man is an Island* is a unique, personal account that takes a humanitarian stance on immigration detention.

'essential reading'
Sydney Morning Herald

'evocative but never obtrusive . . . powerful'
Saturday Paper

'a rare insight'
Adelaide Advertiser

Cindy Wockner is the National Investigations Editor for News Corporation Australia. Her articles appear in newspapers across Australia, including the *Courier-Mail*, the *Daily Telegraph*, *Herald-Sun*, *Adelaide Advertiser* and *NT News*. Before writing *The Pastor and the Painter*, Cindy co-authored two books, *Bali 9: The Untold Story* and *Evil in the Suburbs*. Cindy reported on Indonesia for over a decade, including seven years as a foreign correspondent, and she has extensively covered the Bali Nine case and the executions of Andrew Chan and Myuran Sukumaran.

 @CindyWockner

If you would like to find out more about Hachette Australia, our authors, upcoming events and new releases you can visit our website or our social media channels:

hachette.com.au

 HachetteAustralia

 HachetteAus

www.ingramcontent.com/pod-product-compliance
Ingram Content Group UK Ltd.
Pitfield, Milton Keynes, MK11 3LW, UK
UKHW041959230426
12048UKWH00008B/434